ALL GOD'S
CHILDREN

ALL GOD'S
CHILDREN

Inside the Dark and

Violent World of

Street Families

RENE DENFELD

PublicAffairs
New York

Published in the United States by PublicAffairs™, a member of the Perseus
Books Group.

PublicAffairs books are available at special discounts for bulk purchases in the
United States by corporations, institutions, and other organizations. For more
information, please contact the Special Markets Department at the Perseus Books
Group, 11 Cambridge Center, Cambridge, MA 02142, call (617) 252-5298,
or e-mail special.markets@perseusbooks.com.

Designed by Brent Wilcox
Text set in 11 point Adobe Caslon

Library of Congress Cataloging-in-Publication Data
Denfeld, Rene.
    All God's children : inside the dark and violent world of street families /
Rene Denfeld.
       p.   cm.
    Includes bibliographical references and index.
    ISBN-13: 978-1-58648-309-8 (hardcover : alk. paper)
    ISBN-10: 1-58648-309-9 (hardcover : alk. paper)
    1. Gangs—United States.   2. Murder—United States.   3. Violent crimes—
United States.   4. Juvenile delinquency—United States.   5. Street youth—
United States—Social conditions.   I. Title.
HV6439.U5D46 2007
364.1'0660973—dc22

                                                            2006037157

10 9 8 7 6 5 4 3 2 1

For

Bill

Contents

A Note from the Author

In the summer of 1992, I became aware of a group of street kids squatting under a bridge in downtown Portland, Oregon. I lived only a short walk from their camp.

As a young reporter, I was curious about the group and visited their squat several times. I observed the kids as they roamed the neighborhood, panhandling. Among them was a boy with longish brown hair and a square face, known on the streets as Highlander. His real name was James Daniel Nelson, and he was just sixteen.

One day in August 1992, as I walked down toward the squat, I noticed police. There was James Nelson, showing detectives the crime scene of his first murder. The newspaper I worked for at the time covered the case. Among the documents we collected were then confidential police interviews, photographs, and autopsy reports.

Ten years passed. I wrote two books, and my partner and I adopted three children from the state foster-care system. I also kept tabs on the street culture and watched as the society these youths created grew and expanded.

One day in June 2003, I opened the daily paper. There was the boy I knew as Highlander—only now he was twenty-seven, and he had killed again. Along with his name were those of twelve other street kids. Their victim was a sweet-faced young woman who had a lot in common with my children: she had a terrible beginning with foster care but had been adopted by a family who loved her deeply. It would turn out that her parents even shared the same caseworker, Beth Girard, as one of my children.

In my home office, I opened the boxes with the street kid research inside, going all the way back to 1992. I pulled out photographs of the square-faced Highlander and the grimy camp he had called home: Checkpoint Charlie. I remembered what it had been like to be a twenty-four-year-old reporter, visiting that squalid squat. And here we were, nearly eleven years later.

But this book is not about my history with this case. This author's note is all you will read about my intersections with James Daniel Nelson. This book focuses on a much more important subject: the phenomenon of street families.

Over the years, I have interviewed many street kids, including James Daniel Nelson. I have crawled through squats on my hands and knees, and I have listened as the street kids shared with me their lives and their codes of justice. I have visited the accused in prisons, jails, and mental hospitals. I have collected studies, shelter reports, and statistics. I have interviewed police, detectives, district attorneys, defense attorneys, social workers, counselors, investigators, families, victims, anthropologists, criminologists, and sociologists—anyone who could lend insight into the street kid culture. Not all the names of those who contributed to my knowledge made their way into this book, but I greatly appreciated their help.

Because of the nature of this subject, I made efforts to verify claims as much as I could. When told of the assaults on Sara Baerlocher, for instance, stories recounted in these pages, I confirmed the events with the victim, the district attorney, police, and some of the youths involved. In some instances, this verification process was difficult or impossible. I have tried to indicate when a story or allegation is based on a single person's account.

A few notes about my methods: this book is not fictionalized. Dialogue is either taken directly from the person quoted or as recalled by witnesses. This book is not based on a true story. I have tried to ensure that it is a true story.

The reader should know that this book contains details of graphic violence. I wrestled with this as a writer. I did not want to sensationalize crimes. Finally, I shared my feelings with a police officer involved in the case. He replied, "If you just say 'she was beaten,' then that isn't really the truth. Tell the truth." The truth is that these are not crimes of passion. They are, for the most part, organized, elaborate, and brutally sadistic.

Every book is a collaborative effort; the writer is only the vehicle for an idea. I was blessed with the trust of many involved in this story, even when it pained them to speak or when they knew their behavior was beyond explanation. Others were gracious enough to take time from their professional schedules to help me with my research.

Without the help of the following people, this book would never have come into being. I owe the utmost thanks to Becky and Sam Williams, Multnomah County district attorney Norm Frink, Portland Police homicide detective Barry Renna, Multnomah County district attorney Robert Leineweber, Attorney Timothy Dunn, Portland police officer Anthony Merrill, Portland Police criminal intelligence investigator Matthew McDonald, Attorney Steven Krasik, Portland Police homicide detective Rich Austria, Portland Police commander and detective Larry Findling (retired), Portland Police sergeant George Burke, Attorney Mark Cross, Portland Police criminal intelligence investigator Stephanie DeKoeyer, Portland Police public information officer Gregory Pashley, Attorney Kirk Roberts, Portland Police records manager Debbie Haugen, Portland Police programs specialist, Records Division, Veronica Nordeen, legal investigator Sandra Gillman, assistant to the district attorney Jill Chedister, anthropologist Marni Finkelstein, Larkin Street director of older youth services Sarah Porter, youth consultant Jerry Fest, Janus Youth Access and Reception Center manager Favor Ellis, Outside In executive director Kathy Oliver, *San Francisco Chronicle* reporter Kevin Fagan, Robyn and Ken Hale, Kelly White, Portland State University associate professor of sociology Dr. Randy Blazak, Connie Moore, Portland State University professor of black studies Dr. Darrell Millner, author John Hagan, foster-care transition specialist Ginger Edwards, Portland City Club research director Wade Fickler, documentary filmmaker Kristen Zuhl, fetal alcohol syndrome specialist Diane Malbin, author Sherrie Eldridge, Foster-Works director Fred Krug, reporter Mike Magrath, security guard Andrea Timm, investigator Steve Tyler, Rob Taylor, Union Pacific conductor Randy Russ, video specialist Aaron Eugene, KUFO night host Cort Webber, warehouse worker Brock, adoptive parent and legal aid attorney Julie Stevens, author Todd Grimson, Debbie and Jamie Alberts, Mary and Larry Bright, and the patient staff at the filing room of the Multnomah County Courthouse. I owe a very special thanks to *Tribune* reporter Jim Redden.

In addition, I relied on the work of several people who deserve special credit: Portland Police homicide detective Shirley Parsons, Portland Police crime specialist John Courtney, Portland Police homicide detective Tom Nelson, Multnomah County medical examiner Dr. Edward Wilson, Portland Police homicide detective Michael Hefley, and Portland Police homicide detective Robert Norman.

Very special thanks go the editor who was eager to embark on this project with me, Kate Darnton of PublicAffairs, and the agent who believed in this book from the get-go, Sally Wofford-Girand. I'd also like to thank Margaret Kopp at Brickhouse Literary Agents, Jaime Leifer at PublicAffairs, Laura Stine at Perseus Books, freelance copy editor Jennifer Kelland, and the executive editor of PublicAffairs, Clive Priddle.

Finally, in memory of the deceased who are discussed in these pages: Hal Charboneau, Michelle Woodall, Leon Stanton, Richard Crosby, Nicholas Moore, Io Nachtwey, and Jessica Kate Williams.

Come lions and lambs, come calves and leopards . . .
Come, children of God.
We are God's children. We love peace.

—MENNONITE LITANY

Prologue

The Union Pacific train left the Albina train yards along the lower tracks a little after five in the morning on May 23, 2003, southbound out of Portland, Oregon. Randy Russ, the conductor, checked the tracks from his position in the right side of the train cab. His engineer checked the tracks on the left.

The railroad tracks curve as they follow the Willamette River, and the trains are kept to a speed limit of six miles per hour. This gives engineers plenty of time to look for trash, or even cars, blocking the tracks. Homeless people camp under the dirty tangle of freeway ramps and bridges, and there are often discarded clothes, beer bottles, and damp blankets along the rails.

Russ felt the railway police did a good job of patrolling the tracks. Those transients who tried to camp on company land were charged with trespassing. But much of the area near the tracks was not railroad property. It belonged to the state of Oregon, and that was where some of the street kids set up their camps.

As the train passed under the east end of Steel Bridge, Russ's engineer spotted something from his side of the cab. It lay stretched out a good hundred feet from the tracks, near a stairway retaining wall.

"Oh," Russ recalls his engineer saying. "That doesn't look good."

Russ looked over. What he saw, he said, looked like a female mannequin. She was lying on her back. Her right arm was flung up over her head. Her legs were open, but her heels had curled back in. She had been badly burned.

Immediately, he radioed the dispatcher. It was 5:23 in the morning. "You have a body here in East Portland," he said. "Under the Steel Bridge overpass."

About a year before, Russ remembered, he had been conducting a train under another Portland bridge and passed two detectives working on a stabbing. The pillars, he recalled, were splashed with blood. As a conductor, Russ was well acquainted with the underbelly of the country. In Arizona, he had worked the trains when Rafael Resendez-Ramirez, dubbed the Railway Killer, was being sought. Russ knew a lot about the transients who rode the rails—trainhoppers, they called themselves. Some were okay. Some were not. He got to where he could tell, by looking in their eyes, which ones were dangerous, and he told those to stand back away from his train, or he would radio them in. Russ had seen a lot in his years on the rails. But nothing like this, he thought. He would never forget this sight.

A short way down the line, the radio burst back at him. Russ was told to stop the train. Police had cordoned the area behind him, and all rail traffic would be stopped for four to five hours. The entire network was frozen.

———

Detective Barry Renna of the Portland Police is a tall, careful man who measures his words as if seeing them strung at the end of a sentence, weighing his statements against the concerns of the victims, of the accused, and of the justice system at large. In passing, he resembles the actor Sam Neill, only with a little more care worn into his face. He has been a police officer for almost thirty years, most of them in Portland.

What Detective Renna found near the tracks was a light brown–skinned female wearing what had been blue jeans and a light blue shirt. She was lying in a pool of blood. Her head had been beaten to the point that her features were nearly obliterated. The skin above her eyes was split open in several places. There were gaping holes in her throat about an inch in diameter. Her curly brown hair was partially torn from her scalp, and her ears were filled with blood.

The lower half of her body was so badly burned that her jeans had burned right off her legs. Only a scrap of panties was left on her belly. They had what appeared to be a pattern of little cherries on them. The skin of her legs was charred black and had split open from the intense heat in several places, revealing moist pink flesh.

The pale blue shirt she had been wearing was pulled above her waist and soaked with blood. The fabric smelled strongly of lighter fluid. The front of the shirt bore shoeprints, as if someone had been jumping on her. At her feet was a burned gray blanket, and off to her left was a large square of discarded cardboard. The cardboard also had shoeprints across its damp surface.

Detective Renna noted these details as the crime team photographed and videotaped the victim, turning her body to photograph the knife wounds in her soft, wide back. Some details were incongruous. Looking closely, Detective Renna noticed grass clippings on the bottom of her sneakers. There was no grass in the area.

The police strung up crime scene tape. The sun had come up completely by now and the Willamette River sparkled in its light. People riding their bikes on the nearby esplanade stopped and watched as the police worked. A news station helicopter appeared, whipping the clear blue sky. The police put up a freestanding canopy "in an effort to block public view of the deceased," as the crime specialist on the scene recorded. The burned gray blanket, with one piece attached to the victim's right shoe, was placed into an arson can.

Detective Renna knelt next to the body. The smell of death and burned flesh would linger in his nostrils for days no matter how many showers he took. He felt a sense of déjà vu: here was another body, found under another bridge.

If the places where people had been killed in similar circumstances were marked on a map, there would be little flags all up and down the river: the Marquam Bridge, 1992; North Portland, 1992; St. Johns, 1992; Old Town, 2000; the Ross Island Bridge, 2001; and now this: the Steel Bridge, 2003.

"So many things were unknown at that time," Detective Renna recalls. They didn't know who the victim was. They didn't know if she had been murdered at that location or brought there after her death. They didn't know anything.

At almost eleven in the morning, police finally cleared the scene, loading the charred body into a white morgue van. There was a large pool of blood where she had lain, bright red on the sharp gray rocks. The crime scene specialists sprayed this off with high-pressure hoses.

And then, Jessica Kate Williams was gone.

———

The members of the Thantos street family were sleeping soundly in their squat across the river under the Front Avenue overpass. There were thirteen of them, ranging in age from sixteen to twenty-seven.

The dirt of their squat was damp with runoff and greasy with oil. Years of refuse had been tamped down into the dirt: opened tin cans, molding wet shirts, and shards of yellow glass. Hundreds of twist-off beer caps lay flecked over the rutted earth. The family had placed cardboard over the ground to protect against the damp. The street kids slept under coats and sleeping bags.

In the middle of the squat, they had scratched a circle in the dirt. This was their magical circle, a place to practice martial arts. They called it the Circle of Seven. A Wiccan star, the star of chaos, was drawn on one wall.

The overpass roof was a good twenty feet above them. When cars passed overhead, the concrete boomed and shuddered, and there was the whining creak of rebar. Heavier trucks made the whole structure groan and thud, passing with a deep, repetitive *chucka-chucka-chucka* sound, before they were gone with one snapping final boom over the edge of the ramp. It was dark in the squat, but the sides let light filter in. Birds had pulled straw into round concrete holes in the underside of the overpass. Night animals had left dozens of three-toed tracks, and the droppings of rodents were embedded in the sour dirt.

The concrete pillars around the family were marked with graffiti. *I die every day for my freedom. Wild weed rock on. Big John He Got Some Pussy—no he didn't. Sleepy. Suicidal. Hammerin Henry. Neo was here.*

Some of the graffiti consisted of street names and what the homeless youth call "roll calls," the names of those who occupy the squat at that time. Others were just nonsense. Where someone had defecated at the bottom of a pillar was a scrawled notation and an arrow pointing the way: *eat shit.*

The Thantos Family had only been staying in the squat for three days, but they had organized their camp in military fashion. Clothes went here, sleeping bags there. At the far end of the squat, the ground rose sharply to meet the overpass, and there was a shelf of concrete where they kept their toothbrushes and one pink comb.

Everyone had a designated place to sleep. If someone in the family was being punished, he or she was put on "bed restriction" by the street parents. It was like being sent to your room when you were little.

Dudley Strain, a LaGrande Industrial Supply salesman, arrived to work that morning around eight. He was the first to notice the large group of street kids that had settled into the squat next to the warehouse.

The LaGrande warehouse predated the overpass. The area had once been a vibrant Italian neighborhood known as Lair Hill, with simple-frame Victorians and small yards spilling over with fig trees and rampant with fennel. A 1970s urban-renewal plan had torn out the heart of the neighborhood to lay down the overpass and others like it in a Byzantine effort to streamline downtown traffic. The result had sent the area into dereliction.

Before the overpass was built nearly right over it, the LaGrande warehouse had faced a sunny lot, and two loading-dock doors remained from that time. Now the doors led into darkness. The warehouse employees kept them locked. They had a reason to be cautious: the sunny lot had turned into a fetid camp for homeless people. The city had erected a cyclone fence around the other side of the overpass in a futile effort to keep squatters out, but the street kids had cut a hole in the fence and easily slipped inside. Employees avoided the area after work, saying it was unsafe. When the warehouse worker went to clean the parking lot, he found syringes and human excrement.

Having so many squatters next to a warehouse filled with expensive tools was a bad idea. Dudley Strain called the police and asked them to move the campers along. Twenty minutes later, three Portland police officers arrived. It was 8:20 in the morning, just three hours after the charred body had been found across the river.

The officers walked through the cavernous warehouse to the loading docks. It was safer for them to access the squat through the dock doors than to crawl through the hole in the fence. The warehouse worker cranked the old metal dock door open with a loud whine. When the door was lifted, even he was surprised at the scene. "It looked like Beirut down there," he says.

The police officers cautiously woke the campers and began asking for their names and running their records. The reporting officer, Brenda Dean, noticed that one of the young women of the group took command, issuing orders for the other youths to pick up the squat and to pile their clothes and other belongings in a shopping cart. The woman looked about twenty, with a long whip of blonde hair and a steely gaze. She was tall and heavyset, but she moved her large body with surprising quickness. She gave her name as Cassandra Hale.

Officer Dean had dealt with street kids before. She asked Cassandra if the squatters were a "street family," and Cassandra said yes.

"Who's the mom?" Officer Dean asked.

"I am," Cassandra replied.

"And who is the dad?"

Cassandra pointed at a man in the squat. He had longish brown hair that touched his shoulders and a frown line deeply grooved above his blue eyes. His shoulders were broad, and his arms were thick and meaty. He gave his name as Michael Smith. His date of birth, he said, was February 9, 1976, making him twenty-seven. Officer Dean ran his name, but it came up UTL, or unable to locate.

Officer Dean confronted the man about the false name. He glared at her, giving what she described as a "hateful and evil" look. He insisted Michael Smith was his real name. "He continued to stare at me, and he said he had no ID," Dean noted in her report. In truth, his real name was James Daniel Nelson, and he had just been released from the Santiam Correctional Institution in Salem, Oregon, after serving almost eleven years for murder.

The rest of the street kids were now fully awake and following orders from Cassandra. The warehouse worker watched as the police moved among them, collecting information. He felt older than his thirty-seven years. "They were all so young," he says. "You know, I'm pushing up toward forty and they all looked so *young*."

Young they were, but they were also at a dangerous age, lurking at the edge of adulthood when the body can grow faster than the mind.

Carl Alsup was one of these, a pale boy with a shaved blond head and a pair of aw-shucks ears. One muscular shoulder bore a tattoo of a sun. Carl was only seventeen, but he was a tall, strong young man with an unfolding sense of power in his body, and just that last night he had proved it. Carl gave the officer a fake name, David Edward Moody. Like his street father hero, Nelson, he gave a birth date that matched his real name.

On one of the concrete pillars near her cardboard-paved home, another family member, Danielle Cox, had marked her street name with black pen: *Shadowcat,* it read, in spiky, proud letters. There were cryptic runic symbols next to the name. Age eighteen, Danielle gave her true name to the police. Under uncombed hair, her eyes looked shocked and depressed. Her teeth were dirty, and she wore clothes pulled out of a communal pile.

Only a month before, Danielle had been a college student with a scholarship and a meal plan and a prepaid phone card. She had a caring mother who supported her, a brilliant mind, and a gift at debate that had helped win her accolades. That previous summer she had worked with autistic children and told others about how she dreamed of becoming a teacher. Now, she was living in the dirt under an overpass with a group of angry street kids.

One by one, the police got a name, true or false, from the youths in the squat. They had no reason at that time to connect the group of street kids with the body that had been found across the river, where Detective Renna was still working, crouched at that very moment over the mutilated corpse. They didn't notice the bag of knives hidden in the back of the squat, or the magical Circle of Seven that had been stained with blood from the beating the family had administered to Jessica the night before. They didn't see the water the youths had poured over the Circle of Seven in a hasty effort to clean up. They didn't see the chunks of hair that had been cut from their victim's head, some of which were still floating around the squat. They didn't smell the lighter fluid on three Thantos Family members, including the seventeen-year-old brooder Carl Alsup and the college student Danielle Cox, who had led a bloody Jessica on a long walk across the river, where they had stabbed her, stomped on her head and chest, and then lit her on fire when they suspected she was still alive.

The squat was rank and filthy smelling and full of dark corners. These were just street kids in a street family, sleeping under an overpass. There were hundreds like them in the city.

Officer Dean called in a supervisor from the Oregon Department of Transportation. Surveying the large group of street youth, the supervisor declined to press trespassing charges. He did promise, however, to fix the hole in the Cyclone fence.

The street kids were now free to go. One by one they crawled through the hole in the fence. They dodged the traffic to cross the ramp, where they pulled two bikes out of the bushes, as well as another shopping cart, where they dumped some of their stuff.

For a few minutes, the warehouse worker said, the street kids just stood there, as if stunned. A sprinkler came on in the bushes, and the spray doused them, startling the group. They trundled off, toward downtown and the Square.

———

Every city has a place where street kids gather. In Portland, it is Pioneer Courthouse Square, called simply "the Square" by the street kids. In New York City, they hang in the East Village, but especially in Tompkins Square Park on the benches they call Loser's Lane. In Cambridge, Massachusetts, they congregate by the T-Stop in Harvard Square, an area dubbed "the Pit." In New Orleans, Louisiana, the place to be is Jackson Square, where street families with names like the Drunk Belligerent Crew pass the time. In Madison, Wisconsin, they hang out on State Street, near the university. In Minneapolis, Minnesota, they squat under the uptown bridges by the railroad tracks in street families with names like PIM, short for Prosper in Madness. In Seattle, Washington, street kids numbering in the hundreds hang out in the University District, which they affectionately call the U District, in street families with names like the Drunk Knights. East of Seattle in Spokane, the Rat Pak family hangs out in People's Park, sleeping in a squat called the 420 Flats. In Sacramento, California, street youth hang outside the Birdcage Centre, a shopping mall in Citrus Heights, and up and down Del Paso Boulevard. In Berkeley, the place to be is on Telegraph and Shattuck avenues, near the BART station. In Santa Fe, New Mexico, they hang out in the plaza. In Tucson, Arizona, the spot is Fourth Avenue, near the University of Arizona. In Austin, Texas, over seven thousand street youth were counted in one year on the Drag, a strip of Guadalupe Street that runs along the western edge of the University of Texas.

Small towns also have their share of street kids. Quaint Ashland, Oregon, is home to a popular Shakespearean festival; it is also home to a number of street kids sleeping in Lithia Park. Arcata, California, a scenic town tucked between redwood forests and the Pacific Ocean, has large numbers of street kids who hang out in the plaza near Humboldt State University. The street kids describe Arcata as a "homeless oasis" and a "paradise."

There are an estimated 1.5 million street kids in the United States, and agencies believe their numbers are growing, from Asheville, North Carolina, to San Francisco, California, where street kids are said to be the "fastest-growing" homeless population. The phenomenon is not confined to the United States. Canada and Australia report a growing number of street youth, with an estimated thirty-seven thousand in Australia. As far away as Tokyo, the *Mainichi News* reports that kids are hitting the streets in "numbers unprecedented in the modern era." The newspaper blames the increase on the cleaning up of public places like Yoyogi Park, which makes them more inviting for teenagers "playing lover," which is slang for prostituting themselves.

Flying under the radar of conventional society, these street kids have organized themselves into tight-knit groups they call street families. The street youth you see out panhandling or hanging out, from Manhattan to Seattle, are not isolated individuals. They are part of an extensive, organized, and highly developed culture.

In Portland, there are several long-lived street families with names like the Nihilistic Gutter Punks, or the NGP, as they like to be called, and the Sick Boys. A street family controlling marijuana dealing downtown calls itself the 420s (there are said to be 420 psychoactive compounds in pot, and 4/20 is also the date of Hitler's birthday). There are also about a dozen smaller families with names like the Happy Time Kids, the Brood, and the Pirates. The Thantos Family was one of these smaller families.

Street families sound like gangs, but they're not—or not entirely. Street families are a unique creation of street kids, combining elements of fantasy games, Dungeons and Dragons, prison codes, punk fashion, and pagan religions. The youth have even created a distinct language. They use terms like *spange* (a contraction of "spare change") for panhandling and *oogle* for a new kid on the street. These terms are consistent across the country. A weapon made out of a chain and a padlock is a *smiley*. If you get *86'd*, you have to leave the street youth culture. If you get *taxed*, you are beaten or robbed. Street parents can tell their followers whom to have sex with. This is called *gremlin rights*.

In a unique but extensive study of the culture in Canada, professors John Hagan and Bill McCarthy interviewed street kids in

Toronto and Vancouver. They found that over half (54 percent) of street youth were members of organized street families. Taken conservatively, this study would suggest at least half a million youth in the United States are involved in street families.

Street families are a criminal subculture that has grown with little notice. There has been no national recognition of their existence. Only a handful of researchers, such as Hagan and McCarthy, have ever studied their culture. And yet, street families are so common as to be a matter of fact among the agencies that deal with them. In San Francisco, some street families are defined by one domineering alpha male who controls three or four women, according to Sarah Porter, the director of older youth services for Larkin Street Youth Services, an agency serving homeless youth. Porter describes the family arrangement as highly patriarchal. Other San Francisco street families are large crews who sleep in Golden Gate Park, such as the San Francisco Scum Fucks, or SFSF as they call themselves, a hard-drinking street family that prides itself on being filthy brawlers.

In some cities, the street family concept is loosely defined, with all the youth feeling they belong to one giant family. In other cities, the street kids divide themselves into smaller, well-defined groups. In Vancouver, British Columbia, one street family formed out of pregnant young street women who attended prenatal classes together. In Des Moines, Iowa, a street family formed around a shared "profession": stripping wire from abandoned buildings to sell.

Some street families, like the Hollywood Drunk Punks in Los Angeles, are permanent residents of a city, while others come and go with the seasons. In New York City, street families develop among the nomadic street youth who arrive for the summer and then disperse when the weather turns bad. For the time they are together, they call themselves a "family," and they will refer to their leaders as "mom and dad."

Street families are characterized by their highly defined familial organization, their language, their secrecy, and, more than anything, their rules. The youth call this "code." Code defines their world. "It's like a society with rules," Cassandra explains. "Always doing things for each other, taking care of each other." She pauses, then says with a hard look in her eyes, "Nobody goes against family."

If you "go against" a street family, the result can be violent punishment. In the two months since their creation, members of the Thantos Family had attacked and beaten one member for allegedly breaking a family rule. They had attacked another member and cut off all her hair. They had plotted to kill at least three other people and had killed at least one of their dogs. And in the end, they had assaulted and murdered Jessica Williams because, they said, she had broken code.

This is the story of the Thantos street family, and the story of the subculture that created it, from its tiny beginnings in 1992 to its current status as an entrenched, subterranean society. It is the story of a new, disturbing society created by teenagers, a lawless world of secrecy, retribution, and incomprehensible violence.

PART ONE

1992

"Aren't there any grown-ups at all?"

"I don't think so."

The fair boy said this solemnly; but then the delight of a realized ambition overcame him. In the middle of the scar he stood on his head and grinned at the reversed fat boy.

"No grown-ups!"

—WILLIAM GOLDING,
LORD OF THE FLIES

1

James Daniel Nelson was born on February 9, 1976, in Tennessee. One of his first memories is of sitting at the kitchen table and drinking alcohol with his mother. According to Nelson, she finally quit drinking when he was eleven. "I was abused my whole life," he says. He watched his parents abuse each other, and, in turn, they abused him. "I lived in violence."

Early on, Nelson claims, he had learning disabilities, which he believes resulted from his mother's drinking while she was pregnant with him. An evaluation of Nelson as a young teenager did find a significant scatter in his cognitive abilities. In some tests, he scored as high as seventy-five out of a hundred. In others, he scored as low as sixteen. Nelson struck the evaluator as a concrete thinker. Yet, he struggled when he was asked to plan out strategies in advance. He had trouble in school. "I couldn't focus," he says.

Before he reached fourteen, Nelson was committing crimes. His juvenile convictions included theft and attempted burglary. At first, his crimes netted him minor sentences: informal probation, and when that didn't work, formal probation, and when that didn't work, group homes.

The first accusation of a serious violent offense occurred when Nelson was fourteen. A mentally retarded high school classmate told police that Nelson and a friend of his talked her into cutting class so they could go hang out. She said they lured her into a nearby tunnel, where Nelson raped her by pulling down her pants and forcing his penis inside her. She later recanted this story and said the sex was consensual.

Five months later, another mentally disabled girl at the school made a similar claim. This time, the victim said that before the rape, Nelson talked about satanism and told her she was a "sacrifice." According to Multnomah County district attorney Norm Frink, Nelson had been reading *Necronomicon,* a cheap paperback claiming to be a translation of the bona fide Book of the Dead, or ancient black magic. For an occult-minded teenager like Nelson, the book was entrancing: he could learn how to cast "binding spells" on his enemies. This time Nelson was charged with several counts of rape and was convicted of sexual battery. A photograph taken at the time shows a smiling boy with a shock of brown hair. He was just fifteen.

Nelson was sent to the B. T. Collins Juvenile Hall in Sacramento, California, known simply as "the Hall." The Hall remains today, a sturdy expanse of concrete buildings on twenty-five acres. A 1998 grand jury investigating the Hall found filthy kitchens and heavy use of intrusive searches by the staff, but praised other aspects of the institution, including its educational programs. Close to eight thousand juveniles pass through the doors of the Hall every year. Some stay as long as two years. Most are in for nonviolent property offenses, but about a third are held for violent crimes.

Because of his sexual-battery conviction, Nelson would have been considered one of the more violent offenders. At the Hall, he got in trouble for fighting and lying, and in February 1992, he was kicked out of the sex-offender treatment program. Nelson refused to take his sex crimes seriously. His parole officer, Gary Steele, said he had "not accepted responsibility for his offense or admitted guilt."

Nelson turned sixteen and was transferred into a smaller group home in Sacramento. He promptly ran away. He was caught and sent to another group home in Yuba City, California. He claims there were mostly blacks there, and "they were fighting left and right." Once again, he ran away, this time with a friend.

By sixteen, Nelson was nearly a grown man. He stood six feet tall and weighed 174 pounds, with a strong, muscular build. He wore his chestnut brown hair down to his shoulders. Under straight eyebrows, his eyes were a dark, steady blue. He was a good-looking boy if you could get past the flat expression in his eyes. He came off as a cocky braggart, but he didn't seem particularly violent—at first.

Nelson says that he stayed with friends in Sacramento for a few days, then took a Greyhound bus to Portland, Oregon. He claims he heard about Portland from street kids he had met during his journey through the juvenile justice system. When he arrived in Portland in June 1992, he owned a pair of gray Levis, a white shirt, a blue flannel shirt, a pair of coveralls, and a pair of black jeans cut into shorts. He carried a dog chain, about two to three feet long, to use as a weapon.

A study conducted by the Vera Institute of Justice found that the majority of juveniles who run away from state care escape from group homes and that the effort to find these runaways, even those convicted of serious offenses, can be indifferent, especially if the juveniles cross state lines. Once the Greyhound bus carrying sixteen-year-old James Nelson crossed into Oregon, he effectively disappeared.

In Portland, Nelson found a street culture at the tail end of significant change. Youth agencies estimated that there were about two thousand homeless youths in the Portland area at the time, with perhaps three to five hundred hardcore street kids living downtown.

A decade before, to be a homeless youth was to be a child prostitute. A 1985 study by the Portland City Club found that at least two-thirds of homeless youths were prostitutes. Their average age was fourteen, but a local shelter recorded boy prostitutes as young as ten. On a strip of Third Avenue called "the Wall," dozens of child prostitutes waited for customers in broad daylight. Portland was so notorious for boy prostitutes, it earned the derisive nickname "Boy's Town."

Then, in the mid to late 1980s, cities from Portland to Cleveland, Ohio, began to clean up their downtown cores, sweeping out the porn shops and steam baths and arresting the pimps in the bus stations. The fleabag motels were turned into boutique hotels, and hockshops became steakhouses. In Portland, the Wall was torn down and replaced by a parking garage for a nearby Saks Fifth Avenue. In New York City, police cracked down on child prostitution in Times Square.

At the same time, funding for youth shelters increased dramatically. The federal Runaway and Homeless Act of 1974 was reauthorized, and the government began funneling millions of dollars into agencies serving homeless youth, offering shelters reimbursements for meals and money for job and education programs.

While these changes greatly improved life for homeless youth, they didn't eradicate the presence of teenagers on the streets. For runaway youth such as James Nelson, the cleaned-up streets offered a new playground. They could invent the society they wanted, free from the interference of adults. No longer defined by the pimp or the pedophile, they could define themselves. Isolated from other influences, they would create a fantasy world all their own.

———

When he stepped off the bus in Portland, Nelson headed straight to Pioneer Courthouse Square. It was as if he had a homing device.

Nelson swaggered into the Square in late June 1992, carrying his backpack of clothes and dog chain. He told the other youths that he was the infamous Scorpio killer. He said he was the Nightslasher. He said he communicated with aliens and that he had psychic powers. He said he was a Ninja master who had killed sixty-five people. Listening to all this loud talk, some of the kids of the Square thought he was a "dumbass," as one girl later told police.

A congenial open-air pavilion built in 1984 as part of the downtown renovation, Pioneer Courthouse Square was hailed as "the city's living room." The definition was apt for the street kids who practically lived there, day and night, lounging on the brick steps, panhandling along the sidewalks, and hanging out on the benches near the Starbucks.

One of the dominant figures in the Square that summer was Black Panther, whose real name was Michael Lynn Tinnin. Tinnin was a young man of nineteen with a thick scruff of dark hair, cut short on top with a long Mohawk tail in back, a flattened nose, and an edgy demeanor. His skin was sun-darkened, and he had dancing black eyes.

Tinnin had what the youths at the time called an "old-timer" reputation. He was no hesher, no summer bunny. He lived the life. Rather than sleep in a shelter, Tinnin made his camp out of doors under a bridge. His street name was tattooed on his left shoulder— *Black Panther*—and the words *Live and Let Die* were tattooed on his right shoulder. Tinnin wore a silver ring in the shape of a skull that was connected by a thin chain to a skull bracelet around his wrist. In his pocket he carried a switchblade, and on his waist, he wore a silver dagger in a gold hilt. He carried a wooden staff, about four feet long. He told the other kids it was carved out of ironwood. He had etched *Black Panther* into its side in runic-style letters. The handle of the heavy staff was wrapped with black electrical tape, and the sides were decorated with bits of human hair affixed with more black electrical tape. When he walked, Tinnin used the staff for emphasis, the hanks of hair swishing in the breeze.

Tinnin was quite the storyteller. He had one story about his identical twin, with whom he shared exactly the same name, though the twin was called Junior. They looked exactly alike, except the first Michael Tinnin had a scar on the left side of his chin, and the twin had a scar on the right side of his chin. Junior's street name was Snow Leopard. This was in contrast to Black Panther, as in white and black, good and evil.

Apparently this story floated. One girl told police she had dated both of the twins. One twin would go walking off, she said, and the other would appear. Then, one day the mysterious twin called Snow Leopard disappeared. He had gone to Utah, the girl was told, leaving her to date just one boy.

Others believed Tinnin had a bionic eye. They knew this was true because when he pressed the side of his temple by the bionic eye, his eyes went all batty. The bionic eye could see long distances.

Tinnin had a regular girlfriend who was respected because she could "stand up under pressure," meaning she could be beaten without complaint. Her bruised arms and legs proved it. Tinnin had the girl's name tattooed on his left arm. On his wrist, he had a tattoo with the number sixty-nine. At times he also went by the street name the Eliminator.

Nelson and Tinnin hit it off right away. The two developed a contentious, competitive, yet appreciative relationship. It was an extended game of one-upsmanship, with the stakes growing ever higher. Sooner or later, one of them would have to make good on what he claimed.

Tinnin said he had killed people in California.

So what, Nelson boasted; he had killed people everywhere.

Tinnin bragged he had killed for money. I've "completed contracts," he said.

Nelson countered that he was the Zodiac killer. He had escaped from Alcatraz. All of his murders were done for pleasure, he said. No payment was required.

At one point, Tinnin told other street kids he had known Nelson four years earlier, and they had killed people together. Nelson denied this at the time. "I never met Eliminator, well, Black Panther, till I came to Portland," he said in 1992. "He told a bunch of people I used to live in Portland. I used to live in California, in between California and Tennessee." Over a decade later, Nelson reversed himself, saying he had known Tinnin before, that they had met in Salt Lake City, Utah. "I would have been twelve," he now claims. According to court records, however, Nelson would have been living in California at the time.

Nelson quickly became familiar with the places street kids hung out. There was the Pioneer Courthouse Square, of course, but there was also O'Bryant Square, a small, dirty plaza on Stark Street, which the kids called Paranoid Park. A growing number of youths also hung out on the Willamette River waterfront, where a new memorial to the Japanese Americans interned during World War II had been built in 1990 near the west end of the Steel Bridge. The low, rocky sculpture was a popular spot for street kids, who hung out and dealt drugs, leading to its nickname, Pothead Hill.

Nelson could have stayed at local youth shelters, such as the Greenhouse, run by the Salvation Army, or the Porch Light, a shelter in the same building. The Greenhouse offered its own high school equivalency program with diplomas and even a prom for its graduating youth. For medical care, many youths went to Outside In, a low-income health clinic in a ramshackle old house at the top of downtown with funky old couches in the living room and a lived-in feeling. Outside In offered free pap smears, birth control, and shelter beds. The director, Kathy Oliver, had been running the agency since 1983.

For food, other street kids introduced Nelson to places like the Sisters of the Road café, a charity restaurant in Old Town where, for a dollar, he could get ample plates of beans, burritos, pastas, salads, and veggies, all with a side of very good cornbread. For another quarter, he could get juice or coffee. If the street kids didn't have any money, they could work for the meal by busing tables or washing dishes. There was plentiful food at the youth shelters as well, including the Greenhouse, and at the St. Francis Church, a soup kitchen across the river. Tinnin's girlfriend didn't like the food at St. Francis, so they often ate at the Greenhouse.

The street kids Nelson met at the Square had plenty of safe places to eat and sleep, as well as programs for work and education to get off the streets if they so chose. But they didn't choose. The street kids Nelson met disdained the programs. The programs were for the heshers and the summer bunnies. They counted themselves as among the hardcore: they chose to sleep outside in a permanent camp near downtown called Checkpoint Charlie.

Checkpoint Charlie was next to the Willamette River on the southwest side of downtown, where miles of deserted industrial land stretched from the Marquam Bridge to the Ross Island Bridge. Portland is a city of bridges—there are seven in the city proper—and along the river corridor are miles of abandoned industrial districts left over from the time when shipping ruled the city. The industrial districts give the city a gritty feel not far from its blue-collar roots.

The thriving industrial district along the river had long since been leveled, and all that remained was buckling concrete foundation pads with twisting rebar, choked in a sea of dried grass, wild bachelor's buttons, and scrubby trash trees. When the wind blew off the river, the wild fennel shook their umbel heads, and the air filled with their heady licorice smell.

Deep in the lost fields were massive concrete pipes and strange bunkers covered with graffiti. An abandoned and rotting house hung precariously off the shore on pilings, and a forgotten grain ship was moored out on the river. The muddy water near the ship was laced with rusted, barbed strands of broken shipping cable poking out of the murky depths. The ship was tagged with graffiti and littered with trash.

Older homeless people had been camping along this stretch for years, but, generally, their camps were isolated, a tent here or there, maybe a handful of tarp-covered shelters grouped together at the most. The older homeless were largely quiet, keeping to themselves, lugging buckets down to the river for fresh water to boil over their campfires.

The street kids changed that. At least a dozen kids were camping at Checkpoint Charlie that summer before Nelson arrived. Their ages ranged from fifteen to twenty. They were, on average, a few years younger than the street kids who would have come a decade later. They went by street names such as Coaster, Black Heart, Foot, Evil, Blazer, Angel, Grover, Breeze, Black Panther, Bitch, and Giggles. Many shaved their hair into Mohawks as a sign of allegiance to each other. Nelson kept his long brown hair uncut.

At the squat site, huge concrete pillars rose out of the ground to support the Marquam Bridge. The street kids had spray-painted the words *Grim Reaper* on one pillar in the middle of the squat and decorated it with a graffiti skull. Another pillar read *I wish the pain would stop*. The Marquam Bridge rose high enough above the camp that rain could blow in unimpeded, but the youths were reasonably well protected. Nearby was the leveled ground from what had once been an electrical plant, and metal plates on the ground still led down damp stairs to forgotten basement storage areas.

The group worked hard on their squat, protecting it from other street youths in nearby camps with whom they were warring that summer. They made traps by filling holes with barbed wire, then covering them, so that if an intruder stepped in the hole, "They fell in barbed wire," one of the girls said. The edges of the camp were called the "perimeter." At night the men patrolled the perimeter.

On the dirty, condom-strewn sand along the river's edge, there was plenty of driftwood for fires. There was even a shallow little area in the river where the youths could swim. The water of the Willamette was cleaner than it had been, but after every hard rain, the overburdened sewer pipes dumped their excess raw sewage directly into the river. Signs near the overflow pipes warned *Combined Sewer Overflow*. One was right near the camp. On rainy days, the pungent smell of human sewage wafted from the river.

A defunct, graveled service road ran directly near the camp. Across the road were the remains of a tannery that had ceased operations in the early 1900s. In its location, marshy lowland had formed into a series of oily puddles where blue herons hunted fruitlessly for minnows. Tanneries typically use caustic chemicals, such as coal tars, formaldehyde, and cyanide-based finishes, to strip hair from hides. Later, the city came, plowed up the muddy lake, covered the poisoned land with black plastic anchored with tires, and left it to stew in the sun.

Checkpoint Charlie was the perfect spot for a squat. The street kids could stroll up the river and be downtown in ten minutes; yet, the camp was far enough away to escape supervision. No security companies patrolled the area, and police rarely visited the homeless camps.

The group invited Nelson to move in with them. He hid his belongings in a secret hole covered with a metal plate. He spread blankets on the ground, like the other street kids. And he was home.

———

Mimicking the other street kids, Nelson took a street name. He called himself Highlander, after the B movie starring Christopher Lambert as one of a race of immortal warriors. The use of fake names is common among criminals, and street kids eagerly adopt the custom. The names make them sound dangerous. "The reason we have a street name is because we have lots of warrants and stuff with the law," a street youth named Adam Linday, called Linx, said in 2003. "That way . . . we aren't sitting there yelling each other's names," he explained.

The street names also serve a more personal purpose, one that speaks to their secret desires. By calling himself Highlander, Nelson created a new identity for himself. He *became* Highlander, an immortal warrior, and to call him anything but Highlander was to deny his supposed fighting prowess. The same was true of the other youths of the camp: Tinnin *was* the Black Panther, the stealthy warrior with a bionic eye.

The street kids rarely used their real names. They immersed themselves in their new identities until those adopted identities started to seem real. Even after they had been sleeping together and hanging out together for weeks, most of the street kids didn't know who each other really were. Asked the real name of Highlander, some of the youths thought it might be James. Or maybe it was Richard. No, that was the name of the vampire Nelson claimed to be, one said. The street kids didn't question each other's street names. If Nelson said he was Highlander, then that was who he was.

Most of the males at the squat took masculine warrior names, though a few had goofy names, including one boy called Grover. The girls took melodramatic names, such as Black Heart, or names that were warnings; one of the girls was called Bitch. By taking the name Highlander, Nelson was making an announcement. He was a warrior, fearless and proud. He was a force to be reckoned with. He was not some goofy kid. He had ambitions.

Street kids know their lore like any other subculture, and Nelson says that street kid identity crystallized in Portland in 1988, four years before his arrival, when the Portland Street Kids, or PSK, was created. The PSK was not a street family per se. It was more of an umbrella organization, a collective identity, for the street kids of Portland. Virtually all the street kids in the city came to identify themselves as part of the PSK.

Three cultural trends heavily influenced the street kid identity: punk culture, anarchist politics, and Dungeons and Dragons–style fantasy games. Street youths took to the punk look with a vengeance, adorning themselves with Mohawks, scowls, and torn clothing, but they didn't necessarily embrace the punk creative ethic. Instead, they found nihilistic solace in the new anarchism coming out of the United Kingdom into the United States through the Class War and squatting movements. Street kids across the United States eagerly adopted anarchism, or at least their interpretation of anarchism, especially the belief that "squatting breaks down the traditional exploitation of people by landlords," as anarchist squatting leader Rick Van Savage claims. Squatting outside under bridges became more than a cheap way to live outside the law: it became a righteous political statement.

At the same time, Dungeons and Dragons–style fantasy games had become popular among teenage boys. Playing pretend was no longer for little kids. Growing up, many of these boys had immersed themselves in hours of elaborate role-play involving medieval characters, magic, and spells. Adolescent males who hit the streets brought with them this interest in real-time fantasy role-playing, including adopting mythical identities and acting out complicated plots on the streets.

Together, these three influences formed the foundation of street kid culture: punk kids living in squats with names like Highlander, Black Panther, and Evil, playing endless imaginary games of intrigue, romance, and violence.

When they weren't in their camp or downtown, the street kids wandered the lower Lair Hill neighborhood. Walking straight up from the squat, they wound through a small industrial district, passed a deserted Greyhound service depot, and walked up Water Avenue, where there was a strip of beat-up houses. At the top of Water Avenue was the Front Avenue overpass that broke up the neighborhood. That's where Nelson and his street family would camp eleven years later. It was only a short walk from Checkpoint Charlie.

Another group of street kids camped nearby, under the Arthur Street ramp, where a long series of shallow caves had been tunneled. The homeless squatters there had set up the caves as houses, draped with tapestries and outfitted with camping stoves.

The lower Lair Hill neighborhood was home at the time to an eclectic community of artists, writers, and musicians, the kind of people who didn't mind living in the middle of an industrial zone. It was a cheap place to live, and if a few bums camped out under the overpasses, no one much cared.

The street kids injected a new note to the neighborhood. Nelson and his group stalked the area, panhandling. They walked in flapping long leather coats and Mohawks, carrying wooden staffs and knives at their belts, materializing suddenly in the 7-11 store on First and Arthur or roaming down deserted industrial streets in large packs to

accost strangers walking alone. One mild summer day, they carried a
March of Dimes placard. Where the quarters had been there were
only empty slots. They approached people they passed, asking for
contributions. There was a forceful aggressiveness implicit in their
appeal. This was not begging.

On another occasion, they knocked on doors along Water Avenue.
One asked for money, while the rest of the kids huddled on the sidewalk, snickering. These were not the pathetic child prostitutes immortalized in the Seattle documentary *Streetwise*. These young
people were organized and healthy and strong. They didn't look like
victims at all.

2

During that summer of 1992, the street kids camping at Checkpoint Charlie did more than form a loose association. They organized themselves into a street family, possibly the first documented modern street youth family. By moving into their camp, Nelson joined their family. He was not a leader—not at first.

At first the group called itself the Predator Group. Other times, it was known as the Company. Finally, the simplest name stuck: they called themselves the Family. To cement their bonds, the street kids in the Family called each other "brother" and "sister." By joining the family, Nelson became a "brother" to Tinnin and the girls of the camp became his "sisters."

"If I say, 'you're my sister,' then you *are* my sister," Nelson explains, pointing a finger for emphasis, as if simply saying it made it true. And for him, it was true. In interviews, the youths of the Family often indicate their disrespect for each other—for instance, one girl called Nelson a "dumbass"—but they stayed together, if only out of a sense of commitment and obligation created by their familial identity. You can walk away from a friend. It's not so easy to walk away from a brother or sister.

While they shared some similarities with criminal cults like the Manson family, the Family camped at Checkpoint Charlie that summer was a new phenomenon. Unlike the Manson family, the street kids were not reliant on a single charismatic leader. When one street kid fell out, another could step into his or her place. Any young adult with a desire for power could become a leader. And any street kid willing to obey could become a brother or sister. It is important to note that Nelson did not create the Family. The street kids were identifying as a "family" at least a month before he ever came to town.

In 1992, the Family didn't call their leaders "mother" or "father." They used the term "commanders" instead, according to police interviews. The youths did refer to a street woman in the Square as Mama D, however, so the concept of calling a leader "mother" or "father" did exist.

Creating a mock family was a natural progression for the street kids camped out at Checkpoint Charlie. Already isolated in their camp and downtown, they had come to align with each other closely. In some ways, they were tapping into a tradition as old as time, from godparents to blood brothers to the Big Brother and Big Sister programs. Sociologists use the term "fictive kin" to describe such made-up relationships.

In the United States, the African American community has strongly influenced the concept of fictive kin. "Because slaves arrived without members of their original kinship networks," writes Pearl Stewart, a professor at Montclair State University, "it was necessary to 'create' those ties." Adults on plantations would informally adopt children separated from their parents. Men and women who didn't know each other came to address each other as "brother" and "sister." These patterns continued long after slavery was abolished. Informal adoption, for instance, continues today, with many African American children being raised by grandparents, uncles, aunts, and fellow church members.

By the 1970s, the concept of fictive kin had crossed over to white youth culture, where it became hip to call each other "brother" or "sister." Hippie communes, cults, and other alternative lifestyles also rejected traditional concepts of the family, which were also challenged by stepparent relationships, adoption, and blended families. The rise in divorce may have played a role as single parents explored finding "family" among friends.

John Hagan, the Canadian professor who has studied street families, points out that fictive families have long been part of our cultural fabric, from Fagan's band of young criminals in Charles Dickens' novel *Oliver Twist* to biker gangs. At different times, for different reasons, groups of individuals coalesce and become formal and organized. This happened in the 1990s with street kids such as the Family.

By the time James Nelson ran to the streets at the age of sixteen as a convicted sex offender, the concept of fictive kin had already infiltrated the street kid culture. This generic feeling of kinship would help establish a new society.

The Family taught Nelson all about living on the streets. The first lesson was the street kid code. Every brother and sister in the Family—every street kid, as a matter of fact—was expected to memorize the code. Street kid code is like an unwritten law book, constantly revisited and revised. One cannot live on the streets for more than a few days without hearing the code. It is passed down with great seriousness from one street kid to another.

Rule number one is No Snitching. Rule number two is Respect the Old-Timers. Rule number three is Never Talk to a Cop. There are more rules, too. It is against the rules to use someone's real name. It is against the rules to flirt with the girlfriend of a street brother. It is against the rules to talk about where people sleep. It is against the rules to steal from a brother or sister. There are so many rules in the code, as a matter of fact, it is hard to keep track of them all, and the rules have a way of changing depending on who is the offender and who is the enforcer.

Michael Tinnin, for instance, seemed to beat his girlfriend with impunity, while another street kid was severely punished for merely "using" his girlfriend. The code is harsh and endless, fluid and yet inflexible, but one aspect of the code is consistent: the punishment for breaking rules can be severe. "It's a violent culture," Nelson explains. "It's got rules. You break them—you're through. Taxing is usually because you've wronged someone."

Taxing is the way the code is enforced. A tax can be a stolen backpack or a beating. For a minor code violation, like failing to respect an old-timer in the Square, a youth might be told to hand over all his belongings. For a major code violation, like talking to a cop, the tax might be a thrashing. But the absolute worst code violation is snitching. For snitching the tax is death.

Having so many harsh rules would seem contradictory in a society that prides itself on anarchism. But for the street kids, anarchy doesn't mean having no laws. It means making your own laws. "Street culture has its own government," explains Joshua Brown-Lenon, a future follower of Nelson, in 2003. "It has its own rules. Some of us say, screw the [real] laws. We'll fight for our own laws."

The code governs their romantic relationships as well. The street kids in the Family would become boyfriend and girlfriend for a few days or weeks, then move on to the next partner, until it seemed they were playing sexual duck-duck-goose. But as rapid-fire as their romances were, the Family members expected each other to playact by the traditional rules of marriage. The Family did not approve of homosexuality or any other nontraditional couplings.

A girl called Angel was one of these brief flings for Nelson. She was a fifteen-year-old runaway and one of his sisters in the Family.

She had shaved the sides of her head in the Mohawk that identified her as part of the Family. Nelson didn't think she had earned the street name Angel yet, so he referred to her as Black Angel because of her bad childhood. It was romantic: the Highlander and the Black Angel.

In the Square, Nelson hooked his long dog chain to a collar around his girlfriend's neck and led her around. She followed obediently, like a puppy. Later, she explained the chain to police detectives. "It was kinda like ownership, like you're mine," she said.

Nelson liked to boast to Angel about how dangerous he was. According to police interviews, she remembered his saying he killed baby animals and liked sacrifices. Dying meant new life forever, he said. He told her that he was looking for the Hades key to open up the dimension world. He was on the quest from hell to find his black book of the dead. He referred to Satan as his father. She thought, okay, *whatever*. Nelson had a special name for his dad Satan that was like a mumble. Angel couldn't understand *what* he was saying.

In the Square, Nelson was given a dagger by a youth who was staying at the Outside In agency and didn't want it anymore, according to police records. Nelson tucked that dagger with another one into scabbards on his belt. The daggers had five-inch blades. Nelson named one dagger the Hades Key. He scratched the name into the handle. The other dagger he called the Problem Solver. Sometimes he called it the Problem Maker, depending on his mood.

At some point, the old-timer called Mama D supposedly confiscated these daggers from Nelson as a punishment for some slight. He got one dagger back. His girlfriend told police the knife was a piece of crap. It was sharp, but nothing much beyond that.

Two older men, Grant Charboneau and Gregory Paul Wilson, appeared in the Square that summer. Neither was homeless. Instead, they were part of an important and largely unrecognized aspect of street kid culture: slightly older men who hang around the youths, trying to impress them, bed them, and, in general, prey upon them.

Charboneau was twenty, a pale-faced young man with a scraggly beard who, until recently, had lived with his grandmother in St. Johns, a working-class neighborhood in North Portland. He owned a truck, a shiny red 1989 Ford pickup with a stereo system and a flatbed in the back. He hung out on the sidewalk outside the Greenhouse shelter that summer, trying to impress the homeless youths who stayed there, according to local reporter Mike Magrath.

Grant carried a staff, just like Tinnin, only Grant's staff was made out of a three-foot piece of steel rod, about an inch around, which he had sharpened to a point. He called this sharp metal rod his "sword" at times. Grant held his sword while he talked to the street kids.

A psychologist would later describe Grant as having a personality disorder that allowed him to "float into an illusory world." He fancied himself a cowboy or a movie tough guy. Sometimes he wore a white Stetson. Sometimes he wore a black one. On the streets, he bragged that he knew martial arts. Not only that, he had had commando training. He talked about "eliminating" people. He said he was a secret agent on a secret mission. He had secret plans and secret clearance. He told the street youths he was running a special operation, a very secret mission for the Organization.

Just what was the Organization? What was this mission? No one seemed to know, and more importantly, no one cared to ask.

Talking about all the wild claims, Nelson shrugs. "People make shit up." He explains why. "It's all a status thing. You build your rep so no one else will challenge you." By claiming he was a top-secret military operative, Grant was indirectly challenging the other youths to dispute him. If they did, a fight would be on, and few wanted to tangle with a man carrying a sharpened metal rod. But by accepting his wild statements, the street kids allowed Grant to take a dominant role. The more preposterous claims they allowed to pass, the more they became his passive, unquestioning followers. Through such lies, the males of the Square jockeyed for power, and through such silences, the rest of the street kids supported and encouraged their fabrications.

It's unclear how much the street kids really believed each other. Later, some of the kids would say they never did believe Nelson when he said he had escaped from Alcatraz prison, which had closed thirteen years before he was born. In fact, they said they hadn't believed anything the big-mouthed boy said. But at the time, no one directly disputed him either. It was more fun to let him talk, and besides, if they called Nelson on his fibs, then all bets were off, and all of their own lies might be exposed. And so, the house of cards was built.

The outrageous claims represented an important shift in the street kid culture. In the past, homeless youths often did fib, usually to protect themselves from present hurts—a child prostitute, for instance, might say he was really an aspiring actor—but few maintained an ongoing imaginary identity as a military spy or an immortal warrior unless they were mentally ill or prepared to be laughed off the streets. Through their fantasy role-playing, these street kids sent the culture spinning in an entirely new direction. As truth took a backseat to fiction, the question became, Where would the fantasies end?

Nelson was smitten with Grant, a man who was everything he wanted to be: a secret agent, a leader who commanded respect among the street kids of the Family. "He told me he was one of the 101st Airborne Rangers," Nelson says. On the streets, Grant called himself the XO. This was short for executive officer for the mysterious Organization. His second in command, the CO, the commanding officer for his secret organization was his friend Gregory Paul Wilson.

Wilson was an anomaly in the street kid culture, and not just because he was thirty. He was a dark-skinned black man. His relatives couldn't figure out *what* he was doing hanging out in the Square with a bunch of white street kids. "The boy's a fool," one said. They couldn't understand why he would hang around that "crazy white son-of-a-bitch" Grant.

The overwhelming majority of street youths are white. This was true in 1992 and remains true today. Only 6 percent of street youths in Portland shelters are black, according to a 2002 shelter count. "Practically all the kids in the street culture here are white," says Marni Finkelstein, an anthropologist who spent two years studying the street kids of Tompkins Square in New York City. Finkelstein published the results of her study in her 2005 book *With No Direction Home: Homeless Youth on the Road and in the Streets.*

Considering that minorities are overrepresented in every other homeless category, from families with children to older adults, the lack of racial diversity among street kids is remarkable. Finkelstein points out that few African American teenagers are into punk music, anarchistic politics, or Dungeons and Dragons–style games. Black males also feel uncomfortable hitchhiking, which is the primary means of street youth transportation. When minorities do appear in the culture, they tend to be biracial females. Very few dark-skinned black women call themselves street kids.

Portland State University black studies professor Darrell Millner suggests there are other, deeper reasons for the segregation. The same fictive kin concept that draws white teenagers together on the streets keeps African American youths tied to their communities. "When black youth have a problem with their parents," Millner says, "they go live with their grandparents. Or they live with their uncle or their aunt." White teenagers, on the other hand, are more likely to strike out on their own. "Going out on your own is a feature of the domi-

nant culture," Millner says. "It's a cultural legacy that whites participate in more."

In many cities, like Portland and Seattle, homeless youth agencies
are located where the white street kids cluster, not where the bulk of
minority homeless youths reside, which is within their own neighborhoods. The system has evolved to assist the runaway white youth
who hits the streets, not the genuinely homeless black teenager who
stays trapped in the poverty of his neighborhood.

Gregory Wilson, as a black man, appeared to be drawn to the
street culture for the same reasons as the younger white kids: he liked
to play fantasy games. With his muscular physique, baggy pants
worn military trooper style over high tops, and his perfectly trimmed
mustache, Wilson looked the part he claimed to be: a secret military
agent. At times, he said he was a Navy Seal. He flashed around a military identification card, though the youths said they didn't catch the
name on it.

As the CO of the mysterious Organization, Wilson had top-secret
conversations on the streets with his XO and friend, Grant. He
talked in a low, slippery voice that earned him his other street name,
Whisper.

The two older men hung around the Square during the summer of
1992, telling tall tale after tall tale to impress the street kids of the
Family. They didn't follow the street kids back down to their camp at
Checkpoint Charlie to sleep at night. They didn't need to. Grant already had his own place, his father's home in North Portland.

3

James Nelson can't be blamed for starting the killings in his first street family. As the XO of the mysterious Organization and a leader in the Square, Grant Charboneau had orchestrated their first murder over a month before Nelson ever set foot in town.

The murder plan was hatched after a boy named Leon Michael Stanton joined the Family that spring, about two months before Nelson arrived in Portland. Until he met the Family, Leon was a high school student at Columbia River High School across the Columbia River from Portland, in Vancouver, Washington. He was a skinny, gangling boy with perfect white teeth.

In April 1992, Leon was hanging out in Pier Park in North Portland when he met Grant, who lived nearby. The young teenager and the twenty-year-old man hit it off. Leon appeared to idolize Grant, going on long drives with him in the red truck. Grant may have taken Leon to hang out in the Square, and Leon was introduced to the street kids of the Family.

Leon tried to impress the kids of the Family by bragging about all the drugs he had supposedly done. He said he had done so much acid he was on "perma fry." The other teenagers seemed less than impressed. They called the skinny boy Fred, a street name as inconsequential as Leon appeared. Like others in the Family, Leon shaved the sides of his head into a Mohawk, keeping the limp brown hair on top tied in a ponytail. He wore khaki shorts and high-top black sneakers. On one bony knee was a circle-A anarchy tattoo. He was not an imposing boy. He looked his age, which was only fifteen.

About a week or two after they met, in late April 1992, Grant took Leon driving past his father's house. Harold Charboneau was just forty-two and a popular figure in the St. Johns neighborhood. Everyone called him Hal. He was a self-sufficient man, a proud military veteran with a modest ranch home. Though he was a double amputee, Hal didn't let the lack of legs keep him from getting around. Every day he pushed his wheelchair down to the neighborhood restaurant, waving at everyone in his working-class community along Lombard Avenue. Hal was a heavy drinker and an even heavier smoker. The walls of his tiny home were stained a rich, dark yellow from nicotine.

Grant was not close to his father. Apparently, the two had been estranged for some years. Grant complained about Hal to the youths in the Family, claiming, for instance, that his father had tried to drown him when he was two.

Idling the red truck at the curb outside his father's ranch house, Grant told his new friend Leon a sad story. He said that he had tried to reach out and have a relationship with his father, but that Hal had snubbed him. "I made two attempts to try to get some relationship going with him," Grant recalled telling Leon, "and he made it quite obvious that he was happy the way things were."

Leon responded with anger. "I ought to mug him. He'd been an easy target," Leon commented, according to Grant.

"You might just wind up getting knocked on your ass," Grant said. "You push yourself in a wheelchair for twenty-five years, you're going to have some thick arms."

The two looked over the ranch home with the tan siding and small porch. A simple poured slab of concrete served as a wheelchair ramp. A set of aluminum windows looked over a few spindly rose bushes, and two plastic newspaper cylinders dangled by the door, one for the defunct *Oregon Journal.*

When they left, Grant made a comment: "When my dad dies, the house will probably be mine." Leon understood.

Soon after their conversation, on May 1, 1992, Leon Stanton, carrying a buffalo skinner knife—a large, razor-sharp knife used to skin hides—crawled in through a bathroom window in Hal Charboneau's house. He had a friend with him. They crept down a narrow hallway covered with worn tan carpet. Three bedrooms were in the back, all off the hallway. Hal lay sleeping in the first bedroom, his wheelchair parked next to the bed.

According to court records, Leon stabbed Hal with the skinning knife while the man lay in bed. Blood sprayed on the walls. Afterwards, Leon poked around in the fridge, looking for beer and food.

Leon went back to see if Hal was dead and discovered that he was still alive, soaking in a pool of blood. Leon began stabbing him again, and Hal sat up in bed and asked calmly, "Why are you doing this to me?" Leon put his hand over Hal's mouth, shoved him back down, and kept stabbing. He asked Hal how it felt, and Hal answered, "It feels so cold."

After Hal was dead, Leon rifled his wallet and found five bucks. He found a coin collection and took that. He stole a ring out of a drawer. On the way back out, he left a shoeprint in the tub.

———

Homicide detective Larry Findling of the Portland Police was assigned to work the murder of Hal Charboneau. He and a crime team spent two days in the house processing evidence, at one point climbing through the crawlspace to look for other victims and even digging up the backyard in a hunt for evidence, but nothing seemed to explain the murder.

It was natural for Detective Findling to look closely at Hal's son, Grant. "The first place we look is at family members," Detective Findling says, "because in most murders, it's someone they knew. I'd say 95 percent are killed by someone they know."

At first, Grant acted like he might cooperate. Detective Findling asked permission to take a pair of his shoes, so they could check them against the print in the tub. Grant obliged. Then, he hired a lawyer. Detective Findling says the lawyer called him directly and told him not to speak to his client anymore. Grant was done cooperating.

Within a few weeks of the murder, Grant moved into his father's house. Detective Findling didn't think Grant had a legal right to take the house; he simply moved in. Grant was the next of kin, and other family members didn't express much interest in the modest home, which would have fetched little on the real estate market at the time.

Grant invited Leon to move in as well. Apparently, moving in with the XO was Leon's payment for killing his father. Leon invited along his new girlfriend, a sixteen-year-old Family member named Skyler Dorsey, who was called Breeze. Skyler had a middle-class background and a father who was an attorney. She claimed to have had "consent" from her parents to live on the streets and planned to be legally emancipated. When she wasn't sleeping with Leon, she stayed down at the family squat, Checkpoint Charlie.

In the house, Leon got drunk, and he and Skyler had sex. Afterwards, the two teenagers lay together, and Leon confessed he had stabbed Hal. Skyler recalled asking her new boyfriend, "How could you kill someone?" Leon, she said, responded, "Have you ever killed anybody? It's a fascinating thing. I'm fascinated with it."

Skyler suspected that her boyfriend had committed the murder "because he looks up to Grant and thought he would score some cool points." She didn't seem to care too much, either way. She laughed about it later, suggesting maybe Leon stabbed Hal because he was "psycho."

Grant invited some of the other Family members to stay at the house at times, but not all the street kids were invited. A core group of perhaps five hung around the home. The rest continued to live at Checkpoint Charlie. Downtown, Grant gave away some of the coins from his father's collection to street kids in the Family, but he wore the ring that had been stolen. He kept his father's silver-dollar collection in a BB case under the front seat of his truck.

Detective Findling continued to investigate the murder, interviewing people who knew Grant. He had nothing to link Grant directly to the murder. The street kids who now hung around the house would not talk to the police.

At the house, Grant and the street youths lived mostly on popcorn. For variety they had garlic-powder popcorn, onion-powder popcorn, and plain old buttered popcorn. The house reeked of onion and garlic powder. A dog ran around, defecating on the carpet.

There was a small living room and a tiny kitchen. The street kids sprayed cleaner on the walls of the living room to take off the nicotine stains, but the yellow dripped down, leaving long, tear-shaped stains. The garage was snout style, opening directly into the driveway. It was crowded with old boxes and Hal's extra wheelchairs. The street kids didn't bother to get rid of the dead man's belongings. The medicine cabinet still held his prescriptions.

In his spare time—and being unemployed, he had plenty of spare time—Grant made weapons. He made a club out of a broomstick, with six-inch sharpened pieces of wood attached to the top. He wrapped rope around the handles of swords. He visited a local spy shop and hunted for secret devices. A slap glove (a glove with metal inserts or lead shot in the knuckles) showed up in the house. Grant built a beer-bottle bomb he called "Alfa Bravo," made of two Budweiser beer bottles taped together and filled with unknown chemicals. He boasted that the device could wipe out everything within thirty feet, according to police records. He kept the bomb under the couch where the youths sat, eating their popcorn and watching action movies. In the back of his truck, Grant kept another homemade "bomb." It consisted of more Budweiser beer bottles tied together.

Watching movies one night with some of the youths, Grant twirled a knife in his hands, which he called his pig sticker. He told the others his father had been murdered. He said that his father had testified against a drug dealer and that was probably why he was killed. He said he would kill whoever had done it.

No one bothered to wash the blood off the bedroom walls where Hal had been slaughtered. "It was really nasty," one of the girls later told the police. Leon slept in the blood-splattered room, according to one of his street sisters in the Family. After the murder, the group christened Leon with a new name, Blades, though they still sometimes called him Fred.

Nelson, arriving in town after the murder, was not immediately invited to the house. He joined the kids camping at Checkpoint Charlie. In the Square, Nelson observed Leon's close relationships with Grant, the XO of the Square. Nelson knew exactly whom to challenge for the role of second banana to the boss. He had no respect for Leon. "I could whup his ass any day of the week," he crowed.

The friend who had run away to Portland with Nelson decided he didn't like the scene. Nelson and this "family" he ran with would sit around and talk gibberish, he told police later, while the others would write down their interpretation. Lo and behold, the interpretations would match. Other times they would try to move objects with their minds.

The friend related one incident that he said had happened under the Steel Bridge. Nelson caught a pigeon and bit into it. Another Family member called Evil helped him clean up all the blood. After seeing that, Nelson's friend decided it was time to get out of town.

He returned to California on July 4, less than twenty days after he had arrived. Nelson decided to stay. He was having too much fun.

———

The Family called it "playing Rambo"—all the exciting games the kids played. That summer of 1992, it seemed, everything was perfect for play. The Square constantly replenished the Family with news of code violations that required taxing and punishment, and Grant and his friend Gregory Wilson were around to make sure the rules were enforced. No one seemed to know how these rumors got started. It didn't seem to matter. The point was the Rambo games.

On a hot day that July, word whipped around the Square that one of the leaders of the Family, a young man with the street name of Coaster, had kidnapped a mentally retarded girl and made her his sex slave. Until that day, everyone had seemed to like Coaster, and no one had thought his girlfriend was a sex slave. She had slept at Checkpoint Charlie, after all. She wasn't exactly a stranger to them. But the street kids of the Family were hungry for excitement, and the incendiary news of a street sister being made into a sex slave offered it. There was a storm of talk about Coaster, and everyone aired his faults.

The stories quickly built on each other, until finally Nelson was claiming that Coaster had raped and killed his sister four years before, according to police statements. That did it. The Family decided to "excommunicate" Coaster from their group. The Rambo game had begun.

Internal Family dynamics may explain why the group could turn so quickly against one of its own leaders. Nelson and Tinnin, both bombastic and power hungry, may have wanted a piece of Coaster's power. Getting Coaster out of the Family would let them move up the ranks and take more of a leadership role.

For Grant Charboneau, the Rambo game against Coaster fit his fantasy military persona, which the street kids who worshiped him had given the stamp of credibility. Grant soon announced a "rescue mission" to save the so-called sex slave. Late that night, two men, one white, one black, crept through Checkpoint Charlie. The white man was dressed in a full military combat suit and carried a three-foot sharpened metal staff. The black man carried a bottle and knife.

Coaster had apparently heard of the rescue mission and had already vacated the camp. In what may have been a case of mistaken identity, the two commandos attacked a homeless couple sleeping in another camp. They stabbed the man in the back and swung the metal staff at his head, crushing his throat. The homeless man stumbled his way to a hospital. An emergency tracheotomy saved his life.

Inside the Family, some of the kids talked openly that Grant and Gregory Wilson were the attackers. According to Skyler, Leon's girlfriend, Grant hit the innocent homeless man with his "sword" because the man supposedly "jumped him."

Coaster was eventually sighted on the freeway, trying to hitch a ride out of town. Some of the Family went to fetch him and forced him back to Checkpoint Charlie for his taxing. The Family gathered around Coaster in a circle at the camp and attacked. The men held Coaster's arms so the women of the family could punch and kick him. The beating was severe.

After the beating, Coaster left town for California and was not heard from again. Police were unable to locate him. With Coaster gone, Nelson and Tinnin became two of the more dominant members of the Family, and they began to take it upon themselves to run "missions." The so-called sex slave, meanwhile, disappeared from the camp. Some said that her cousin or someone else came downtown to fetch her. It didn't matter because there was already another exciting game of Rambo to play.

This time the Rambo game involved Nelson's girlfriend. The fifteen-year-old runaway called Angel claimed she had been raped down at the camp around July 18. Exactly who raped her was not clear.

Nelson and Tinnin, the Black Panther, took charge of looking for revenge, and they stomped off to canvass the camps along the river. They didn't find the right guys, so they raided another homeless camp instead. They taxed the camp bags of clothes, makeup, and what was said to be a Walkman case full of drugs. Stories about the amount and kind of drugs they had stolen quickly changed. At first, it was a Walkman case full of cocaine. Then, it was a kilo of cocaine. Then, it was two kilos of cocaine. Pretty soon it was a kilo of heroin. Then, it was two kilos of heroin.

Unfortunately, the raided camp belonged to a homeless Mexican man. The Family appeared terrified of Mexicans, and now the talk of the Square was that the Mexicans would exact revenge. All day long the Family buzzed with worry. The Mexicans were coming. The Mexicans were coming with their friends. The Mexicans were going to show up with guns.

The next evening, the Mexican transient whose belongings were stolen did show up at Checkpoint Charlie, according to interviews with family members. He and a few friends stood down the beach, yelling. They wanted his clothes back. The Family freaked out, with the brothers and sisters running back and forth through the camp. Finally, the Mexican man and his friends gave up and left.

Now the Family was overjoyed. They thought that the Mexicans had left because the Family had protected their camp so well with the barbed wire holes. They built a huge bonfire that night on the beach to celebrate.

A new girl from Olympia, Washington, crouched by the fire. She had her mother's permission, she said, to live on the streets, and it was true that her mother let her come and go, giving her money when she showed up at home. The Family christened her Autumn. She was only sixteen, and she was pregnant.

Nelson sat by the fire and channeled demons for the new girl. He closed his eyes and put his ring finger and thumb together and meditated for a moment. Then, he opened his eyes and spoke in a deep voice. The voice said that hell was hot, and Satan was strong, but Highlander was even more powerful than Satan. Nelson kept talking about some Necco thing, the girl said. She said later that it was "really stupid, actually."

Still, the Rambo games were intensely exciting to the Family. One of the girls later explained to detectives that the games were just "like playing GI Joe with real action figures." The Rambo games brought excitement and purpose to long summer days. The street kids of the Family didn't go to school. They didn't work, play sports, have hobbies, or engage in any of the other activities that occupy most teenagers. They had little or no contact with their real families or other friends. They were isolated in their own world with very little to occupy their time.

Every family needs to feel a commonality, and without the bonds of blood, marriage, or adoption, the brothers and sisters of the Family used the Rambo games as the glue to hold them together. The Rambo games gave meaning to their lives and provided them with the heady sensation of living without any limits. There was no telling where a Rambo game might lead.

Members of the Family had already committed one murder, with the stabbing of Hal Charboneau, and no one had been caught or punished. They had beaten Coaster and defied the Mexicans. The mood in the camp was sharp and joyous, and the Family was primed for something even more exciting.

4

Only days after the Rambo game with the Mexicans, Nelson was in the Square when he received word that another kid was being excommunicated from the streets. This time it was a girl everyone knew as Misty Largo.

Nobody was quite sure how long Misty had been around. She could have been in Portland anywhere from six to twelve months before she was killed. What everybody knew was how much they all hated her. Misty, they said, was fat, ugly, and had a big mouth.

Her real name was Michelle Woodall, and she had arrived from Flagstaff, Arizona, where her family had filed a runaway report. When she turned eighteen, the report no longer mattered. Michelle had only sporadic contact with a brother back in Arizona, according to court records. She was heavyset, with a rose tattoo on her ankle and the fair, reddish skin of a natural redhead. Her orange hair was cut short and waved off her face. To the other kids, it looked like a boy's haircut. It was not a cool style. Michelle was not invited to shave her head in the Family Mohawk. She was not, in fact, invited to join the Family.

Michelle wasn't welcome in Checkpoint Charlie, either, so she stayed at the Greenhouse. She graduated from their high school program and attended their prom for homeless youths. At the graduation, she wore a borrowed black dress with a heavy white collar. The staff took a graduation photograph of Michelle, with her plump, red arms held stiffly and a fake red rose pinned to her lapel. She had put on makeup, too much aqua green around her blue eyes, and fake pearl earrings. Her skin was shiny. It was a sweet, nervous, sad picture.

Her age fluctuated according to the person she wanted to impress, and Michelle always wanted to impress somebody. One day she would say she was seventeen. The next day she was twenty. She flirted with the men of the Family, which angered their girlfriends. She seemed to have no respect for the street kid code. Her efforts to get attention landed her in trouble again and again. Everyone in the Square, it seemed, had a reason to hate the girl they called Misty. The girls of the Family said Misty had nasty diseases from sleeping with so many men. They gossiped that the men of the Family were afraid to sleep with her, though some of the men did. They said she was "yucky" and a "slut."

On the streets, Michelle's only friend had been Coaster. It was said that Coaster had protected Michelle and defended her. Now that he was gone, Michelle was suddenly vulnerable. She had no idea how vulnerable.

The Rambo game started in the morning. Gregory Wilson, the black commander called Whisper and the CO, allegedly had taken Michelle to bed. This was according to Grant, who later told police Wilson was trying to get information out of Michelle about other street kids by having sex with her. The two slept together on or about July 25.

Michelle thought the bedding was true love. She didn't know it was only "fornication," as Grant put it later to the police. In the morning, she found out she had been used. Angry, she stormed out of the house, saying she was going to tell on Grant and Gregory. She went downtown to the Square, where she began complaining loudly about Grant and the Family.

The word hit the Family that Michelle was talking about them, and the reaction was electric. Gossip exploded around the Square. Misty, it was said, was *telling people their real names*. She was *saying where they lived*. That was it. Misty, the Family declared, had broken the street kid code. She was a threat to the mission—what mission, no one still seemed to know, but Michelle was definitely a weak link.

The story circulated that Michelle had told the Mexicans about the stolen drugs and where the Family lived. As unlikely and backward as this sounded—most of the kids seemed to know that it was Nelson and Tinnin who had stolen the alleged drugs—the story was readily adopted as the new, unvarnished truth. "Then, Misty proceeded to get us in a fight with the Mexicans," Tinnin's girlfriend explained to police. "We had pretty much calmed it down, calmed the situation down to where they were not looking for us anymore. Misty gave them false information and led them directly to us."

In truth, the Family seemed to be looking for a target for a new Rambo game, and Michelle, because she had a "big mouth" and was a "bitch," was the perfect target. It wasn't enough to let her leave town. Her excommunication would require ritual. The order was passed down that the girl called Misty was wanted for interrogation.

Hearing the news that Misty had been excommunicated, Nelson was excited. Grant, he was told, was on his way downtown. The two of them could hunt down Michelle together for her "interrogation." Nelson was eager to help. It wasn't just the Family that took part in the hunt. The entire street kid community, it seemed, galvanized to look for Michelle. By nightfall, "just about everybody in the downtown community, all the street people, were looking for her," Grant told police.

Around midnight, Nelson and Grant caught Michelle walking down a street. They marched her by knifepoint down to Checkpoint Charlie, where Grant had parked his red truck on the graveled service road. No one stopped them on the way or called the police.

At Checkpoint Charlie, the street kids surrounded Michelle. It was dark, but the camp was lit by reflections of the bridge lights. Tinnin kicked Michelle in the stomach, knocking her down in the sand. She got up and took off running down the service road, desperately trying to escape, but she wasn't fast enough. Michelle was caught and led at knifepoint to Grant's truck. She was driven to the house in St. Johns.

At least seven members of the Family accompanied the group to the house for the interrogation. Nelson was not one of them. For whatever reason, he was not given the honor. Nelson stayed behind in the camp.

———

At the house, the Family wheeled one of Hal's wheelchairs into the living room and told Michelle to sit on her hands in it. She was told not to fight back or make a sound, according to police interviews. If she jerked her head or made any noise, she was told, she would get another slap. If she cried, they would all beat her with their fists at the same time.

Michelle was terrified, according to reports. One youth described her as having a "froggy" voice as she begged to be allowed to leave and return to Arizona. She told them she would leave town right away if they let her go. They told her to shut up.

The street kids of the Family did not seem touched by Michelle's open fear. Instead, they acted indifferent. Michelle had been excommunicated, and in their world, that meant she no longer had rights. She was a pariah. It is possible they were so deep in the Rambo

games that Michelle was just another one of the "GI Joe action figures." After all, they were preparing to interrogate Misty Largo, a fic-
tional street character, and not Michelle Woodall, a real person. And
the street kids that lined up that night to do the job were not their
real selves but fantasy figures with names like XO, Whisper, Giggles,
and Breeze. As one of the girls later explained to the police, "It was
like playing Dungeons and Dragons. . . . They were just really cruel
to her."

Forensic psychiatrist Dr. Keith Ablow, author of *Anatomy of a Psychiatric Illness,* writes in the *New York Times* that he sees an increasing number of teenagers displaying "a profound detachment from
self." With scripted speech, hollow behavior, and a lack of ethics,
these teenagers act "like actors playing themselves." Dr. Ablow believes such teenagers are suffering from an identity disorder with
roots in a "society that has drifted free from reality," influenced most
recently by reality television and online gaming.

Such adolescents and young adults see life as a game they are playing. In some instances, they become uncertain that they even exist,
either in a moral or physical sense. Extreme fads of piercing, cutting,
and tattooing may reflect a desperate effort on the part of these
teenagers to anchor themselves back in reality by inducing physical
pain to their bodies.

The youths of the Family displayed this sort of detachment as
they began torturing Michelle. The girls did most of the initial torture, calling her names as they slapped and punched her. "Hey, you
bitch," said Skyler. "You slutty bitch." She waved the weapon made
out of a broomstick at Michelle. "This would hurt if I hit you alongside the head," she threatened. "Why'd you lie? You're such a tramp."

As Skyler later admitted, "I was getting a power trip." In a setting of absolute permission and power, it was fun to torture the
traitor called Misty. The girls "taxed" Michelle her shirt, saying she

had stolen it from one of them. Michelle was left in her bra. Then, they taxed her bra as well, and Michelle was left in the wheelchair with her breasts hanging out. They gave her a towel to cover herself up because they said it made them sick just looking at her. The girls seemed intent not just on hurting Misty but on degrading her as a woman.

In the wheelchair, sitting on her hands with her breasts exposed, so terrified that one of the girls said she was too scared to cry, Michelle was beaten, punched, and slapped, both by hand and with the slap glove, for a period of hours. "It went on a long, long time," Detective Findling says, his eyes clouding. At one point the girls were afraid Michelle was making too much noise, so they wheeled her into a back bedroom for further torture.

There was some talk of the men getting sport from Michelle. "If you get a sport, it means you get somebody to give you a blow job," Grant explained to the police. He thought that Gregory Wilson might have gotten some sport from Michelle. Others denied it. Michelle was left alone in the room with some of the men of the family, but sexual abuse was never proven. "They were laughing and giggling, ho-ho-ho," said one of the girls.

For much of that long night, the Family beat Michelle. The torture worked up their appetites, and so they took a popcorn break. One of the men made bowls of popcorn for everyone. By the time the sun came up, everyone was exhausted. Michelle was bloody nosed, and her face was a welter of red marks. She slumped in the wheelchair. The Family decided to take a nap. Michelle was left in the wheelchair and told not to move. No one seemed worried that she would try to leave.

Michelle may have weighed the likelihood of being killed for trying to escape against the hope that the Family would let her go. They had let her friend Coaster leave town. Maybe they would let her leave too. Despite her brassy behavior, Michelle was, at heart, a passive young woman. She slept for a few hours that morning in the wheelchair with her chin slumped against her chest, according to the street kids.

After the Family woke up from their naps, Michelle was treated, in the words of one witness, "like a slave." They told her she had to do what they said, or she would be beaten. The girls gave her orders, calling her a bitch as they went. "Bitch, vacuum the floor," the woman called Giggles ordered Michelle, according to police interviews. "Bitch, do the dishes." The men, watching television, ignored the whole scene.

The dog left his droppings on the carpet, and one of the girls made Michelle pick up the feces with her bare hands. When chores were over, Michelle had to take a position on the couch, with her hands crossed over her bare breasts, her face turned up toward the ceiling so she couldn't make eye contact with her captors. She was still without a shirt, according to accounts by the street kids.

Around noon, Grant announced that he had to go downtown to "gather intel." He took a few of the Family members with him, including Skyler. She said the two of them had a conversation about killing Misty. "I asked Grant if they were gonna kill her, and he say yes, and he said, 'Do you want to stay?' And I said, 'No, I don't want to be there.' So I went downtown." Grant dropped Skyler off at Checkpoint Charlie. While he was there, he picked up her boyfriend, Leon, who was hanging around the camp, and returned to the house.

Back at the house, the Family members present included Leon Stanton, Grant Charboneau, Gregory Wilson, and a few others, according to police interviews at the time.

Killing the traitor called Misty was more difficult than they expected. First, the street family tied Michelle firmly to the wheelchair using heavy cords so she couldn't try to escape. They decided to poison her. They made her eat salty popcorn so she would be thirsty. Then, they ground up a nitroglycerin pill they found in Hal's medicine cabinet and dissolved it in water. They thought the medicine would give her a heart attack. Michelle drank the water as ordered. "If you have a brain in your head, you're gonna die," one of the Family members allegedly threatened her as she drank. They waited, but Michelle didn't have the desired heart attack.

One youth went into the kitchen and found a big trash bag. He returned and put the bag over Michelle's head. They tightened the bag around her neck, trying to cut off all the air, but still, Michelle wouldn't die. "At this time, she's kind dazed," Grant explained. Frustrated, they took a long piece of speaker wire from a spool near the stereo and took turns choking her with the wire. They pushed their feet on her body for extra leverage while they pulled the wire tight around her neck.

The Family members would occasionally check to see if she was still breathing, listen to her heart, and touch her skin to see if it was getting cold. They could see her chest moving, the life staying firm inside her. One youth punched her in the throat and on the sternum. Finally, she "gurgled and choked and stopped breathing," according to court records.

The Rambo game continued as the group cleaned up after the murder. The street kids bragged that their commanders "were both in the military so they know how to sanitize things," as one girl said. Baby powder was sprinkled over the house. The body was wiped down with a wet washcloth "to wipe off any possible fingerprints or skin fibers."

At some point, the body may have been disfigured. Leon "gouged" at her flesh with a knife here and there, slicing her up, according to Grant. He "did the eye socket thing" and gouged out her eyes, and cut a hole in her belly. Grant, the XO, allegedly took a splitting maul and whacked Michelle in the head, cracking her skull open, or so he told other Family members. Allegedly, he later boasted that her head "popped like a watermelon." The watermelon story became popular on the streets and was repeated by other street kids.

The corpse was wrapped in a piece of plastic and loaded into the back of the red truck. Grant and Leon drove it to a railroad track across the river in lower industrial Northwest Portland, where an expanse of gravel led to a culvert pipe under a railroad. The two stuffed the body inside the concrete drainage pipe and went back to the house, where they cleaned up and did a load of laundry.

———

Even after participating in a horribly cruel, protracted, bloody murder, none of the Family members seemed repulsed by what they had done. One of the girls told another sister that she was "kinda grossed out" when they took the plastic bag off Michelle's head, but that was as deep as their reactions ran. Asked if the other street kids in the Family had murdered Michelle because they were afraid of disobeying their leaders, one of the girls answered succinctly: "No, they were enjoying it too much."

Instead, they joked about their crimes. "There's a lot of sarcasm about it," Skyler said later to the police, "because . . . oh, for me, I was just kind of sarcastic about it for myself and to please other people." Like an actor playing herself, Skyler was more concerned about what the other family members thought of her performance than with the moral gravity of what she had done.

The Family was also part of a larger street kid culture that was forming into a society, and this new society condoned what they had done. On the streets, other kids seemed to know about the murder. They agreed the woman called Misty had brought it on herself by breaking code. "Basically Misty died because of some of the things she was saying. She had too big a mouth and she was telling people where Grant lived," Skyler summed it up.

A month later, a staff worker at the Greenhouse shelter realized she hadn't seen Michelle Woodall, known to them as Misty Largo, for some time. Misty had disappeared after graduating from their high school program. But street kids disappear all the time, and the shelters can't call the police on every one that turns up missing.

No missing person report was filed. There would be no awareness that Michelle Woodall was gone or dead at all, not for the outside world at least. It was almost as if she had never existed.

5

If he was feeling left out of all the killing, Nelson soon had his chance to make up for lost time. The day after Michelle's murder, Grant drove his truck down to Checkpoint Charlie to have a private talk with Nelson. Nelson had proven his loyalty and eagerness by helping kidnap and walk Michelle through downtown at knifepoint. Now XO had a mission especially for him.

Grant wanted to talk about Leon Stanton. He was worried that Leon was going to squeal about his involvement in the murder of Michelle. There was no reason to believe Leon would snitch. He had been involved in two murders, first Grant's father's and now Michelle's. He would have no reason to incriminate himself.

The real motive for targeting Leon came with Nelson, who had never liked the boy called Fred and Blades. Killing Leon would give Nelson street credentials and make him an old-timer, a street youth worthy of respect. Nelson may have been jealous of Leon, too, because he had actually done what Nelson had only boasted about doing: murder someone. Nelson was finally getting a chance to make his bragging true.

Grant fed Nelson's fire. "He's gonna run around and tell everybody about Misty," Grant said, according to Nelson. "I told him he must be crazy. He goes 'No, we'll be bad asses.' He wasn't gonna listen to me."

Nelson replied, "Then, it's settled. I'll kill him."

"Okay," said Grant.

According to Grant, Nelson asked him how he should kill Leon. "I'm not going give you a damn blueprint," Grant snapped.

The Family turned as easily against Leon as they had against Coaster and Michelle. None of the youths seemed concerned they could be next. There was a sense that summer that none of it was real, that none of *them* could ever die. Skyler Dorsey, for instance, appeared completely unworried that she could be killed. Asked why she stayed with the Family even after the murders, the middle-class girl explained, "I didn't really have any place to go except back home, and I didn't really feel threatened."

The word passed around the Square that day: Leon was a "security risk." The Family bought this story as easily as they had bought the story that Misty had led the Mexicans against them, and they reacted with predictable outrage. Tinnin stomped around the Square, saying, "I want Leon here, tomorrow, at noon. I'm going to kick his ass all over this Square," according to police records.

That night, Leon showed up at Checkpoint Charlie, spreading his blankets in the bushes to sleep with the rest of the Family. He had heard he was targeted for excommunication, and he was nervous. Nelson crouched down next to him, and the two had a quiet conversation. Leon appealed to Nelson for mercy. "Highlander, you didn't expect *me* to turn on the Company," he said. Nelson was evasive. He played both sides of the fence. "I don't think Whisper [Gregory Wilson] is really a Navy Seal," Nelson said, according to his statements to police. "He doesn't sound like he knows what the fuck he is talking about. I know he's probably killed a few people, but . . ."

Leon talked to one of his street sisters. "I have a bad feeling that they're gonna do something to me," he said. He decided he would be safer at the house, according to court records, so he rolled up his blankets, packed all his gear, and headed there to sleep. He planned to run to Seattle the next day.

The next day was too late. That morning, Grant told Leon he was needed in a fight downtown. It was July 28, 1992, just two days after Michelle's murder. Leon was dressed in a black Metallica shirt, khaki shorts, and black high-top sneakers. Grant took him down to the squat. In the path at Checkpoint Charlie, Tinnin was waiting, with his wooden staff in his hands, the human hair fluttering in the breeze.

Tinnin began to beat Leon with the staff. He broke his finger and cut his face. He struck Leon in the ribs three times, and Leon fell to the ground. Leon curled in a ball and cried as Tinnin struck him with the wooden staff over and over again.

"That's enough," a girl watching said nervously, according to police reports.

"He deserved it," another replied.

After the beating, Grant announced he and Tinnin were leaving. But first, he gave Nelson orders to kill Leon. Nelson was thrilled. It was just like being in the military, he said.

Only a few Family members were left at the camp: Nelson, Leon, and Leon's girlfriend, Skyler. It was time to "pick off the bone," or kill someone who had already been worked over, as Nelson explained. Nelson pulled his dagger out of his sheath.

He later recalled the conversation for police. "Do you know what XO wants me to do?" Nelson asked Leon.

"Yeah. I know he wants you to douse me," Leon allegedly said. "But if you kill me, I'll go to hell."

"Tell them Highlander sent you," Nelson said and stabbed him.

Leon fell. Skyler rolled Leon on his back. She held his hands above his head so Nelson could stab him more easily.

On the ground, Leon begged and pleaded with his girlfriend. "I love you," he told Skyler. "Help me."

"Drop dead, Fred," Skyler replied.

Leon Stanton never spoke another word. Nelson stabbed him with the knife over and over again. "I stabbed him in various other pressure points throughout the chest and made sure he was dead," he told the police. At one point, Nelson took his dog chain and used it to strangle Leon, pressing and twisting into his neck, letting him have a little air, and then strangling him again. "He kept loosening it and giving him air and tightening it again," Skyler recalled. Leon stared at his girlfriend as he died. She ignored him because she was busy "rooting Highlander on," as she later explained.

When they were done there was another corpse. The Family had been responsible for three bodies in three months, with two of them in as many days, and Nelson had just committed his first murder. He had been in town for about a month.

Nelson grabbed handfuls of bloody grass out of the dirt and tried to burn it. He wrapped Leon in old plastic that was around the camp and strung wire around his body. He dragged the body into the brush and piled weeds and old Christmas trees on top to hide it.

The killing had made Nelson hungry. He told Skyler to keep an eye on Leon's body while he went downtown to get a bite to eat. At the Sisters of the Road café, he ate a big plate of spaghetti. He stopped at the Square on his way back. He had blood on his shirt. He told a girl there he had killed a Mexican.

By the time Nelson got back to the camp, it was evening. Other members of the Family had shown up and were swimming in the shallow area under the bridge. Leon's body was stiffening in the bushes. There was a pool of blood, fresh and very red, in the camp.

Late that night, Grant parked his truck on the service road. They used scrap wire to truss Leon's corpse to Tinnin's staff like a deer on a pole. A homeless man in the bushes watched. He later told police that when they dropped the body in the back of Grant's truck, it "spewed" blood. Nelson sat in the back of the truck with the body. "I bet you're wondering what that is?" a girl recalled him boasting. "That's a dead body, and we're going to bury it."

Skyler was also along for the ride. She remembered Nelson making jokes, like "Don't disturb my friend here, he's *dead* to the world," and "I wonder how Fred is doing in Seattle. I hear it's *dead* up there." Nelson slung his feet up on the corpse, using it as a footrest. "He was kind of regarding it as his trophy," Skyler said.

This time they buried the corpse in a North Portland industrial lot. The men of the Family were tired, it was late, and they dug a shallow grave. They untied Leon from the pole so Tinnin could have his magic runic staff back, now anointed with corpse juju, and dropped the body in the grave. They scooped the pale, sandy dirt back over the body, and Leon Stanton, age fifteen, rested under only a few scant inches of light brown soil, his face turned toward the ground.

Afterwards, they took Nelson to the house, where Skyler washed his bloody clothes and shoes. Nelson had just earned his invitation into the inner sanctum. Like Michelle Woodall, Leon just vanished, and no one seemed to care. None of the shelters appeared to notice, and no reports appear to have been filed.

———

If Grant was worried about someone squealing, it should have been Nelson, who seemed intent upon telling everyone he could about his first murder. "Do you remember Fred?" he asked one boy who was new to the Family and was hanging around Checkpoint Charlie. "We killed him," Nelson said. Nelson strutted down to the waterfront, where he told a group of street kids that he had killed not only Leon Stanton but also Michelle Woodall. In the Square, he told a girl he had killed Leon because of direct orders from his father, Satan.

At night, the Family built another roaring bonfire on the beach, and Nelson brayed, "That's another soul I collected." In front of the fire, he channeled a demon for Skyler. Now that Leon was dead, she and Nelson had decided to be lovers. Nelson closed his eyes and began talking in a low, deep voice. He petted Skyler's hair and asked what it was, as though he had never felt hair before. Then, he opened his eyes and asked her what had happened.

Skyler thought it was stupid, but she wore his chain anyhow, just like a letterman's jacket. It was the same chain Nelson had used to choke her boyfriend.

Over a week passed. At Checkpoint Charlie, the brothers and sisters slept near the bloodstained ground where Leon was killed. At the Square, they hung out, passing the time of day. With his nemesis out of the way and a murder under his belt, Nelson assumed an alpha role in the Family, issuing commands to the other youths. He would hide his knife far away in the bushes and then make one of the pregnant girls go out searching for it. When she got back, he would invent a new errand for her to run. He was full of himself about the murder and bragged about it constantly, until the other street kids grew irritated and found excuses to stay away from him.

When Nelson began telling the other street kids in the Square he had written a death list of people he wanted to kill, however, they responded with alacrity. The word was he and Tinnin were going to kill everyone who knew about the murders. This caused immediate panic in the Family, and some of the street kids seemed to awaken to the possibility that they, too, could be next.

On August 6, 1992, five of the lower-ranking members of the Family, convinced they were on Nelson's death list, decided to break code. The punishment for snitching was death, but they were worried enough to risk the punishment. They snuck down to the Central Precinct, where they were informed that Detective Findling and the other homicide detectives were out. The receptionist told the street kids they could come back later. They refused to leave. They waited until the homicide detectives came back.

The detectives heard an implausible story of a "street family" and secret missions and murders. There was no record of any "Misty" or "Fred" that had gone missing, and the street kids didn't even seem to know the real names of the victims or their killers. It was all Highlander this, XO that, and Black Panther this.

The street kids insisted they could prove their story. One led the detectives to where Leon's body was buried in the industrial lot outside of North Portland. In his shallow, sunken grave, Leon's body was already badly decomposed. The medical examiner who autopsied Leon Stanton counted eleven stab wounds, five of them perforating the heart.

Over the next few days, Nelson heard the cops were looking for him. He was finally caught in the Square. When he emptied his pockets, there was a Greyhound bus ticket and a pamphlet for the Society for Creative Anachronism. "There's a lot of shit going on," Nelson told the officer right off the bat. He insisted his name was Highlander. He even signed his waiver of constitutional rights with the name, in cursive, *Highlander*. He also claimed to be called the Shadow Master.

This Highlander was eager to talk, pointing the finger at everyone else. He claimed he had nothing to do with the murders. He said he had watched Leon get beaten, but he claimed he had not participated in any attack. In an interview room, Detective Findling let him ramble. His impression of Nelson was he was "not very bright" and "had no conscience whatsoever."

Later that afternoon, Detective Findling took Nelson down to Checkpoint Charlie, where the brazen young man narrated his fanciful version of events as the police filmed him with a video camera.

With his self-conscious swagger, Nelson showed the detectives where the Family kept their belongings. The police took a pair of bloody jeans, a piece of chain, and blood samples from the camp.

Helping the police with their investigation was the closest Nelson would ever come to real secret-agent operations, and he was excited. As the day wore on, he told Detective Findling he would wear a wire into the house in St. Johns to record Grant and the others. That evening, police equipped Nelson with a wire and sent him into the house. Detective Findling camped out in a neighbor's house across the street, watching through the curtains and listening to his radio. When he heard Nelson was coming out, he ran outside to arrest Grant. In the tense minutes that followed, Nelson strolled nonchalantly down the street, walking away from police custody, as Findling recalls with a chuckle. Nelson was two blocks away when police realized he was gone. They quickly brought him in.

In his interviews, Grant called the detectives "sir" and eventually admitted to his role in the murders. He led the police to where he had stuffed Michelle Woodall's body in the concrete culvert pipe. She was badly decomposed from the summer heat and covered with maggots.

Michael Tinnin, the Black Panther, admitted in his police interviews that he really didn't have a twin. There was no Snow Leopard after all. There was also no bionic eye. After his arrest, police got a call from a shelter staff worker. She remembered how Tinnin had threatened a girl with a large hunting knife right outside their doors. This had happened, she estimated, a few weeks before the murders. She had not called the police at the time.

Meanwhile, Nelson confessed to the murder of Leon Stanton. He insisted he had killed Leon because he was afraid of Grant. "I was afraid of XO. I was afraid XO would kill me," Nelson told Detective Findling. The detective didn't believe him. He thought Nelson had wanted to kill someone.

At one point in the interview, Detective Findling almost pled with Nelson, trying to find some sign of remorse. "Now look inside your heart now, alright?" he asked. "Look inside your heart and look inside your head. Is there any other reason than XO [Grant] telling you to kill him that you decided to kill him?"

"No," Nelson replied.

"You look for help, you run away," Detective Findling suggested hopefully.

"Yeah," Nelson replied without conviction.

Another detective in the room, Tom Nelson, persisted: "Isn't it true you go around and brag a lot about the thrill of killing?"

"No," Nelson replied coolly.

Detective Findling recalls how shocked Nelson was when he heard he was under arrest for the murder of Leon Stanton. Nelson apparently thought that since he had helped out the police by wearing the wire, he would not be charged with any crimes. "He thought that it was a wash," Findling laughs. At that point, Nelson may have realized he had been thoroughly finessed, first into helping the police with their investigation, then into confessing his own crimes.

Grant Charboneau was found guilty on three counts of murder for hiring Leon Stanton to kill his father, killing Michelle Woodall, and ordering the murder of Leon Stanton. Originally sentenced to death, his sentence was overturned, and he is now serving life without parole at the Oregon State Penitentiary. The once wispy young man bulked up in prison and now sports huge shoulder muscles. Gregory Paul Wilson, charged with the murder of Michelle Woodall, became one of the more complex criminal cases in Oregon history, with appeals, reversals, and overturned convictions. At this writing, he is still incarcerated, and his attorney is moving toward yet another trial. Michael Tinnin served a short sentence and was released.

Several members of the Family were never prosecuted, including Skyler Dorsey, who had participated in the torture of Michelle, held her boyfriend's hands while Nelson stabbed him to death, and gone on the burial party. Skyler was almost carefree in her police interviews, laughing and acting as if nothing untoward had happened. She could have been tried for kidnapping and assault and quite possibly for murder. Instead, she was not charged with anything. Detective Findling was not pleased with how the district attorney's office handled her case. "I believe she wasn't held fully responsible for her acts," he says.

Skyler was back in high school within a few months, bragging about how she had supposedly knifed Leon herself. According to other students at the school, she said, "I'm so glad he's dead. I'm glad I killed him." Police investigated the incident and forwarded it to the district attorney, but nothing came of the report.

According to a prosecutor involved in the case, Skyler ended up going to college and is presently doing well with her life. She apparently found a way to transition back into normal society. She may have been the only Family member to do so. Other teenagers involved in the Family have had rocky adulthoods, including some who have subsequently lost their own children to foster care, according to a district attorney.

Nelson pled guilty to murder and was sentenced to eleven years as an adult to be served in Oregon prisons. He testified at the sentencing for Grant, where he described in chilling detail how he killed Leon Stanton. While waiting to be transferred from the juvenile home to prison, Nelson allegedly attacked other inmates and the guards.

At the trial, Detective Findling sat with the group of detectives who had worked the case. They hoped out loud that after Nelson served his time, he would be returned to California because they felt sure he would kill again. "He's a cold little bastard," Findling says.

The murder spree of the Family generated only a brief flurry of media interest. The lurid nature of the murders led to local media speculation about Dungeons and Dragons, but within days the story faded.

The agencies that had served the street kids dismissed the Family as an aberration and defended the street kid culture as benign. "Given the manner in which society has left these kids to settle their own devices, it's surprising the number of murders is so low," a Greenhouse supporter told *PDXS* newspaper. He said the street kids "do a surprisingly good job of forming their own community."

Detective Findling feels differently. He points out there are few things more potentially dangerous than a group of teenagers running amok without adult supervision. Add in weapons, a taste for violent fantasy play, and a punitive street code, and you have a recipe for adolescent savagery. "You might as well pour gasoline on them and strike a match," Findling says.

6

Nelson went away to prison, but the street kid culture did not dry up and disappear. Instead, over the new few years, a nascent community rapidly became a national subculture.

In Portland, the first major street family came into being in 1998 with the Nihilistic Gutter Punks, or the NGP. The NGP made themselves a logo, which some members had tattooed on their bodies: an X with the letters "N," "G," and "P" in the upper three sprockets and the chaos star (a sun with arrows) underneath. At times they used two syringes crossing underneath a skull for the X. This was to signify methamphetamine use.

The NGP family soon claimed between seventy and a hundred members. The family grew too large to squat together, and smaller families began to splinter off the main group. One of the first splinter families was a local chapter of the Sick Boys, which was formed in late December 1998, according to local street kids.

According to a street youth named Travis Harramen, a member of the Portland Sick Boys, the family originated in Orange County, California. Sick Boys is the name of a British punk band, as well as the name of a well-covered punk song by Social Distortion. The lyrics go:

Sick-boy, in his faded blue jeans
Sick-boy, black leather jacket scene
Sick-boy, he's always in trouble
With the law don't ya' know . . .
Sick-boy, likes to get into fights
Sick-boy, he'll go drinkin'
With the boys all night.

The Sick Boys created their own logo: a sick-looking face with Xs for eyes and a stitch for a mouth. Sometimes they add a circle-A along one side, the international symbol for anarchy.

Other families rapidly appeared; including the 420s and the Portland Drunk Punks and even a group glorifying the murder of Michelle Woodall called the Fat Bitch Killers, whose members claimed to have murdered a "fat bitch in a wheelchair." Within a year, virtually all Portland-area street kids would claim to belong to one street family or another. Joining a family became a customary and expected part of living on the streets. The street kids also identified as Portland Street Kids, or PSK, in much the same way as a gang member might claim to be an Original Gangster but also a Crip or a Blood.

As the youths split into smaller factions, the families developed increasingly severe initiation rites. New members of the Sick Boys were beaten into the family and, at times, were told to inject eighty units (a large syringe) of methamphetamine into the neck, a shot that is now known as a Sick Boy. The female members of the Sick Boys were called Sick Bitches, and they had to commit assaults and robberies in order to earn the right to wear "Bitch Bangs," or the short fringe of hair that female street youths sometimes keep when they shave the rest of their hair off. If they wanted to tie objects in their Bitch Bangs, the Sick Bitches had to commit more assaults. The harsher the initiations, the more the street kids clamored to join, if only to prove how tough they were. One street kid was glowing after his initiation into a street family, despite the fact that he had a dislocated shoulder from the beating.

Until the arrival of the street families, Harramen says, most street kids had the simple common goal of "getting so drunk you puke on your shoes." The old street youth culture was built around getting drunk and getting laid. When fights broke out, the kids were usually too drunk to do much harm. Travis describes a sense of "unity" among the street kids, who were all enjoying drunken nihilism together. He believes two factors changed that drunken unity: methamphetamine and the street families. Travis went to prison himself in 2002 for blinding another street kid in an attack.

Perhaps as the inevitable result of the burgeoning families came what the street kids openly refer to as the 1999 "street wars." The street wars are virtually unknown outside the culture but had devastating impact on the street kids. "It got really, really bad, with fights and killings and attempted murders," Joshua Brown-Lenon, a Thantos Family member, says of the street wars. "Before the street wars, everyone was one big family," he claims.

Street family members disagree on what started the street wars. Harramen claims the wars began when a street father of a major family was accused of giving another youth a "hot shot," or a fatal shot of heroin. Mayhem broke out between the families. Travis says it got to the point where "[i]f someone came into your squat uninvited, you'd stomp them out. . . . No one could trust no one, so everyone naturally cliqued up to protect themselves. A lot of minor fights, brawls, robbings, and lots of dope wars—my dope is cleaner, mine is better, etc. This not only happened in Portland but also every place meth touched in the Pacific Northwest and the West."

Other cities experienced the same escalation of violence as street families spread. In Minneapolis, skirmishes between street families erupted in 1996, with groups attacking each other with boards and knives. "When we weren't battling with outside parties, the Crusties would turn on themselves attacking the weaker members of its dysfunctional tribe," wrote Sean Otero, a street youth called Frhate, who later died of an overdose. "Smaller, less aggressive kids and females were often victimized by the bigger meaner drunks. Rape was not uncommon, but the victims seldom knew who their attackers were because they would pass out from excessive alcohol use, and when they woke up realized they'd been violated."

In San Francisco, the growth of street families created a ganglike atmosphere. "I thought for a moment that I was part of this 'family,'" a former member of the Scum Fucks street family recalled, "until I realized I think for myself and have had better luck surviving on the street without a gang mentality that produces violence."

Where one street family existed other families mushroomed, if only for "protection" from the others, as Nelson frankly puts it. By the end of the 1990s, street families had appeared in most major cities and in many small towns as well. They were springing up all over America.

═══

Tempe, Arizona, a hot little desert town with a population of 158,000, is home to Arizona State University. In the 1990s, street families coalesced among the hundred or more street kids mingling on Mill Avenue alongside the university. The street kids liked Tempe for its warm, dry weather and the generosity of the local college students. Panhandling, they said, was especially lucrative.

In an extensive 1998 report for the *Phoenix New Times,* journalist David Holthouse followed a local street family called the Dank Krew, a play on the word *dank* (a kind of marijuana), as well as the smell of unwashed street youth. "Street kids in Tempe are almost all white, aged 14 to 26," he wrote. "A few grew up in the valley, the rest are from points across America. Most drink and smoke pot, and roughly half are junkies who picked up the needle once they were on the streets, not before. They call modern society 'Babylon.' A lot of them carry knives or bludgeons, and a few are dangerously violent."

Holthouse found that "violence is a near constant subtext among the street kids on Mill." The youths fought and made homophobic comments to each other. A favorite threat was to claim they would rape their victims anally so violently it would be "like throwing hot dogs down a hallway."

These were not peaceful, gentle, open-minded teenagers merely looking for a warm place to stay. They were angry, homophobic, and violent street criminals who had chosen their lifestyle. In one instance, the Dank Krew family attacked a man they concluded was a "faggot." As soon as one of the attackers was released from jail the next morning, he promptly got into another fight, breaking the victim's sunglasses into his face. This he described as "funny." He showed up to his meeting with Holthouse with blood on his shirt. "That's what happens when you fuck with the Dank Krew," he told Holthouse. "I get your blood on my shirt."

Bart W. Miles, a professor of social work at Wayne State University in Detroit, Michigan, spent time with another Tempe street family called the Scum of Tempe, for his study "Street Life on Mill." The Scum family went by the usual street names, like Seven, Forty, Tweety, and Cowboy. Every weekend, as in other cities, the Scum of Tempe gathered with other street kids for a large drum circle, where they pounded on drums, sang, chanted, and smoked marijuana. Miles saw the drum circle as more than just entertainment for the youths. He believed it was a "major form of homeless identity," allowing the street kids to socialize and introduce new members to the culture. While the Scum family claimed to be less violent than other street families, they talked with ease about taking disobedient members "down to the tracks" and beating them up. For them, the lingo was "taking them off the streets."

In their 1999 study of street families, Canadian professors John Hagan and Bill McCarthy found that youths in street families are far more criminal than other homeless kids. One out of four street family members in their study admitted to crimes that qualified as attempted murder, such as attacking another person with a weapon with the intent to kill. Hagan and McCarthy say the reason is what they call *tutelage*. The street family acts as a mentor program, training and encouraging the street kids into violence, even murder.

This happened in Denver, Colorado, when street families with names such as the No Sanity Left Kids, the Denver Drunk Punks, and the Old Skool Kings cropped up around the Sixteenth Street Mall in the late 1990s, particularly in Skyline Park. Lounging on benches stenciled with anarchist graffiti—Property Is Theft—the street kids talked about Karl Marx and George Orwell and bragged how they were hardcore.

At least four hundred hardcore street kids were living in Denver by 1999. Various assaults, rapes, and other crimes had been associated with them for years. But in the fall of 1999, there was a spate of murders so grisly they shocked even the local street community. Seven older homeless men were murdered. Two were decapitated.

At first, the assumption was that the murders were hate crimes against the homeless. But the investigation soon centered on a local street kid family involved in a turf battle with older transients over panhandling spots. The youths, who were mostly around age eighteen, went by the usual street names, such as Crazy, Little Chris, and Trip.

One of the family members explained that they had been angry with an older homeless man who had taken a prime panhandling spot. One night they found the transient sleeping on a steam grate in

Skyline Park. "There's that bitch," one yelled, according to court documents. They stomped the man "until his ribs turned to mush." Two weeks later, the street family lured another transient into the woods near Cherry Creek, beat him severely, and left him for dead.

Once in jail, one of the leaders sent threatening letters to another member. "Remember street rules," he warned. "Snitches are bitches that wind up in ditches with stitches. I live by that rule boyz and snitches aren't part of the family."

Despite the evidence, including confessions, some local agency workers seemed convinced that the youths were being railroaded. "These kids are good kids," one outreach worker told the press. "Not one of them wants to be out here." Homeless advocacy groups used the case as an example of "hate crimes" against the homeless. The *New York Times* cited the slayings in an article on hate crimes, depicting the killers as a "pack of young men picking on homeless people for thrills." No mention was made that the young men were street kids or involved in a street family.

The same response occurred in Boston in 2001, when a group of street kids murdered a woman hanging out in "the Pit" in Harvard Square, a block away from the famous university. The Pit is a low, sunken square with brick steps adjoining the subway station. Planned as a gathering place for musicians, it has become a popular hangout for street kids. In Cambridge, the street kids call themselves Pit Rats, and their number has increased over the years, while the general homeless population of the area has declined. A local agency, Bridge Over Troubled Waters, has reported a 50 percent increase in street youth since 1994.

According to Cambridge police, the Pit is a "hotspot for homeless crime." In one year alone, police documented one murder, two rapes, one kidnapping, four robberies, and eight aggravated assaults associated with Pit Rats. The street kids have been accused of harassing male students they suspect of being gay and punching and kicking a Muslim student down a flight of stairs.

Harvard University has a defensive relationship with the Pit Rats. Even after a skinhead street youth was arrested in the attack on the Muslim student, some defended him as misunderstood and falsely accused. An opinion piece in the student newspaper, *The Harvard Crimson*, blamed "obnoxious Harvard students" who are "out-and-out rude" to the street youth, who "don't begrudge Harvard students their relative wealth and opportunity." It is the college students, the author wrote, who are committing the hate crime of intolerance.

Inside the Pit, the street kids are less kind to their benefactors. They are contemptuous of rich students, gays, and, most especially, the "Listo Bums," or older homeless men. These, they joke, should be killed. "Bam. Eliminated from the gene pool," one Pit Rat suggested to the *Boston Globe*. "If you are still out here when you're forty and up and you don't have a home, you should be put down by society."

Though Harvard University has created its own homeless agency for the Pit Rats, many choose to panhandle instead of getting services and sleep outside in the local graveyard. That was where a naïve young woman from Hawaii named Io Nachtwey slept in 2001. Io, nicknamed Rook by the street youths, was sweet and funny and very Hawaiian in disposition, it was said; she could not say no to a friend. "Rook in particular was a very inspirational, creative, bright person. A very smart, intelligent person," David Clark of Youth on Fire, an agency for street kids, told the press. "She didn't have a lot of experiences on the street."

Born into a transplanted American family living in Maui, Io was given a litany of poetic, hopeful names: Io Nani Liberty Illuminata Rukmini Christina Bernier-Nachtwey. Her father was strict. He wouldn't let Io wear jeans, but he did dance with her at her high school graduation, raising his arms in celebration, according to the

Boston Globe. Family pictures show a tiny, almost doll-sized girl with pale skin and long, slightly curly, blonde hair.

Despite her delicate appearance, Io was an outgoing girl who was voted best female dancer her senior year, which was no small feat at the King Kekaulike High School in Maui. She was extremely bright and could converse in several languages, including Russian, German, Spanish, and Italian. She always carried a white backpack full of language tapes. Io was also innocent, according to news reports. She confessed to friends that before her high school graduation, she had never kissed a boy.

It was after she enrolled in a Maui community college that Io began to question her strict upbringing. She migrated to Maine to live with her grandparents. She soon left, landing in a shelter for the night. There she met her soon-to-be boyfriend, a street kid who went by the name Leppy. It was an overnight transition to the streets. Io and Leppy hit the road and soon landed in the Pit, where they slept in the graveyard with the other Pit Rats. Within days, Io was offering a smile in exchange for spare change, her white backpack slung over her shoulder.

Io and her boyfriend soon connected with a street group run by two brothers who called themselves the Kings. The brothers had criminal histories ranging from petty theft to stabbings. They had impressed the other street kids of the Pit by giving away money. They had several followers, including the grandson of the city's former police chief, an admitted heroin addict.

Two girls of the group befriended Io. One was the daughter of an upscale Milton family, the other the daughter of a hard-working single mother from Malden. Both families appeared to love their daughters. The parents of the Milton girl had gone to court to try to keep her home, but once she turned eighteen, there was nothing they could do.

By the time Io, now called Rook, became involved with them, the street family counted at least six members, and its leaders were talking about expanding into a "gang." The Kings had no actual gang connections. It was all just talk.

On Halloween night 2001, the Kings called a meeting of street kids in a cheap hotel room. At least a dozen street youths attended, including Io and her boyfriend Leppy. At the meeting, the new members were told they would have to perform a series of thefts as an initiation. The new recruits left, fired up by their missions. By the next day, however, many had second thoughts. The word in the Pit was that the brothers weren't real gang members. They were liars and to steal for them might be risky.

According to news reports, the Kings were angry that no one had followed orders. They decided to make an example out of one of their reluctant recruits. The group kidnapped Io and took her to a secluded place along the Charles River to "interrogate" her. Io tried to bargain her way out of being killed by having sex with one of the men in a tunnel. Instead, she was raped. The two young women who had befriended her held her down while she was stabbed to death. Her body was dumped in the Charles River.

The Kings were not done. They returned to the Pit to kidnap another street kid. The police were called, and through a stroke of luck, they pulled over the car containing the kidnapped youth. He was saved.

The murder of Io Nachtwey caused a sensation in Cambridge. Almost immediately, Io was characterized as a runaway teen who had been murdered by a gang of outsiders from "tough" neighborhoods who had come to prey on the innocent homeless youth of the Pit, though a 1999 sample found that 83 percent of Pit Rats were also from outside the Boston area. The heritage of the brothers—they were Hispanic—seemed to play a role in the way they were depicted as somehow different from the other street kids in the Pit.

Suggestions to tackle the "Pit problem" by filling in the square met with a storm of criticism. Those pushing for action feared they would be labeled elitist. Defenders of the Pit argued that it was a colorful, safe place for street youth. If there was violence, then it was rare. "There are bad things that happen there, but you wouldn't want to sanitize it," the president of a defense fund said.

In April 2005, the four men who murdered Io Nachtwey were convicted and sentenced to life in prison. The two young women who had befriended Io and then held her down to be stabbed were given sentences of twelve to fifteen years in exchange for their cooperation. The National Coalition for the Homeless included Io's murder in a 2001 report on "violent crimes committed against homeless people." Io was cast as "broke and homeless," while her killers were said to be a "criminal gang."

Nothing much has changed in the Pit since the murder of Io Nachtwey. Crime has risen and fallen, following the migratory youth in the square. There was a stabbing in 2005 and the usual assaults and robberies.

Of all the factors explaining how the street family culture became so consistent across the country, including the nomadic nature of the youths themselves, one influence has been overlooked: the Internet. The Internet has had a profound impact on the shaping and solidifying of what had been a transitory culture.

In the 1990s, street youth shelters began offering free computer access, and a number of Web sites either created by street kids or catering to them quickly appeared. The sites had names like roaddawgz.org, digihitch.com, hippy.com, and punkconnect.com. Street kids could enter a shelter and, within moments, be in touch with other street kids across the country. Aspects of street family culture from anarchist beliefs to squat rules became uniform from coast to coast.

On digihitch.com, a portal claiming five thousand members, a query about New Orleans can run to pages of answers from street kids, complete with tips on how to find good squat (ask in Jackson Square), the rules of the street (don't panhandle your first day), and how the police react to street kids (be careful "flying a sign," or using a cardboard sign to beg). A post on hippy.com about Venice Beach includes the local menus (a church that gets donated pastries from Starbucks, a café that delivers hot soup and cookies to the street youths), places to sleep (a place called Hooker Hill or the beach), and even the names of homeless people in the scene to connect with (such as a woman called Crazy Mary).

The Internet fostered the creation of distinct subcultures within the street kid society, such as the gutterpunks. Some of the most savvy and nomadic street kids, gutterpunks are often political anarchists. On the West Coast they travel the I-5 freeway through California, Oregon, and Washington into Canada. That is one "circuit," as they call it. In the Midwest they suffer the Colorado curse: all roads seem to lead to Denver. On the East Coast, they migrate up and down I-95 from Florida to Maine.

Other youths began to call themselves crusties, for their encrusted dirt (a crust is also the scab from a piercing or a tattoo). You can smell a crusty ten feet away, with their matted dreadlocks and ripe, unwashed aroma. Some crusties are stinky because they don't bother to bathe, but others are vainglorious about their stench, believing that (1) bathing is a tool of the Man, and (2) without unnatural perfumes or soaps, the body will eventually cleanse itself. There are Web sites devoted to crusty culture, such as crusthaven.com.

Still other street kids began labeling themselves peace punks, vagabonds, and road dawgs, and an entire culture developed around riding the rails, including groups like the Combat Railfans. For a society that derides labels, the street kids have shown a delight in creating their own.

The Internet also became a recruitment tool. For instance, digihitch.com has a section devoted to sparkies, their term for youths interested in the culture. Teenagers can post questions ranging from the best places to hitch to what kind of shoes to wear on the road. The questions bubble with innocent enthusiasm. Once on the road, however, the tone of the postings can change. A post on digihitch.com warns about "Getting Along with Street Groups," including the advice to identify the leader of a group immediately and offer opinions only to him. The writer suggests keeping "a special compartment of things you are willing to part with" in your backpack to offer as a means to smooth your way out of a bad situation quickly.

———

Back in Portland, police had become well aware of street family crime. A Portland police count of charges leveled against known street family members and street youths from 1998 to 2005 numbers a startling twenty-six hundred. This amounts to over four hundred charges a year, or more than one a day. This is far more crime than is attributed to black or Hispanic gangs downtown. Many of these charges are minor, such as trespassing; others are more serious and include robberies, assaults, and murders.

In one case in 2001, a street family had been "persistently teasing" a blind man at a bus stop, according to police reports, because they thought he was faking his blindness. Six street kids attacked him, stole his glasses and his hat, punched him in the face, and then beat him with his cane.

In another 2001 case, a girl was accused of writing a "binding spell" on the jeans of a street leader. She was beaten and 86'd from downtown, and a family member kicked her boyfriend in the face with steel-toed boots. The girl ran back to the Greenhouse shelter, where according to the police reports, "she told a female staff member what was happening and asked her to call police." The staff refused to call police because they "feared a reaction from the suspects." This was not the only time the shelter refused to call the police.

There are literally hundreds of reports like these: two schoolgirls on a bus who were attacked and sprayed with mace for giving a street family member a "disrespectful" look; a street kid beaten for taking a street name too similar to that of his street father; another street youth accused of stealing a dog collar necklace who was forcibly marched out of the public library downtown to a nearby freeway overpass, from which he was dropped onto the freeway below. Luckily, he survived.

A surprising number of victims have been innocent bystanders. Two arson investigators who chased a suspect into a street family on the waterfront were attacked by at least fifteen youths, one of whom then smashed an investigator in the head with a skateboard. A citizen was robbed at knifepoint for his wallet and CD player. Two teenagers were lured to the waterfront in broad daylight, robbed of their clothing, and left shivering in their underwear. Very few of these crimes were reported in the daily newspaper at the time they occurred. A reader of the paper would have no idea that street families existed or posed any danger.

Larry Findling, the detective who had arrested James Nelson in 1992, went on to become the central precinct commander. In 2001, he asked for funding for a Youth Crime Unit to address street family crime. He was given funding for two officers.

One of the officers Findling chose was Portland police officer Anthony Merrill, thirty-two at the time, with a fair Irish complexion and a gentle, compassionate demeanor. Before they hired Merrill for the job, the police allowed the youth shelter staff to interview him.

Merrill remembered one director quizzing him on topics such as needle exchanges. Both the police and the agencies were looking for an officer who would be more disposed to reason than anger, and they agreed they had found that person in Officer Merrill, who could take street kids spitting in his face without a corresponding rise in temper.

Officer Merrill's job wasn't just to enforce the law but to act as a liaison between the police, the youth agencies, and the street families. He would attend meetings in shelters as a police representative. The street families, he says, would elect some of their own leaders to come talk to the cops. It was all quite formal. Often Merrill was the only police officer who could identify a youth by his or her street name. When another police officer wanted to hunt down a suspect going by a street name, Merrill was the one who pointed him out.

But his most important role, perhaps, was simply to be there, a reminder to the street kids that they did not exist outside of the law. "I tried to be constantly visible," he says. "The waterfront down by the memorial was really popular. On a warm day there might be a hundred street kids there. And there was Four Court Fountain, and the Square, of course." He and his partner crossed the bridges to the other side of the river, visiting the squats.

What struck Officer Merrill most profoundly was the core group of older street fathers who controlled the scene. "Some of these guys leading the groups, they exert this humongous influence over the kids who come downtown. They're street smart, and they know how to work the entire system. They've been doing it for years. Some of these leaders are thirty years old."

He saw a lot of violence. "You would see these suburban kids who would try and come down and assimilate into this culture. They'd be down there and make some mistake, usually unintentionally, and they would be stripped of their clothing and belongings and kicked out of downtown. These people would just beat them. We had several incidents like this." Some of the violence was aimed at him. "You have to be careful getting in those groups. We were attacked more than once," he says. "We'd get called to assist medics on overdoses in the shelters. We'd go in, and the kids wouldn't see that we were there to help. They thought we were going to arrest their loved one, you know, because this is their family. I would be telling them, 'we are here to help.' It was an explosive situation. I can see the agencies feel they can't do their jobs if the kids see them working with the police."

Officer Merrill was called in on two street family murders that occurred while Nelson was still serving his time. One homicide occurred on July 23, 2000. It was a hot summer day, and the waterfront was crowded with street families. There had been a free concert in the park that day, with a DJ spinning rave-type music. One of the street families hanging out had members with names like Assassin, Cartoon, and Gadget. Almost all had criminal records, including one with a rape conviction.

The fight started when a new girl on the streets was accused of "disrespecting" the street family. One of the women of the family swung at the girl with a large police-style flashlight. About seventy street kids were watching, and they began chanting, "Beat her ass, beat her ass," according to police reports.

The targeted girl took off running, and one of the women of the family shouted that she would pay $20 to anyone who caught her. At this news, hordes of youths picked up and began running after the girl. Estimates put the number of street kids chasing the girl at between fifty and seventy-five, with the angry street family in the lead.

The targeted girl ran across Front Avenue and past the Skidmore Fountain, which is under the Burnside Bridge. At Second and Ankeny, the girl dashed across the street and hid in a bar. After a time she came out, perhaps thinking the street family was gone. They were not. They were waiting with the large group of street kids watching, and the girl took off running again, this time across the street, back toward the waterfront.

At exactly the same time, a homeless man named Richard Clayton Crosby was walking across the crosswalk. Crosby was in his forties but so bent and grizzled he could have passed for sixty. Hearing the street kids yell, "Stop her," Crosby playfully, and perhaps drunkenly, stuck out a foot. To the street family chasing the girl, it looked like he was going to trip one of them.

According to police records, one of the street kids shouted at Crosby, "You tried to trip me." At that news, in a savage turn, the street family ran straight at the older homeless man. The men began punching him, and Crosby fell down, right there in the street. The street family circled him and began kicking and stomping him. The rest of the street kids, some fifty of them, gathered in a rough semicircle and watched.

The attack happened so quickly that Crosby didn't have time to run away or even to raise his hands. Within seconds, he was on the ground, surrounded by close to a dozen street kids, and buffeted with kicks and stomps. "You stupid asshole, you done fucked up," one of the street kids yelled as he kicked Crosby, according to his police interview. Another member of the family admitted to the police that he was trying to push his way into the circle so he could kick Crosby too. He said he wanted to be cool and show the others he was "down with them."

In the distance, sirens blared. The street kids took off, running, heading back to the waterfront. Crosby rose unsteadily to his feet, according to witnesses, looked dazed, and then went crashing down, cracking his head on the pavement.

By the time the police arrived, the streets were empty. Crosby was lying in the intersection with a thin stream of blood coming from his head. Officer Merrill recalls leaning over Crosby and seeing that the man was dying, right there in the street. He was pronounced dead at the Oregon Health Sciences University hospital soon after his arrival. The cause of death was blunt-force trauma to the head.

By this time, police were familiar with the street families, and they canvassed downtown that night, interviewing street kids. The detective in the case, Rich Austria, says the lack of cooperation from the street kids made his investigation difficult, but he solved the case within three weeks. The murder of Richard Crosby generated scant media concern. A brief article characterized his death as the result of a "street dispute."

A year later, Officer Merrill was called in on another street kid killing. The victim was another stranger to his murderers. Nicholas Moore—Nick to his family—was a young man afflicted with paranoid schizophrenia. His mother remembers him as a joyful boy, but the onset of Nick's paranoid schizophrenia in his teenage years overshadows those sweet memories.

Dedicated parents who ran a farm in Boring, Oregon, the Moores exhausted every legal remedy to help their son once his illness became apparent. When he was seventeen, they had Nick committed in order to get him to take his medications. When he turned eighteen, however, the Moores lost their legal hold over him. He would often just disappear, leaving his mother and father distraught. "I don't know how many times I reported him missing," says Connie Moore. They tried taking him to court and having him committed as an adult, but the courts ruled that Nick Moore could take care of himself. The courts were wrong. Nick could not take care of himself. He was kicked out of one treatment program after another, usually for behavioral problems.

In September 2001, Nick was referred by mental health services to subsidized housing in downtown Portland. He was placed in the Joyce Hotel, a dank hotel that serves transients, the mentally ill, and drug users. The Joyce is notorious for crime and flagrant drug use. Occupants have complained about toilets filled with used syringes.

On September 17, 2001, Nick was thrown out of the Joyce for threatening the front desk clerk. He found himself on the streets in the depths of a psychotic episode. He drank alcohol and wandered about downtown. He was tossed into the county detox center that evening and spent the night on a cold concrete floor. The following day, Nick was released.

That evening, Nick canvassed downtown, still having hallucinations. It was a beautiful Indian summer night. Nick wandered through the Square and paused to ask for a cigarette from a street kid named Valerie Derscheid. In one of the sad twists of his case, Valerie had grown up in the same rural Oregon town that Nick grew up in, according to his mother, who says she knew Valerie when she was a child. Connie Moore thought Valerie had a nice family. There was no need, she says, for Valerie to be living on the streets.

Valerie was apparently having the time of her life. She had connected with a group of street kids with names like Sasquatch, Sylvester, Taz, Dread, and Ghost. The group was all men, except for Valerie, who, one later said, was a leader in a "subtle, provoking way."

The street kids had squatted together the previous summer in the McLoughlin Caves under the Ross Island Bridge. They had left their roll call, or list of names, on a concrete pillar. They called their cave Camp T-Bird. According to police records, one of them, Taz, carried a serrated knife, the kind advertised on television that can cut through cans. Another youth carried a Gator knife, a small knife with a black handle and a thick, curved edge.

When Nick asked Valerie for a cigarette, she refused to give him one. He began calling her names. That started it. Valerie had been disrespected. She went off to a corner of the Square for a good cry. The other street kids clustered around, soothing her.

The group decided to punish Nick for calling Valerie names. According to one of the youths interviewed by police, the mentally ill young man had violated "one of the main rules of the street." From the Square, the group forced Nick several blocks down to the Willamette River. They told Nick to swim out to a light on the river. It was a long distance to the light, and the Willamette is deceptive, with a strong, surging channel. Every now and then, an unsuspecting swimmer tries to cross the river and drowns. Nick made it out to the light and came back. The group was surprised. The exercise was clearly not intended in fun. His parents later told the police that Nick had always been a strong swimmer.

Frustrated, the group pulled Nick from the water and marched him across a bridge to the east side of the river to the McLoughlin Caves. It was late at night, and Nick was sopping wet and babbling incoherently about his jacket, which his father had bought him. He was worried his father would be mad that he had gotten his new jacket wet.

At the McLoughlin Caves, the group forced Nick up a short sandy slope covered with brambles of blackberry vines. Here the homeless had tunneled an amazingly intricate series of caves under McLoughlin Boulevard. The caves extend deeply along the boulevard, a wandering maze of sandy red-brown caverns with carved dirt platforms for sleeping. Footholds are carved in and out of the caves for easy access. Once you are in the caves, only one narrow path leads in and out.

The group led Nick deep into the caves, where they came to their Camp T-Bird site. The cave was dark, but they could see from the city lights shining off the river, reflected by the overpass. The homeless camping in the other caves would claim to hear nothing that night.

In the cave, the group began "interrogating" Nick. They started beating him, and Nick accidentally knocked Valerie down. This enraged the group, and the assault began in earnest. Nick was muzzled with a filthy sock. The men took turns stabbing him with a six-inch knife they passed around. For at least twenty minutes, the street kids stabbed Nick over and over again.

Nick begged, pleaded, and said he was sorry, his words muffled by the wet sock. "Die, just die, motherfucker," one street kid called Sylvester chanted. When Nick was dead, they rolled him back down the bushes outside the caves and threw the knife in the river. After the murder, some of the street kids were elated. Two of them slapped palms, high-fived, and boasted that they had committed "the perfect crime."

Back downtown Valerie went to the Greenhouse shelter to get some pain relievers for her sore muscles from being knocked over by Nick. Some of the men sat down on the sidewalk and had a discussion about how great knives are. "They are the best weapons in the world," one of the kids proclaimed, according to police interviews. A few days later, two of the killers took another street kid back to the caves and reenacted the murder for him, a sort of Court TV on the streets. No one called the police.

The detective called in on the murder of Nick Moore was the same detective who would later work the Jessica Williams case, Detective Barry Renna. Detective Renna remembers arriving at the scene and seeing Nick's brutalized body dumped in the bushes, as if he were human garbage. A wet sock found at the scene would test positive for his saliva. The Nick Moore case, Detective Renna says, stayed with him. He hesitates when answering why. "I think it was his illness," he finally says. "And that dirty sock in his mouth. It was the same with Jessica. It's so hard when these things happen to vulnerable people."

Detective Renna worked the Moore case for over a year, pressing hard even when there seemed to be no leads. He kept returning downtown, tracing Nick's path that night, and interviewing truculent street kids. He met a brick wall of silence. "The stigma of being a snitch was a factor in this case," Renna says. It would have been easy to shuffle the case over to the unsolved file. Nick's murder was not the object of political pressure, and the Moores were working-class people who lacked the sophistication to orchestrate a media campaign.

Connie Moore was upset by what she considered a culture of indifference downtown, from both the homeless youth agencies and the media. It was as if her son's murder didn't matter. Frustrated, the Moore family plastered downtown with a hundred flyers featuring Nick's photograph. The street kid who had witnessed the "reenactment" saw the flyer and realized that the actors had been telling the truth. He confided to a Greenhouse worker, who in turn, called the police. It was a major break, but the witness only knew the suspects by their street names.

Detective Renna knew that the shelters record both the real names and the street names of their clients, and this would enable him to track down the suspects. He found the Greenhouse helpful, even though they made him get a court order to read their files. Once the records were in hand, it was easier to match the street names with real identities. Officer Merrill was called in to help identify the street kids.

Connie Moore was disappointed that Valerie Derscheid was given only twelve years in prison. She thought Valerie had played a major role in the murder of her son by inciting the others. "She got in a place where she had power over these boys," Connie says.

Because of crimes like these, Officer Merrill exulted when a teenager managed to extricate himself from the street family culture before he harmed others or was harmed himself. Sometimes a young person would approach him on the streets and ask, "Remember me? I'm not on the streets anymore," and Officer Merrill was always glad to see that they had left the streets unharmed.

Others were harder to deal with. "How do you reform people?" he asked. "A lot of these guys want to be out there. It's complicated by mental health issues with some, and of course drug addictions. But some would not use the services."

Around the beginning of 2003, about a year and a half after his unit was created, Officer Merrill was transferred to another division. The funding for the Youth Crime Unit had been cut, in turn cutting the connection between the chaotic world of street families and the rational world of law.

Some of the youth agencies and the police would continue to work together, and other police units would fill in as they could. Local businesses created the Portland Patrol Incorporated, a private security firm to patrol the Square. But no one would be out there, constantly visiting the hot spots, wearing a badge, and expressing concern for the street kids. The street families were largely unsupervised, and they knew it.

It was early 2003, and in eastern Oregon, a parole date was fast approaching.

PART TWO

2003

We are all droogs, but somebody has to be in charge. Right? Right?

—ANTHONY BURGESS,
A CLOCKWORK ORANGE

7

It was spring once more. On March 24, 2003, James Daniel Nelson was paroled from prison. He had served a few months shy of eleven years.

Over a decade behind bars had coarsened Nelson's face and given him a prison build, heavy with muscles. His hair was thinning on top, and he wore wire-rimmed glasses prescribed while he was incarcerated. He looked older than twenty-seven. Deep wrinkles were embedded in his forehead, and the beginnings of a goatee dotted his chin. It would grow into a short, lush, brown beard and a mustache he kept neatly trimmed, one of his better features. He still had the same flat, cocky expression in his eyes, only now they looked like the eyes of an adolescent boy trapped in the face of a grown man.

There was no media notice of Nelson's release, and no rehashing of his crime. After ten years, the Family's murder spree had been forgotten.

Nelson had not been idle in prison. He continued to view the world as a place of fantasy and conflict, and this was reflected in his disciplinary record, which ran to over a hundred pages. Some of these infractions were minor, such as possessing pornography and making homemade Dungeons and Dragons pieces out of Tylenol tablets, which violated prison rules against fantasy role-playing games.

Other infractions were more serious. In one incident, Nelson was angry that the prison cafeteria workers were not wearing hairnets. "They need to be wearing hairnets and gloves," Nelson shouted out his cell door. "We will grieve them all." He incited the other inmates to near riot, instructing them to shove towels down their toilets to flood the floor. On another occasion, he was caught breaking the fire sprinkler head in his cell in order to create a disturbance. Nelson was honing his people skills. "Hey, Nelson!" one of the inmates yelled. "Anything you do, I'll do too!"

Several of his infractions were racially motivated. Nelson attacked one African American inmate in an assault that guards suspected was racist. He fought another inmate because they were in different factions of a white supremacist gang, he said, and the other inmate was a "race traitor" and a "sellout." When a guard tried to break up the fight, Nelson punched him in the head and broke his glasses, cutting his nose. He targeted those he considered Jewish. When a guard serving breakfast one morning asked him, "How are you this morning, Nelson?" he replied, "Fuck you, you Jewish cocksucker."

There were months when Nelson spent more time in the disciplinary unit than in his regular cell. Even in lockdown, he found ways to extend his stay. When a nurse walked the segregation floor, Nelson catcalled out his door that she was a "true redhead" and told her to "come here and suck my cock, give me a blow job, you bitch." Some months he wracked up five or more infractions.

Then, in 2001, two years before his release, Nelson's prison file shows a near cessation of violence. Nelson says he had promised his mother, who was dying of cancer, that he would stop fighting (she passed away while he was in prison). "I was trying to change," he says. "I was trying to leave violence behind." It is also possible that Nelson was nearing his release and realized he didn't want to commit any crimes inside that would lengthen his stay.

Whatever the reason, Nelson acted as if he had turned a page. He attended dozens of educational classes and religious services. "I took every program I could," he says. Several of these were religious services on Wicca, or modern witchcraft.

Ever since he was an adolescent, Nelson had been interested in the occult. It was perhaps ironic that the prison system gave him the chance to explore this fascination. A series of legal rulings, beginning in 1964 and enacted in federal statute, protect the rights of inmates to practice whichever religion they choose. As a result, prisoners are free to follow every faith from Wicca to satanism.

In Oregon, as in other states, prisoners may choose from a menu of religious services, usually hosted by outside ministers, shamans, and Wiccans who come to the prison. Nelson chose pagan classes. Among the religious ceremonies Nelson attended was a winter solstice ritual run by a self-proclaimed druid named Roy Lakey, owner of the Moonshadow pagan supply store in Portland. Lakey says he cannot recall Nelson.

Nelson's prison manual taught him that witchcraft is a "magical based" philosophy. Followers worship the Goddess, a fertility figure associated with the moon. Her consort is the Horned God, a man with antlers who represents death and rebirth. Wiccan inmates are allowed to write their spells down in journals called Book of Shadows. The manual says they use a "ritual knife" in their ceremonies. This knife is to be black hilted and double-edged, but not sharpened.

In his classes, Nelson may have learned to say "Thou art God" and "Thou art Goddess" to other convicts since the faith promotes the idea that everyone is divine. He may have also heard what sounded a lot like the credo of the streets, the Wiccan Law of Threefold Return: "What is sent forth will return threefold to the sender, good or evil."

Most Wiccans are peaceful. Lakey says that he is adamantly opposed to racism and violence. However, the European focus of druidism and other pagan faiths has encouraged some extremists to promote a racist viewpoint. As Mattias Gardell writes in *Gods of the Blood: The Pagan Revival and White Separatism*, racist pagan sects are on the rise inside prisons. These faiths include Odinism (named after the Norse god) and Wotanism (an acronym for Will of the Aryan Nation). These new sects are a heady combination of white supremacist ideology and pre-Christian pagan divinity. They exalt a warrior mentality, racial pride, and a belief in Valhalla. Their followers usually worship Norse gods and wear the Hammer of Thor, the Norse god of thunder, as an approved religious medallion. They see themselves as Aryan warriors protecting the fair maidens of Nordic heritage.

White supremacists imprisoned for hate crimes have eagerly adopted these new sects as a means to spread their beliefs. David Lane, once a leader in the Order, a terrorist neo-Nazi organization that went on a spree of assassinations and bank robberies, is one of the leaders of this racist pagan movement. Lane was imprisoned for murdering Denver, Colorado, Jewish talk show host Alan Berg. Inside prison walls, Lane promotes Wotanism. He explained to Gardell that he created Wotanism for "religious concepts that would preserve our people." Christianity, he felt, preached too much love. He wanted a creed that would "stir the warrior soul."

Other white supremacists have successfully spread their ideology from within prisons. In Lompoc, California, white supremacist Richard Scutari runs a kindred called the Sons of the Noble Wolf, a "brotherhood of incarcerated heathens." Scutari holds classes for fifty or more prisoners at a time, where he teaches about heroes such as Adolf Hitler.

In Oregon, racist pagan sects include Richard Kemp's Kindred in Sheridan's federal prison. In a photograph, Kemp's Kindred pose proudly with a large Thor's hammer made out of what looks like electrical tape and cardboard. Around their necks they wear Thor's medallion. Other groups include the European Kindred, or EK, a white supremacist gang active in several Oregon prisons.

Prisons are surprisingly porous institutions, and what happens behind prison walls is transferred to the outside culture through ex-convicts and their families. It was in prisons, for instance, that the Aryan Nations got their start. As convicts like James Nelson take their new beliefs back into the street culture, racist paganism is spreading. In Oregon, skinhead groups such as the Volksfront are now largely racist pagan. Graffiti tags for the racist EK prison gang have appeared in southeast Portland.

When he left prison, Nelson took with him articles about Adolf Hitler and a list of books on witchcraft. His ability to expound on esoteric faiths would impress the younger adults on the streets, many of whom already wore Celtic tattoos and claimed to be Wiccan, though they weren't always entirely sure what that meant.

Nelson was placed in the Harbor Light agency on Burnside Avenue, right in the heart of the downtown street culture in which he had killed before. Run by the Salvation Army, the shelter is one of the few to offer a short-term transitional housing program for parolees. The agency is a plain brick building next to the weekly Saturday market under the west end of the Burnside Bridge. The shelter, like many adult shelters, is austere. A simple door advertises weekly tuberculosis testing. In the men's section, Nelson was given a bed and a small dresser. He had access to educational services, a chiropractic clinic, and computers.

In fairness, Nelson had tried to avoid returning to Portland. He had applied to have his parole transferred to Sacramento, California, to live with his brother and stepfather, who said they were willing to have him move into their house. The transfer application was pending decision from California.

The conditions of his parole were simple. Nelson was to not drink alcohol, carry a weapon, or contact Leon Stanton's family. There was no mention of avoiding street kids. After checking in with his parole officer, Nelson was free to wander the streets.

———

It must have felt strange to have left more than ten years before and come back to find nothing had changed. The same square was there with the same-looking street kids hanging out on the same scratched benches. The same agencies still served the youth: the Greenhouse, Outside In, and the Sisters of the Road café. The same hangouts were popular, including O'Bryant Square, still called Paranoid Park; the Japanese memorial, called Pothead Hill; and Four Court Fountain on Third Avenue, now called Four Corners. The same squats were still under the same bridges. Under the Ross Island Bridge, there was the McLoughlin Caves. At the end of the Steel Bridge was a cavern called the Hole. The Arthur Street Ramp squat was still there, as were other squats in the lower southwest.

Only Checkpoint Charlie itself was gone, recently cleared to make room for future condo developments. A Marriott hotel stood where the tannery grounds once stewed. The dirt path to the squat had been paved over, and little shrubs were planted in military rows along the shore. The city had built a circular lookout point over the ground where Leon Stanton had died, with a low, black, iron fence and two tall lampposts. The ground was paved with buffed triangular stones. There were no benches to sit on, but the lookout afforded a lovely view of the river with blue herons flying to their nesting grounds on Ross Island. The Marquam Bridge still rose overhead, and when big trucks passed, the pigeons roosting in the supports scattered over the river.

Rising in the middle of the lookout was the large round pillar that had once cemented the Family squat. The graffiti had been scrubbed off, but in the bright sunlight, one could see faint marks where the words *Grim Reaper* had been painted over.

Walking up Fourth Avenue a week after his release, on what he said was April 1, 2003, Nelson came across a festive scene: the Portland Peace Encampment, which had begun only five days before Nelson's parole date, soon after the bombs began falling in Baghdad. Antiwar protestors had decided to camp in Terry Shrunk Plaza, across the street from City Hall, where they could draw the attention of passing cars and politicians. The plaza was only a block long, with a gentle hump of trees and grass. The peace activists had unrolled their sleeping bags and set up tents. "We're camping here until the war is over," one protestor announced.

The peace camp made the news, and the protest took on the aura of a party, with drumming, meditating, and signs asking people to "Honk for Peace." When a call went out for smokes, only American Spirit menthols would do. When a certain protestor needed gluten-free food, a call went out for that, too. Tables were set up with elaborate spreads of food, all donated by concerned citizens: fresh sandwiches, organic blue-corn chips, and tubs of salsa.

The appeal to street kids was obvious—free food, free love—and within days, a number of them had moved into the camp. There was some grumbling about this among the activist ranks. One organizer complained about the "freeloaders, people looking for handouts." Others defended the street kids as having an important perspective.

Nelson, fresh from prison with his cellblock shoulders, made a splash in the encampment. Street kids clustered around him, listening to his angry diatribes. When Nelson talked, it was all fuck this and nigger that. He bragged to one street kid about how he had never spent cell time with a black man, and he complained loudly about "niggers." He sounded like a man who had spent the last decade behind bars. He was openly racist and sexist, and yet no one told him to leave the peace camp.

Nelson was not the only racist running around the streets. A notorious local skinhead, Dennis Mothersbaugh, had been hanging out downtown in the Square. Mothersbaugh had been released from jail a month before, and he sported a long criminal history. He was said to use the youth shelters, and he boasted many friends among the street kids, whom he allegedly tried to recruit for his white-power gang.

While some of the street kids claimed to be against racism, when it came down to it, their convictions never ran deeply enough for them to reject the skinheads in their midst. In the Square, ethics were always situational, except, possibly, in the case of male homosexuality. It was still almost impossible to find an openly gay, male street kid, though gay and bisexual girls were now accepted.

The street kids were not turned off by Nelson's coarse language or raw beliefs. On the contrary, they were drawn to the older man who said he had been an original Portland Street Kid way back in 1992, when some of them were still in kindergarten. Nelson told them he had gone to jail after killing the man who raped his sister. The street kids were impressed. Within a few hours, literally, Nelson had a core group of street kids hanging on his every word.

Not all of the street kids took to the newcomer. Some thought Nelson was a "vulgar" man. One claimed Nelson had tried to bully the others by making semi-threatening remarks. "He told me I had a purty mouth," the young man said contemptuously. "He thought he was a big, badass guy."

Nelson immediately picked up the changes in terminology since he had left. Respected street kids were no longer "old-timers" but "old school." Instead of "heshers," new kids on the scene were "oogles." The teenagers slumming for the day were no longer "summer bunnies" but "hot topics" (Hot Topic is the name of a punk-style clothing store) or "goths in a box."

What the Family had called "Rambo games" were called "the dramas," a term that would be heard across the country. Getting "excommunicated" was out; instead, street kids were more commonly "86'd." A hangout was now a "hot spot." A miscreant youth would still get "taxed," and that tax could include a number of penalties, including a "pocket check." The leaders whom the Family had called commanders were now referred to as "mom" or "dad." Code was still code, though it was also called "the rules." A snitch was still a snitch and always would be.

Jerry Fest, the former director of the Portland Social Service agency Janus Youth Programs and the author of the 1998 *Street Culture: An Epistemology of Street-Dependent Youth,* says he is often asked to write a dictionary of street kid slang. He always declines because he knows the next year will bring about a new crop of terms and his writings will be soon out of date. Street kids are the ultimate cultural appropriators, picking and choosing their terminology from across the pop-culture board and endlessly adapting their language to new trends.

——

Nelson began creating his new street family in the peace camp that very first day. It seemed as if he went to the camp planning to recruit followers, but it is also possible that the street kids who threw themselves eagerly at Nelson gave him the idea. They were looking for a leader as much as he was looking for followers, and in the synergy of that first day, everyone got what he or she wanted.

One of the first street kids he met in the camp, Nelson says, was seventeen-year-old Carl Alsup, an impressionable boy with a shaved blond head and stick-out ears that made him look a little bit lost.

Even his friends described him as a liar, a moody boy with a temper who "told so many lies he believed them himself." Among his stories were outlandish claims that he had murdered people, that he had spent time in prison, and that he was a contract killer. He told other street kids he could have people killed "with one phone call." Carl would lie about the silliest stuff, too, like how much an eagle's nest weighs or how many miles there are from one point to another in Alaska. He seemed to have a fondness for facts and figures, especially when they were not real. He would just make up garbage and see how people reacted.

Carl's mother, Kelly White, was once a Dallas, Texas, police officer. A frail-looking woman with red hair and the same deeply embedded blue eyes as her son, Kelly has two younger children at home. Court documents indicate a history of emotional struggles.

Kelly and Carl's father divorced when their son was young, and Carl bounced from home to home, living with his father, mother, and grandparents. During the few years he lived with his father, his dad allegedly abused him. "Ricky [Carl] was a victim of physical abuse from my first husband," Kelly claims, and court records back her account. Carl told an official that his father "rammed me into walls, smashed my head into the wall, hit me across the face with a one-by-eight board." A witness has confirmed that the father was a heavy drinker who struck his children. Kelly also claims that Carl was sexually abused at age five by an older child.

As a child, Carl lived in ten different homes in at least four states. He passed from school to school, migrating among relatives in Alaska, Oregon, Arizona, and Utah. Family photographs show a skinny, angular boy with blond hair. He seems hyper in the photos, often clowning for the camera, but a few pictures capture a softer side of Carl. In one photograph, he hugs a dog in the backseat of a car, his smile uncertain.

In 1996, when he would have been ten, Carl was placed briefly in foster care, according to an investigator who worked on his case. He was later returned to his family's care. By fourteen, he was an angry, violent boy. He moved back in with his mother, whom he routinely told to "fuck off," according to police reports.

Kelly reported Carl as a runaway on several occasions. She says she did everything she could to help her son, including tough-love interventions. On January 4, 2001, when Carl was fifteen, his mother had him arrested. Carl had thrown burning superglue at his younger brother, causing second-degree burns. His mother called the police, who took pictures of the burns.

Carl was referred to anger management through a juvenile diversion program. The program didn't work. Carl continued to run away and verbally abuse his mother. By this time, his mother was living in Lake Oswego, a wealthy town outside of Portland. The zip code did nothing to improve her son's behavior. When Carl turned seventeen, he ran to the streets. He found the streets fun, and nobody, it seemed, could make him return home.

Kelly White feels the criminal-justice system failed to take her son's descent into violence seriously. "I begged him for three days not to leave home but he did," Kelly says. "He had a home." She pauses. "My son is a follower. He always has been."

On the streets, Carl wore the same thing almost every day: a long-sleeved black shirt, black jeans, black work boots, and a work jacket. It was the standard uniform of a skinhead, and with his hulking body, shaved head, and thick lips, Carl looked like just that, a dangerous, immature, and scary skinhead.

According to Nelson, Carl had wanted to join the Sick Boys street family, but the Sick Boys were not interested in the boastful boy. "Carl couldn't get into the Sick Boys. They didn't want him," Nelson laughs. Other street kids confirm this account. One says that after rejecting Carl, the Sick Boys family contemptuously referred to him as the Little Blondie Boy.

Carl was looking for a street family who would accept him, and that day in the camp, he found it in Nelson. Carl would become to Nelson what Nelson had been to Grant Charboneau, a hero worshiper and eager acolyte. A close friend thought Carl wanted to be a tough guy and would do anything to prove he was. Nelson was his big chance. "Carl thought Nelson was a righteous guy," Carl's mother says, tears standing in her eyes. "Nelson told the kids he went to prison for killing the men who raped his sister. To them, he was a righteous guy."

When he met Nelson that first day in the peace camp, Carl already had a street name. It was Wreath. He had gotten the name, his friends say, from his middle name, Richard, which morphed into Ricky, then shorthand to Reith, and then Wreath.

With him Carl brought his girlfriend, Crystal Ann Grace, who went by the street name Jade. Crystal had thyroidal eyes and pale skin. On the streets, she wore a gray hoodie over her short auburn hair. At times she liked to be called Venus, another exotic misnomer.

Crystal Grace was a smart young woman who had taken college classes and had recently been employed, both in a jewelry store and in the dental laboratory her parents owned. She claimed to have volunteered with Alzheimer's patients. Like many of the other street kids, Crystal also said she had attention deficit hyperactivity disorder, or ADHD. Her family declined to be interviewed for this book, but police described them as "normal."

The day before Nelson's release, on March 23, 2003, Crystal stopped into a youth shelter and was evaluated for services. The shelter staff noted that she "seems to be a very articulate and intelligent person." Her parents, Crystal said, had kicked her out for partying too much. She explained that she had gone out on a Friday night and didn't come home until Sunday. Her being gone for two whole days didn't sit too well with her mother. When her mom laid down the law, Crystal left. She was twenty.

The youth agency referred Crystal to numerous educational and job programs, but she did not seem to follow up on any of the help they offered. Instead, she hung around the peace camp with her younger boyfriend, Carl. Almost immediately, Nelson began calling his two new followers "my kids."

———

Sara Baerlocher first saw the peace camp from her window in the county jail on Third Avenue across the street from the plaza. She watched the protestors on the sidewalk below with longing. "The sun, the wind, the rain," she sighs. Tall and voluptuous, Sara Baerlocher was twenty, with long, straight, nearly black hair, pale, creamy skin, and full lips. She didn't wear makeup, and she didn't need it. She claimed to be part Cherokee though she didn't have tribal membership.

According to Sara, she was in jail after having a big fight with her father. They had been arguing about "teenage stuff," she says, though Sara was twenty at the time. Police charged her with harassment and unwanted contact on March 30, 2003. Sara's father, Richard Baerlocher, a postal worker, lived in a ranch-style home in southeast Portland. The family had moved from Oklahoma some five years before, and her parents had divorced. Sara made no allegations of parental abuse. Her father was a big, friendly man, and the two usually got along well.

After spending a day or two in jail, Sara was released on or about April 1, 2003, the same day Nelson claims he arrived in the camp. Donning her street clothes—a thin skirt and cotton top—and shivering in the spring cold, Sara headed across the street to check out the protest. It had been raining, and the streets were damp and cold.

The peace camp welcomed Sara with open arms. There was plenty of food, and even showers. The people were so nice, and there were cute guys there, too. Being in the camp, she says, also meant you got to "protest against something you kinda don't like."

Sara found a boyfriend that first day, a man hanging around the camp. The two started going out right away. Sara uses the term *boyfriend* loosely. A boyfriend could be someone you met that morning. Sara denies having sex with the man and says she had realized by the end of that day that the man was a "creep."

By then, Sara had met James Nelson. She remembers it vividly. Nelson was wearing jeans, tennis shoes, a gray jacket, and a baseball cap. He wore that hat so often Sara didn't know for some time that his hair was thinning on top. He had a tiny, squiggly scar under his right nostril that looked, Sara giggled, like a tiny piece of snot had gotten stuck there. Sara thought this was cute. Soon Nelson grew out his mustache, and the scar was covered.

Nelson was charming, Sara says. And he was suave, not a word Sara usually used. Nelson was suave—and Sara was smitten. She broke it off with the other man immediately. Right from the start, Nelson seemed so romantic, and clever—not the evil sort of clever, just clever. "He was a very handsome man." She wasn't alone in admiring Nelson. "The girls swarmed around him." The only people who didn't like Nelson, Sara remembers, were the peace activists who had founded the peace camp. "The guys hated him," which she chalked up to jealousy.

According to Sara, Nelson admitted that he had been looking for a woman. At first, he had his eye on a girl named Destiny who was hanging around with her brother Jeremy. But then he noticed Sara. As soon as Sara broke it off with her boyfriend, Nelson felt free to take her.

The other street girls were angry that Sara walked in and got her man. "A lot of the other girls would talk about me behind my back."

It was a rule of the street, she learned, that you have to wait a full day after dropping one person before hooking up with another. It didn't matter if you had had sex or not. To change boyfriends in one day made you a slut. The street kids called this homie-hopping.

Nelson and Sara became a couple right in the camp, and Nelson introduced Sara to "his" street kids. Sara liked Carl. She thought he was a nice boy, the kind of boy who would make a good daddy. He treated Crystal like a queen. "He was *so* devoted to Crystal," Sara sighs. Her feelings for Crystal were less positive. Sara thought the young woman called Jade was a spoiled little brat who liked to get her way. The two women did not get along.

Nelson told Sara his street name was Thantos. He told her it was from a grandfather in Italy. But another street kid says that Nelson gave himself the street name Thantos after checking out a book on Greek mythology from the library and reading about Thanatos, the Greek god of death. In the myths, Thanatos is described as malignant and cruel: "his heart is made of pitiless iron, when he takes hold of you, the world of light ceases to be."

When questioned, Nelson goes into a long explanation of what the name means, saying it signifies an evolution, how he was "trying to change, trying to leave violence behind." It was a form of rebirth, he claims, part of the cycle of life away from death into life. He wasn't really trying to be the god of death, he says.

——

Sara was impressed with how much Nelson knew about living on the streets, even though he had been in prison for ten years. Nelson had thoroughly researched what the town provided in the week since his release. He had collected flyers from the various agencies, describing what each one provided in terms of food, clothing, showers, and shelter, and he had made little notes along the margins, angrily scratching out those who refused to serve someone his age. "Street parents show you how to survive on the streets," Nelson explains. "They show you where to eat, how to live."

First, he took Sara to get her some warm clothes. He led her to a shelter for homeless women called Rose Haven. While Sara picked out the clothes, Nelson waited for her down the street, leaving Sara with the impression that the staff at the shelter disliked men. In truth, the agencies of Portland are well aware of the older predators who prey on impressionable youths hanging out downtown. Favor Ellis, manager of the Janus Youth Access and Reception Center, where homeless teenagers are evaluated, says she often has to call the police about the older men who hang around outside, looking for vulnerable girls to exploit. Many of these men, she says, are paroled convicts placed in adult shelters downtown.

Warmly dressed, Sara was ready for a new life as Nelson's girl-friend and a member of his street family. Two days before, she had been home, watching the daytime soaps on television and arguing with her dad; now she was living on the streets with a convicted mur-derer as a boyfriend. It was another overnight transition to the street life; yet, Sara acted as if it were natural.

At twenty, Sara still saw herself as a "kid" and a "teenager." Her only employment since high school had been a job at Chuck E. Cheese's. The decline in blue-collar careers in the area meant that the kind of solid postal work her father enjoyed would not come so easily to Sara. She wasn't looking for a home, marriage, and a family anyway. At an age of intense energy and ambition, Sara had nothing to occupy her time and her dreams. She was bored. The streets of-fered to fill her void.

Once she joined Nelson, Sara was christened with a street name. From now on, she was Akasha. In Sanskrit, the name means space, or the primordial source of the all-knowing.

Those first few days, Nelson taught Akasha the rules of the street. As Sara explains, the rules were clear and serious.

1. Don't tattle.
2. Keep your mouth shut.
3. Old school rules. When a street kid becomes old school, you have to do what he says. No exceptions.
4. You can't just declare yourself old school. That mantle is only passed down from one old school street kid to another. Don't ever assume you've earned it.

Nelson, of course, was an old school street kid, and as such, he automatically received obedience. There were more rules, too, that Sara learned as she went. There were, for example, the gremlin rights. "Gremlin rights give you the right to tell people to break up," Nelson explains, "or to not have sex with someone." Only old school street leaders, like Nelson, had gremlin rights.

Sara was pleased and proud to learn the rules of the streets. It was like an introduction to a secret society, she says. She describes street kid culture in precisely those terms: "a whole society." There were the rulers, she says, their enforcers, and then the workers. The rulers were the fathers and mothers of the street families. You had to do whatever they said. The enforcers were the tough guys, the ones next to the leaders. The workers were all the third-rank street youths, the ones who meted out the punishments handed down by the mothers and fathers of the different families.

Yet, this was just Sara's interpretation of the culture, and it is one characteristic of street kid society that there is no consistent agreement on what it all means. In the shifting dynamics of the Square, the kids themselves often couldn't agree on who was really in charge or what the rules really meant or what the consequences of breaking them were going to be. As Nelson explains, the street family culture is "organized chaos." The youths had to stay alert to the shifting sands, or they would be pulled under. You couldn't just show up downtown after even a week's absence and understand the power dynamics. The culture required constant tending.

The street families had divided Portland into territories, Sara learned. To the north of Burnside was Old Town, reserved for the winos and bums. The street youth despised the older homeless. They didn't see themselves as homeless at all—they were street kids, a big difference to them. The crackheads, also despised, got the area down past the railroad tracks. The street kids took all the rest, which was the majority of downtown. Their territories extended across the river to include squats on the east side. The limit, says Sara, was out toward Gresham, ten miles east of Portland, which had its own old school. If you got 86'd from the territories by a street family, you were not to return downtown or to any other area pegged as a street kid territory. The punishment for ignoring an 86 was a beating or death.

Within the larger territories, there were smaller territories, usually defined by squats or hot spots. The Nihilistic Gutter Punks, or NGP, took the squats under the southwest Vista Bridge for a time, and a group of Sick Boys squatted along I-84. The territories shifted according to the power of each family. A more powerful family could easily push a weaker family out of a squat. Some families maintained their territories consistently, as the 420s did with their marijuana-dealing operation on the waterfront.

The street families tagged their territories. A surprising amount of the graffiti in downtown Portland is not from black or Hispanic gangs but from street families. "NGP" tags dot the downtown, along with "PSK" tags for the Portland Street Kids.

When marking their squats, street kids often draw a circle around a letter "N", with two arrows coming off the top and bottom. This is the traditional symbol for squatter's rights. Some squatters believe the symbol is an adaptation of a Nordic rune, with the "N" signifying a lightning strike and symbolizing power and the circle around it representing a dwelling. The arrow off the top symbolizes the rune Teiwaz, or courage in battle. The squatter's rights symbol varies slightly from the East to the West coasts. On the West Coast, the youths often add a small cross at the bottom, signifying the female side, or Wicca.

The leaders of all of the local street families, Sara felt, were two street people called Mama and Papa Wolf, the mother and father of a long-lived street family called the Wolfpack. Papa Wolf, also called Pops, hung around the Sisters of the Road café. He was an older man who positioned himself as an old school street father, much like Nelson. According to police, Papa Wolf has a long history of street kid involvement and is said to have had disobedient teenagers brought to him for beatings. Sara thought that Mama and Papa Wolf were like the president and vice president of the streets. If you had a beef with another street family, you were supposed to take it to them. Nelson scoffed at this. He thought other old school types were more powerful.

That first night they met, Sara slept in the peace camp. Nelson had to go back to Harbor Light to check in. As a paroled convict, he was on tight restrictions, and the adult shelters allowed no leeway with the rules. Nelson didn't like that. He complained that the youth shelters wouldn't let him stay in their housing. The general cutoff for youth shelters is twenty-one, though shelters in some cities have moved the age up to twenty-four or even higher. Nelson wanted to stay at the youth agencies. He seemed to think it was unfair that he was separated from "his" kids.

The next morning, Nelson showed Sara all the good places to get a meal. It was her first introduction into how to work the system. For breakfast there was a newer agency, New Avenues for Youth, which had a reputation for being the "best kitchen in town," according to street kids. There was also the Blanchet House in Old Town, which served three meals a day plus snacks and a two-hour Sunday brunch, as well as the Liberation Street Church on Burnside, which Sara thought had the best breakfast. For lunch, there was Harbor Light shelter where Nelson stayed and Outside In, which served everything from fresh salads made with dark greens to hot tacos. In another agency, street kids were fed breakfast and lunch with donated dishes from the area's top chefs and fresh pastries and breads from the most expensive bakeries in town. At the Sisters of the Road café, a board advertised the specials of the day. Friday was Mexican day, and the youths could chose from three different menus featuring dishes like burritos, Spanish rice, and lettuce. The price of a meal had gone up a quarter to $1.25, but you could still work for the meal in the kitchen.

There were additional options for dinner, including the St. Francis Church across the river. Food Not Bombs, an anarchist organization with chapters across the country, occasionally set up buffet tables on the waterfront. And every Sunday, a group called Potluck in the Park hosted a huge, free brunch in O'Bryant Square. Tables were spread with barbeque, big chunks of cake on plates, baskets of breads, donuts, and hunks of various pies. Sara thought the brunch was delicious, but she complained that they didn't cook their eggs long enough. The Potluck in the Park drew hundreds of street kids. "If you work it right, you could be eating all day," Sara says.

Asked if the food acts as a lure to get engaged in services, street kids often shrug. "It just makes it easier to stay on the streets," a youth named Adam Linday says. In Boston, a van delivers sandwiches and hot chocolate directly to the youths sleeping in the Harvard Square subway station. In Berkeley, charities offer street kids overflowing tables of fresh sandwiches, overstuffed bean burritos, chips, and dips. In Seattle, youths can pick up their meals seven days a week at the Teen Feed, or just wait on the street until the Street Links van drops by, offering free soy hotdogs, sandwiches, snacks, and cups of hot chocolate.

One posting on digihitch.com tells how a street youth ate well crossing Nevada and California, even though he was an avowed vegan. He stocked up in soup kitchens, filling his pack with fresh fruit and bread, and was "stuffed" by truckers, gas station owners, and others who bought him pizzas, breads, soy cheese, and bagels. At a Food Not Bombs gathering, he feasted on a vegan stew and fruit salad. Other street youths directed him to restaurants where he was given fresh peaches, Nutella, and beans. "How do people in this country starve?" he wondered. When he wanted candy, he stole it from health food stores. He was incensed when he was finally arrested for shoplifting Swedish fish candies; he felt persecuted by the police.

Perhaps in pointed response to all this largesse, picking through the garbage for food has become a point of pride among street kids. Street youths in the Square will "dumpster dive" even when agencies are offering hot meals a few blocks away. In her two-year study of Manhattan street kids, anthropologist Marni Finkelstein found that many youths prefer dumpster diving over charity meals, especially when the meal comes from a religious organization. "Almost all of their stories about dumpster diving included a tirade on how much Americans waste food," Finkelstein writes.

Their tummies full, Nelson took his kids—Carl, Crystal, and Sara—to the Square for the main activity of their day, spanging (panhandling) for cigarette and coffee money. Crystal used the old tactic of asking for change for the bus. Others used the common method of sitting pathetically on the sidewalk, intoning the constant,

"Spare some change, man?" With some of her earnings, Sara bought a coffee drink from the Starbucks, sipping as the kids hung out.

Spanging is a culture all to its own, with strict rules: Don't "fly a sign" (use a cardboard sign to beg) unless you know its cool. Don't "go agro" (aggressive) on the "custie" (customer, or mark) if it screws it up for everyone else. And whatever else you do, don't take someone else's corner.

In the Square, Sara knew one girl who made $50 a day. In New York City, a young woman says she averages $40 a day. A runaway in Boston boasts he can make that much in an hour hustling people at the subway station. Street kids use a bag of tricks to make money. A youth in Arizona mastered an Irish accent, which he said boosted his income $40 a night. Having a dog is a tried-and-true method of increasing the score, as many people who will not give money to an able-bodied young person will soften if they have a sad-looking pooch tied with a rope to their pack.

Agencies serving street youth are the first to tell you that panhandling is unnecessary. "Homeless kids don't need to panhandle," Ken Cowdery, director of New Avenues for Youth told the *Portland Mercury* newspaper. "They have the services they need." New Avenues for Youth opened in 1997 with the generous backing of local businesses. It offers shelter beds, educational services, a day program, hip-hop classes, pool tournaments, and even a state-of-the-art music studio. At New Avenues, street kids who want a job are offered internships at eleven local businesses, and those willing to hit the books are given classes and scholarships to college. Up the street, Outside In had expanded from a shabby storefront into a $5.5 million building with winding paths through a flower garden, decorated with colorful murals designed by street kids. The two-story building houses a day program, a medical clinic, an educational resource center, an employment program, a needle exchange, and cozy apartment-style living upstairs. All of this is free to street kids, along with acupuncture and weekly visits from a massage therapist. The agency also provides field trips, art classes, bike-repair seminars, and ice cream socials.

Street kids find a similar wealth of programs in other cities. Seattle, Washington, for instance, offers a variety of programs, including jobs, yoga, and an art sanctuary especially designed as a place for street kids to relax and reflect. Some cities, like New York, are more Spartan, offering the essentials of beds, clothes, condoms, food, and referrals.

Favor Ellis agrees that the street kids do not need to panhandle. Ellis divides street youth into two populations. There are those youths who are truly homeless, and then there are those whom she calls weekend warriors. "I don't think any of the truly homeless youth want to be homeless," she says. The truly homeless youth, she believes, are hampered by backgrounds of severe neglect, abuse, and mental illnesses. Ellis estimates that she calls the police or child protective services sixty times a month about the abuse or neglect of her clients. When she calls the families of some of the teenagers, "their parents say they don't want them." These youths, she says, are the invisible, silent majority of homeless youngsters who use the agencies to graduate into better lives.

The weekend warriors, on the other hand, don't want services because (1) the agencies have rules they don't want to follow, and (2) they don't want to leave the streets. These are the teenagers who are drawn to the Square, pretending they are penniless, and putting forth the worst possible face of homeless youth. The weekend warriors intersect freely with the truly homeless, and at times the two populations can be hard to distinguish, though their backgrounds are usually radically different. Though it might seem that the truly homeless would prey on the weekend warriors, often it is the other way around.

Ellis points out that while a few of those who later joined the Thantos Family were truly homeless, the core of the family, Carl Alsup, Crystal Grace, and Sara Baerlocher, had other choices in life. They may have called themselves street kids, but they were not homeless, and this distinction, Ellis says, is an important one. All three had homes.

——

Surrounded by his three eager new kids, Nelson looked and sounded all the more appealing. Soon, other street youths gravitated toward the group, and within days, Nelson's family grew.

One new member was a young man called T. J. Sara never knew his real name, but he was Thomas Schreiner, a nineteen-year-old with a skinny build, a buzz cut, a pierced upper lip, and a scar over his right shoulder. Schreiner was a heavy methamphetamine user, according to police records. He told police he met Carl and Crystal in April and met their street father, Nelson, soon after.

Like the other youths, Schreiner had options in life, including a mother who lived in town. According to Sara, he made his money by stealing bikes from the open-air Saturday market. That March, during the time of the peace camp, he repeatedly raped a female child who lived outside of downtown. When hanging around the Square, he dated Destiny, the pretty girl whom Nelson first had his eye on at the peace camp.

Schreiner quickly fell into the family routine. "We had the same routine every day," he said. "Wake up, go to Nafy [New Avenues for Youth] and eat, spange all day and give them the money." In New Avenues for Youth, the young rapist rubbed shoulders with younger homeless teenagers and children.

The other new member was a man named Matt Burch, who lived near the top of downtown on Trinity Place in an area known for drug dealing. His basement-level apartment had wide windows that looked out on the sidewalk off Burnside Avenue. Matt was a large, bald young man with heavily tattooed arms and legs. He told others he was a tattoo artist. "Jade [Crystal] was into Goth, and she was fascinated with Matt," Nelson says. "He did all this talk about satanism and how you could become a vampire." Several youths said that Matt was a drug dealer. "Matt sold crystal meth," Nelson says. "Carl was his apprentice," or a dealer-in-training, Sara confirms.

It was the middle of April. Nelson had been out of prison for less than three weeks and already had six followers in his new street family: Carl Alsup, Crystal Grace, Sara Baerlocher, Thomas Schreiner, Matt Burch, and the girl called Destiny. The group began referring to itself as a "family." Nelson was called the "dad."

As a street father, Nelson took naming rights. He decided Matt would be called Leviathan. "He named everyone after different warriors and different gods," Carl said later about Nelson. "He tried to run it like a cult, you know."

The cult part seemed to be out in the open. There was an aura of transparency about the creation of Nelson's new street family. This was not the brainwashing of a band of followers by a sneaky, hypnotic leader like Jim Jones. This was the open designing of an organized tribe, and no effort was made to cloak the power dynamics involved. Part of the fun for the youths, after all, was watching to see how the others performed. It was like a reality show on the streets, with everyone judging whether each member passed or failed.

Everyone knew, for instance, that their new "dad" was "testing" them. Nelson would make up a story, tell one kid it was a secret and not to be shared, and then wait to see if the secret got back to him. That way he would know if someone couldn't be trusted, Sara says. The fact that they all knew it was a test didn't ruin the excitement. The street kids waited eagerly to see if someone fell into the trap.

Another test was one of loyalty. Nelson might order one of his followers to go buy a pack of smokes. That kid would take off running like he had the most important mission in the world. "He gave threats," Sara claims. "He used the kids for everything." No matter what happened, Nelson wanted to hear about it. Every plan had to cycle through him. "The kids were always saying, 'ask James first. We have to ask James,'" Sara says.

Nelson made it clear that if the youths wanted to be his kids, they had to obey his rules. As Crystal said, "You had to abide by James' rules to be a member of the family." This part of the family was especially out in the open. There was no denying that Nelson was the boss.

Lounging on his bench, the spring sun warming his face, surrounded by his new adherents, Nelson had so many stories to tell. He told the youths he was a U.S. Marine trained by the military since the age of five to conduct "urban combat missions." He said he was a Christian. He said he practiced witchcraft. He said he worshipped Lilith, the dark goddess of Hebrew myth who had rejected Adam. He said he had done time in an army boot camp. He told Sara he had been in prison, but that was only because he had killed three men who had raped and tortured his sister. That was back in 1992, he said, and some of the men he knew at the time were Special Operations. Sara believed this.

He said he had murdered a man and buried him under a construction site, and the workers had poured concrete over the body. Sara was sure she had seen this in a movie, but then, maybe that movie was about Nelson. She believed he had a cousin killed in Iraq. She believed his hat was unique of all hats. It was a special hat. And so on.

Sara believed much of this and yet discounted it with a disingenuousness that was disconcerting. She had a deliberate naïveté, a willingness to suspend disbelief when it suited her. Despite all the stories, Sara didn't think that Nelson was a dangerous man. "I thought he was kidding," Sara says.

It was the doublethink of street kid culture, the evolution of the fantasy games that had begun in 1992 and evolved into a mindset. Nelson was both a murderer and a nice guy. He was telling the truth, and he was kidding. He was a killer and a marine who had been trained since age five, and he was the last of the immortal dragon warriors, a Christian, and a Wiccan, too. He was everything and all of the above, and yet he was only kidding.

Destiny's brother Jeremy often passed through the Square. He watched the youths clustered around Nelson and shook his head. "They were like baby vampires learning to feed," he says.

Nelson had left prison with a thick folder of prison papers, including his criminal history. He showed these papers to the other youths, including Carl, who was dazzled by the veracity of his hero's tales. Nelson *had* killed before.

Two things were never mocked in the Square: street names and street lies. In the Square, a youth could be a contract killer, a rare gemstone, the Sanskrit source of all knowledge, or a marine trained in death missions, and no one would point out what they really were: high school dropouts, aimless young adults, and drug addicts.

But what happens when a certified killer comes along?

8

On April 14, Portland Police raided the peace camp. They removed bags of clothing and other items that had been left on the sidewalk, claiming it was abandoned property. Robbed of their favorite hangout, the kids migrated to Matt Burch's basement-level apartment, which took on much the same role that Hal Charboneau's house had in 1992: a place to gather and conspire. Within a few weeks, there would be a dozen street kids in the apartment at a time, watching television and talking late into the night.

Shortly after they had moved into the apartment, Sara says that Nelson came to her and told her that he had found a piece of paper on which Matt had supposedly written her social security number. Nelson told her that Matt was planning to get credit cards with the number and rip Sara off. Sara says she never actually saw this paper, but she believed Nelson.

That was all it took. The "drama," as Sara put it, had begun. Matt would have to be punished. A convoluted plan was put in place. First, Nelson and Carl would frame Matt and make it look like he had used her social security number to get a credit card. To do this they would buy whatever they wanted with Sara's credit. They had a good time making up lists of all the stuff they would purchase: jewelry, clothes, and weapons. Then, the plan went, Nelson would report the purchases as credit card fraud and pin it all on Matt. They would kill Matt, and police would think he was murdered for credit card fraud.

Somehow this all made sense at the time. Sara couldn't quite explain later why the police wouldn't suspect them if the murder happened as planned. Asked about this, Sara laughs and shrugs her shoulders.

As long as the family was planning to kill Matt, Sara says, they added some other names to the list. One was Crystal Grace, Carl Alsup's girlfriend. The other was Thomas Schreiner, the young criminal called T. J. These two had to die because they had been seen flirting. Privately, Sara thought it was just unintentional flirting, the kind that teenagers often do. Put two kids in a room and the sparks fly, she says. But a line had been crossed, and that line was old school rules. If Sara could be labeled a slut for changing boyfriends in one day, then Crystal could die for flirting with the wrong man. After all, she was Carl's girl.

"Everything that happened they [the group] made into something bigger," Sara says. Jerry Fest, the author of *Street Culture,* believes this tendency toward dramatic exaggeration is a characteristic of teenagers who are cut off emotionally from their true selves. The streets fill a void in their lives, a hunger for emotion. "The safest way for them to experience emotion is to create drama," Fest says. "Drama is a huge part of life on the streets. They live and eat and breathe drama."

Nelson has a slightly different explanation for the dramas: "They [street kids] build dramas to get into fights," he says. "It's creating a reputation through the drama." The point, he says, is to create a drama that will escalate into a conflict, and the ensuing fight will then give the youths involved street credibility. It is through the dramas, Nelson says, that the youths build a reputation. Once they have that reputation, "Nobody fucks with you."

Sara was disappointed in Carl. Here he had seemed so devoted to Crystal, and now he wanted to kill her. "He started getting more jealous," Sara says. "He started thinking that men were superior to women." Sara thinks he got this idea from Nelson, who liked to talk about women's place being in the kitchen.

Trying to kill three people at the same time was hard. Sara says they made a plan to get Matt, Crystal, and Schreiner alone in the apartment so that Carl could shoot them through the basement window. Then, they would burn the building down. But the plan never went down. Sara just shrugs when asked why. The street family was distracted by other dramas, she implies. It often happens on the streets.

Like the kids in the 1992 Family, the kids in the Thantos street family didn't seem troubled that the group could turn so easily against some of its own. It was all "kidding" until someone actually acted, and even then it wasn't clear how far a game would go before it stopped being kidding and became real.

———

A new girl began hanging out in Matt's apartment around this time. She was another Crystal, this time Crystal Dawn Ivey (there would eventually be three Crystals in the family). Crystal Ivey was seventeen, a young-looking girl with floppy brown hair and wide, pretty, green eyes set in a heart-shaped face. As a child, she had moved a lot. Her father raised her as a single parent, and he often had to search for work. "I've been to six different schools," she says, "some several times."

In the middle of her eighth grade year, her father moved to Portland, Oregon. He promised that she would attend Park Rose High School for all four years. He kept his promise, but the constant moving and shifting had taken its toll on Crystal Ivey. Her freshman year, she did well, earning good grades and taking Tae Kwon Do. Her sophomore year, she began skipping school and hanging with her boyfriend, "but I made it through that year without too much trouble," she says.

In October of her junior year, the real trouble began. Crystal dropped out of high school. She moved out of her father's home to live with her boyfriend in Springfield, Oregon. On her own at sixteen, she became immersed in the drug culture. "I did a lot of meth," she admits.

Crystal tried hard to pull herself out of her downward spiral. She signed up for night-school classes to earn her high school equivalency degree. The day she turned seventeen, she signed papers to join the army. She was shipped out to Fort Jackson in South Carolina. Two months later, she was given a medical military discharge, she says, for depression. At seventeen, Crystal Ivey must have felt like a failure. She was a high school dropout and a military discharge. She moved back in with her dad. He was sympathetic, but he told her to get a job.

Instead, Crystal started hanging out downtown. That's where she met a young man associated with the Thantos Family. Soon, Crystal was hanging in Matt Burch's apartment with her boyfriend. She met James Nelson, Sara Baerlocher, Carl Alsup, Crystal Grace, Thomas Schreiner, Matt Burch, and the others. She knew most of them only by their street names: Thantos, Akasha, Wreath, Jade, T. J., and Leviathan.

Crystal was assigned the role of "princess." She explains, "We were the 'housewives-in-training.'" She and the other housewives-in-training cooked and cleaned Matt's apartment for practice. Their role in life, she says, was to "make the men look good." They were training for the day they got married and had babies.

The product of a broken home and rootless childhood, Crystal did not find this traditional typecasting insulting. She was the opposite of the hippies of a generation earlier, who had been raised in traditional families and then hit the road seeking freedom. Crystal craved structure, a set position in life, with concrete expectations and rewards. She had found the stability she was searching for, and it was a superficial version of 1950s sitcom families.

A number of studies have consistently shown that the majority of street kids hail from single-parent homes. It is not necessarily the structure of the family, but the number of losses incurred, that drives these teenagers to the streets. "The more transitions children experience in family structure and residence, the earlier they will initiate change on their own," write Les Whitbeck and Dan Hoyt in the 1999 study of runaways across four Midwestern states, *Nowhere to Grow: Homeless and Runaway Adolescents and Their Families*. Teenagers who experience multiple physical moves from relocation, divorce, remarriage, foster care, or other transitions are more likely to end up on the streets than those who stay in one place, building solid connections to their community.

At the same time that she hungered for the security that a traditional feminine role seemed to provide, Crystal grew interested in pagan religions. Like others in the family, she identified herself as a Wiccan. In the Thantos Family, she could explore her fascination with pagan rituals, playing an extended fantasy game where she was a Celtic princess and the men were her protectors, harkening back to a romantic time where women were of the hearth and men were warriors. It was like *The Lord of the Rings*, only with methamphetamine.

By joining a street family, Crystal enjoyed the absolute irresponsibility of not owing society a thing, including her ethics. Of all the street kids in the Thantos Family, Crystal was the most honest about this. "For me it was the freedom," she says. "Making my own decisions, when the guys weren't telling me what to do. I liked living in the apartment. I liked the lifestyle of not really having responsibility. The only rules we really followed were the family rules."

Crystal Ivey was never a big part of the family. She still went home to her dad at night, and the dominant men and women of the family treated her like a servant. When Nelson had to visit his parole officer, according to court records, he took Crystal Ivey with him and made her stand outside the offices, secretly holding his knife for him. Possession of a weapon was a violation of his parole.

If some of the paramilitary talk of the family struck Crystal as odd, she didn't say so. She was not an assertive teenager. Others in the family described her as "wanting to please everyone all the time, and yet, at the same time, not caring." It was the description of a depressed, submissive, seventeen-year-old girl. Crystal was given a street name as diminutive as her role in the family: Nix.

Everyone got involved when a new kid came poking around the Square. "You're supposed to take them in," Sara says. That didn't mean taking the new kids to shelters, and it certainly didn't mean taking them to the police. It meant absorbing them into the street family culture.

The Thantos Family attracted new members almost daily during those weeks of April. One was eighteen-year-old Joshua Brown-Lenon, who came with the street name Scooby. A thin-faced young man with wide eyes set under a buzz-cut of brown hair, Joshua was described as a "weird, out-there kind of guy" by other street kids. "I'm a gutterpunk," Joshua says. "Give me 80 units [of methamphetamine], I'll slam that in my arm." His mother told police he had a "global dysfunction disorder with a possibility of schizophrenia." Joshua claims he was diagnosed as having frontal lobe brain damage as a result of a car accident.

According to court records, Joshua had been convicted of assault with a deadly weapon as a minor. He was first convicted at age thirteen. His only job had been selling hotdogs out of a cart, but in

Joshua's mythology, he had earned up to three grand a week dealing drugs while living at the Hilton Hotel.

Before he met Nelson, Joshua says he was part of the Sick Boys street family, which he describes as "more of a family. We took care of everybody, like a regular family." He admits, "There is a lot of violence. I don't want to say you get jumped in, but you've got to show your heart. You've got to show your loyalties." New recruits show their loyalty by being stomped into the family. For this purpose, the Sick Boys use "Sick Cages," fighting cages made of torn-down cyclone fencing. Police confirm the existence of these cages in several remote areas. One Sick Cage is permanently located in Washington Park, a forested area above downtown known for squatting. The ground is littered with used syringes and with broken glass to make the fights even bloodier. According to one Sick Boys member, up to a hundred and fifty kids have shown up to watch Sick Boys cage fights. In one famous stomp, a man accused of wronging a Sick Boys leader was so badly beaten that he ended up hospitalized.

Like others on the streets, Joshua is quick to say the street family culture is not all negative. "If it was all bad, I would not have been down there as long as I was. I would have gone home," he says. Asked how the culture was positive, Joshua explains, "Say I'm doing heroin and I'm dope sick. And say my partner is dope sick too. I'll give him my last shot so he can feel better."

Anger the wrong old school leader, though, and there will be trouble. "You do something to the wrong guy down in the Square, you get put on bitch status," Joshua says. "You know what that means, right? You got to do everything he tells you. You're on a leash. If he says kiss my feet, you kiss his feet." According to other street kids, Joshua often ended up on bitch status.

That April 29, 2003, Joshua was screened in a local youth shelter. The evaluator recorded that Joshua "seems motivated to find employment and work on goals." Joshua was offered the usual menu of long-term programs, which he seemed to ignore. Instead, he used the shelters as a means to keep himself on the streets. "Youth shelters give you a place to stay, they give you bus tickets, they give you everything," he says. "Nafy [New Avenues for Youth] . . . they give you schooling. You can use whatever resources they have. Outside In, they have a medical department that is just top-notch. . . . They've got acupuncture, massage therapy, so much to offer."

Though Joshua was legally an adult, he didn't like adult shelters and refused to use them. "Places like Harbor Light, they expect youth to fend for themselves," he complains. He was upset that he only had a few more years on the streets before he would be kicked out of the youth agencies.

Joshua took pride in not returning home. "It takes real dedication to not go back home," he says. "There were times I wanted to go back home, you know, when it was raining. But I thought about all the drugs I was doing, and I would have had to give them up. I thought, 'I ain't going to give this up.'"

That April, Joshua saw a beautiful teenage girl with strawberry blonde hair in the Square. The girl was alone and being hit on by an older man. Joshua says he confronted the man. "I said, 'Hey, dude, what are you doing? How old are you? Because she's like sixteen, and how old are you?' Me and my partner, we scared him so bad that dude never came back downtown."

The pretty girl's name was Sarah La'Dona Caster. Tall and slender, with pale clear skin, warm pink lips and silky hair, Sarah Caster was indeed a knockout. She had left home because she had been fighting with her mom. Now, she was downtown in the Square, looking lonely and lost and afraid. She was only sixteen.

Like Crystal Ivey, Sarah Caster was brand new to the streets. Joshua admits that he brought her into the street family culture. "Do

I feel bad about that? Yeah, I do," says Joshua. Other kids thought Sarah was alarmingly naïve. "She had *no* street smarts, none whatsoever," said one youth. Sarah was a pacifist, and she told others she had never been in a fight. "Sarah didn't even like punching people in the shoulder," Crystal Ivey later remarked.

Joshua says the other street men admired Sarah's beauty, and several asked him if they could have Sarah when he was done dating her. He told them no, that Sarah could make up her own mind about whom to date. He was proud of his progressiveness in this regard. Most of the men were not so respectful of the girls, he thought, and would pass them around when they were done with them. The girls, for their part, didn't seem to mind. It was all part of the dramas that made street life so exciting.

On May 5, Sarah Caster walked into a youth shelter and was evaluated for services. She said she felt bad about how she and her mom were fighting. The evaluator was concerned Sarah might have learning disabilities. The screener believed she was a good candidate for family reunification and encouraged her to meet with her mother, but Sarah wasn't ready to go home yet.

In a matter of only weeks, Sarah was swept, briefly and with devastating consequence, into the street family culture. Through Joshua, she met Nelson and his family, and she was invited to stay at Matt's apartment, where she too became a "princess" and led the life of a "housewife-in-training." She was given the name Valkyrie, after one of the beautiful maidens of Norse myth who serve the slain warriors in Valhalla.

⸻

The apartment was often a scene of mayhem. The floor was "wall-to-wall mattresses," according to the apartment manager, and littered with dog feces and syringes. One street girl had three pit bulls, while another youth kept kittens. One of the pit bulls went right through a bathroom door and killed a kitten. According to some of the family, the pit bull was taken outside and killed in retribution.

In Matt's apartment, drugs appeared to be a major occupation, as they are for street kids everywhere. Along the East Coast, heroin is the drug of choice for street kids, but on the West Coast and in the central states, methamphetamine has become more popular. Street youth mix the white crystals with water right in the plastic bag and then aspirate the mixture into a syringe before injecting the liquid into their veins. At times, they even bypass the use of cotton to strain out impurities.

The use of methamphetamine has strongly influenced the violent fantasy aspect of the street family culture. Meth is notorious for inducing complex criminal plans, paranoia, and psychosis, and one hit of the drug can keep a person awake for days, encouraging ever-escalating violent dramas. "Crystal is *the* drug right now," says Joshua. "It's the rush, all the things you can do. You can have sex for hours. I don't know how it is for girls, I assume it's the same, but it brings more pleasure. There's no conscience. You don't care."

Sitting up late in the apartment, the family made up new rules and degrees of punishment. They gave the new punishments code names, so they could refer to them without actually saying what they meant.

SOS meant smash on sight.

STD meant smash to death.

DOS meant destroy on sight.

Nelson assigned some of the family members the role of warriors, according to several of the youths. Their job was to protect the family. These warriors were called death knights. To protect the family, the death knights were given "extensive" martial arts training, according to court records. Ultimately, the death knights were expected to kill someone. Nelson, however, refuses to take responsibility for the death knights. "Carl, Matt and T. J. founded the death knights," he insists.

Carl eagerly embraced the role of a death knight warrior. The boy who desperately wanted to impress people could now say he was a warrior in training. He even took a new street name in celebration of his new identity: D. K., short for Death Knight.

But Sara heard that Carl couldn't take that name because there was already a youth with the street name D. K., and on the streets you can't have two people with the same name. It was yet another old school rule. She thought Carl should stick with Wreath. He ignored her advice.

Everyone in the family now had a role to play. The men were death knight warriors and the women were princesses. Crystal Grace was the leader of the princesses, and Carl was the leader of the warriors. Their father and commander was James Nelson.

The Thantos Family was pushing harder toward violence. Like street kids everywhere, they were armed. Sara, or Akasha, carried a heavy motorcycle chain wrapped into a circle with duct tape, called a smiley chain. She called her smiley chain the Equalizer. Smiley chains had become popular in the late 1990s with the rapid growth of street families and are now found in street kids' pockets and backpacks from Sacramento to Boston. In her two-year study of New York City street youth, Marni Finkelstein found that the majority of kids carry a weapon, "commonly a knife or a smiley, a large lock and chain used to hit people."

Some say the chains are called *smileys* because when you beat someone with one, it leaves smiling crescent marks on their skin. Others say it's because after you hit someone in the head with a smiley chain, all the victim does is smile and drool. Still others say it is because the chain, in repose, forms the curving shape of a smile.

There are two basic ways to make a smiley chain. One is to take a length of bike chain and wrap one segment into a handle with heavy electrical or duct tape. Another is to link a loop of heavier chain with a padlock or pulley to hold the ends together. Some street youths carry their smiley chains slung around their necks or laced through their belt loops, but many keep them tucked away in backpacks and pockets. What can seem like a punk fashion trend is really a weapon.

Smiley attacks can be deadly. In Spokane, Washington, a group of street kids went "bum bashing" for sport in 1998, using their smiley chains to beat an older homeless man. One of the street youths said he did it so "my reputation didn't drop." Their victim died of a traumatic head injury. In Portland, police have recorded numerous smiley-chain attacks.

Other street kid weapons include machetes, claw hammers, num-chucks, and metal pipes. "I remember carrying around a pipe with a nail going through both sides," Joshua recalls. "I'd say, 'You want this going through your neck?'"

Still, the most popular street youth weapon is the knife. Some carry outlandish medieval knives, three-pronged or ornately embel-lished, purchased from designer knife stores. But the most common is a sharp knife concealed in a sheath. Switchblades, butterfly knives, and other tension blades are also popular. "Knives have more impact: they're more deadly," Joshua explains. "Some loosen the screws so you can flip it open real quick."

Street youths take pride in their weapons, often naming them. After his release from prison, Nelson carried a large knife he called the Death Dealer. Only a few family members, including Carl, were allowed to touch their street father's knife, according to reports.

Andrea Timm, a night security guard at the Square, was familiar with the weapons the street kids carried. Many carried the smiley chains, she says. Some of the tougher ones carried "baseball bats or a solid object." She judged how tough a youth was by how hard his weapon was. The shelters are also accommodating toward the weapons. Many have a place where kids can store their weapons, such as a "knife drawer." Joshua explains how it works in Portland shelters: "You hand them your weapons. It's a trust issue. When you leave, you get them back."

The one weapon street youths generally don't carry is a gun. "Most of us are felons," Joshua says. "We don't want to do the time." Nothing brings police heat faster than guns, and street kids are smart enough to know this. If the street families of Portland were armed with guns, they would promptly be classified as gangs and driven out of the downtown area.

With the weapons came the threats. The Thantos Family had a favorite saying: "Snitches get stitches and wind up in ditches." They just loved the sound of it, rolling off their tongues as they hung out in the Square, but the phrase was not original to the group. It was the same saying that the Denver street family used after their stomping death of the homeless man. The phrase is popular with street kids across the country. You can buy punk rock buttons that feature the warning, drawn in red on a black background. A Seattle punk band named Snitches Get Stitches released an album titled *I Liked You Better as a Corpse*. Various eco and animal rights organizations have also adopted the phrase. Earth First used it as a magazine article title.

In graffiti shorthand, *snitches get stitches* is a bar with lines drawn through it, the image of a stitch. Just as the Sick Boys logo uses a stitch for a mouth on a dead-looking face, other street families also use the stitch warning. The logo for the Portland Drunk Punks street family is a whiskey bottle with the letters PDP across the label and a stitch across the bottom. The stitch acts as a warning to other street kids.

Considering his history, it was ironic that Nelson was now repeating the phrase. No one in his new family seemed aware that Thantos, their god of death, had once cooperated with the police and even worn a wire to incriminate his last street family.

Swinging through the Square, talking about snitches and death knights and stomp-on-sight punishments, Nelson and his new street family sounded formidable. But at the same time, some of the other kids in the Square dismissed them as "silly drama queens." Their behavior was typical to the culture. There wasn't much that was unusual about the new Thantos Family.

Inside the family, a different emotion might have been growing: fear. "Nelson took some of the most vulnerable people downtown and made them his loyal subjects," Joshua says. Asked if he meant the other youths were naïve, Joshua replies, "I don't think that word even does it justice. They were afraid. Most of them were afraid. He [Nelson] would say things like, 'All of these people are expendable.'"

This was the culture of control and intimidation masquerading as a "family" that Jessica Kate Williams found when she first started going downtown.

9

Her birth mother had neglected her. How much Becky Williams didn't know, at least not at first. She did know that Jessica had been removed from her mother and placed with a foster parent who was overwhelmed by the infant's special needs. The agency had called Becky and her first husband and asked if they were willing to take Jessica. Sure, Becky said. Bring her on over.

At nine months old, Jessica couldn't suck from a bottle, roll over, crawl, or sit. She could only scream. Becky was told that Jessica's birth mother was an alcoholic, a prostitute, and a drug addict. She had already lost one child to the state, a daughter so brain damaged that she had to be institutionalized.

Jessica, born on June 23, 1980, joined seven other children in Becky's home in Simi Valley, California. "Jessica made eight," Becky remembers fondly. Nearly all her children had been abused, institutionalized, or abandoned. One son, adopted from Korea, was legally blind. Another son had been in psychiatric institutions. Most of the children had been in foster care, and nearly all were considered to have special needs. Becky and her first husband accepted them all. They didn't try to change their children, not even the son who identified himself as gay. They didn't consider it their place to judge.

A simple-looking woman with no pretensions, Becky has a calming effect on those around her. It seems as if nothing can scare her. A recently adopted, raging toddler cannot scare her. Drug effects and sexual abuse cannot scare her. Children seem to sense this the moment they walk through her door. They know they will find acceptance. And because of this trust, even the most troubled children have flourished under her care. Jessica, of all her children, would be the most disabled.

"For the first few years of her life," Becky recalls, "Jessica was constantly screaming, kicking, and yelling." These weren't your typical toddler temper tantrums. They were the rages of a child trapped in a world of confusion and pain.

One night when Jessica was about three, Becky went into her bedroom to check on her. Jessica was gone, and the bedroom window was open. Becky found her wandering the yard. She brought her inside and tucked her back into bed. There was no sense in trying to reason with her. Jessica didn't even speak until she was four. The next day, Jessica's parents nailed her bedroom window shut. That night Jessica went out the front door. Becky locked the front door and slept on a mattress in the hall outside of Jessica's room. Jessica woke up and tried to climb over her on the way out.

Jessica wasn't *trying* to be bad. No one seemed to understand this except her parents. They knew intuitively that something in her brain, the part that controlled impulses, was damaged. Even simple things confounded Jessica. Her mother might tell her not to play in the street and two minutes later Jessica would be out in traffic. Discipline didn't work because Jessica couldn't remember why she was being punished. Becky described Jessica's brain as "like Swiss cheese." There were black holes in her mind, places where information simply vanished.

Jessica, she discovered, could also be a delight, a hair-raising, terrifying, fun-loving delight. Becky had only to look into her wide-set, innocent eyes to fall in love with her all over again.

Her parents began to suspect that the birth mother's alcoholism played a role in Jessica's delayed development. Becky began a long round of visits with doctors and specialists. Jessica was four when Becky got the official diagnosis: her daughter had fetal alcohol syndrome, or FAS.

The effect of drinking on the fetus has been known for thousands of years. Even the Old Testament admonishes mothers not to drink. A 1915 Chicago health brochure warned new mothers, "Babies Die When Mother Is a Drunkard." But the term fetal alcohol syndrome wasn't coined until 1973. The syndrome is now considered a spectrum disorder, much like autism, and as with autism, cases can range from mild to severe. Some victims are of normal intelligence with specific learning disabilities, while others are more universally damaged.

Jessica fell in the moderate-to-severe range of the spectrum. She had the distinctive facial features of an FAS child: a low nose bridge, folding eyes, and a smooth upper lip. These facial anomalies only occur when the mother drinks heavily between days fifteen and twenty-two of pregnancy, when the fetal mid-face is developing in the womb. Most children affected by fetal alcohol spectrum disorder do not have the facial features and, in fact, can look completely normal, even when their brains are severely damaged.

Diane Malbin, founder of Fetal Alcohol Syndrome Consultation, Education and Training Services, an educational group focused on the disorder, shows slides of brain scans of children affected by prenatal alcohol. These she lays down, side by side, with brain scans of normal children. The children damaged by alcohol have smaller brains. In severe cases, the brain is atrophied. It looks like curled, shrunken intestines in a sea of inky black. The corpus callosum, the center for interactive thought, is often smaller or even missing. In less severe cases, the brain is of normal size, but there are black specks dotted across the frontal lobe. These are lesions, literally holes in the brain.

When the mother drinks, alcohol passes directly from her blood into the developing fetal brain, where it kills cells. Damage can occur during the first few months, when a woman might not know she is pregnant. Memory, independent thought, critical reasoning, and comprehension are commonly affected. Physical problems can include poor muscle tone, eye problems, and bad coordination. Jessica had all these problems.

As a person with FAS, Jessica became a great mimic. She saw others around her thinking for themselves, and she would imitate their behaviors, trying to fill the void inside herself. She practiced and pretended her whole life, trying desperately to be just like normal people. But anyone who knew Jessica, says her mother, had to realize she was disabled. "If you knew her, you'd see she wasn't functioning," Becky says.

There is no cure for FAS. Occupational therapy and other interventions help children learn coping strategies. The most important treatment, says Malbin, is acceptance. The world needed to make room for Jessica. Rather, the world needed to make a room that fit Jessica. This didn't happen.

There are far more children born every year with fetal alcohol syndrome than are born with autism or Down syndrome. Fetal alcohol damage is the leading cause of mental retardation, with an estimated forty thousand babies born with the syndrome annually. And yet, the condition receives far less attention and support than other disabilities.

The Williams discovered that there would be no specialists in the schools to help them, no advocacy groups in Washington pressing for funding, and no media outcry for more services. In many ways, Jessica didn't exist on a policy or social service level.

Sometimes, Becky would get the attitude, you adopted her, so you should deal with her problems. Jessica was an unwanted child at birth, and in many ways, outside of her family, she would remain an unwanted child for her entire life.

Becky said, "Jessica, don't go down the block." And there was Jessica running down the block. She was big for her age, a soft, cuddly golden-brown girl with folding, wide-set eyes. There were predators out there.

One lived next door. He seemed like a nice man. He often invited the other children over to play with his own daughters. Jessica, who was in elementary school, went over to his house with her sisters. The Williams didn't suspect a thing, and neither did any of the other neighbors. The man got Jessica alone and molested her. Jessica was afraid to tell. The man had threatened her. Finally, Jessica did break down and told her mother. But no one in the neighborhood believed her story. She already had a reputation as a troublemaker.

By this time, Becky had lost her first husband, killed by a drunk driver, and married her second husband, Sam Williams. A painter by trade, Sam was high on a ladder over a marble floor one day when the ladder slipped. Several surgeries since have left him with a permanent stoop. Sam likes to play the guitar, and his calloused fingers play with each other when he talks.

Becky and Sam pressed charges. More information came out. There were other victims. The man was tried and convicted, but the neighborhood was ruined for the Williams. They moved to North

Carolina, where Jessica had her happiest times. She had a big farm to roam and a horse to ride. The teacher at the one-room schoolhouse seemed to understand her.

Too soon, the family had to move for work, this time to Oregon. Sam Williams remembers driving down the Willamette Valley and seeing the mountains rising above him and how beautiful they were. The family bought a home in Gladstone, just outside of Portland, a sprawling ranch house with a basketball hoop in the driveway, which always seemed to ring with the shouts of children. There they settled into the relentless struggle of getting Jessica through school. They faced daunting odds. According to one study, 60 percent of children with FAS end up getting expelled or suspended or dropping out of school.

Becky remembers the icy stares. That was the worst of it. No matter how often she met with teachers, how much she tried to explain what FAS was, there was always that moment when they realized who she was, the mother of *that* girl. Too many teachers believed that Jessica was just lazy. Or faking. Or that she must have neglectful parents. The Williams, they assumed, just weren't trying hard enough.

The icy stares came when Becky Williams sat at a table with her large, smiling, eager-to-please, yet defiant daughter next to her, and the teacher sat on the other side. The conference always seemed to begin, "Now, Mrs. Williams, have you tried to . . . ?" The Williams had tried everything. They got Jessica tutors. They sent her to after-school classes. They had her tested. Jessica fell into the range of mild mental handicap. She was what was once called a "slow learner." Her intellectual abilities were frozen at the level of a twelve-year-old child, but even that IQ was misleading. Jessica's verbal IQ was that of a child of twelve—she was glib, friendly, and capable of sounding much smarter than she was—but her other cognitive processes, such as critical thinking, were more like a four-year-old's. Confronted with a problem requiring independent thinking, Jessica would literally employ the magical thinking of a toddler: if I close my eyes, it doesn't exist.

Jessica was extremely gullible and easy to fool, and she was almost incapable of abstract thought. Like many with FAS, she couldn't "think in her head," or problem solve. It's a difficult disability for others to understand because most of us have what is called "executive function," or the ability to retrieve and visualize information. It is executive function that allows us to imagine scenes from a book, that lets us add numbers in our head without using our fingers or retrace a road map in our mind. Because of her frontal-lobe brain damage, Jessica lacked these abilities. Her mind was like a computer without a hard drive.

Jessica grew physically, but her memory did not improve. It became harder and harder, for instance, for Becky to get her to take a bath. With her memory problems, Jessica thought she had taken a bath. She would get in her mom's face and yell, "I'm clean! I took a bath yesterday!" No matter how Becky reasoned with her, Jessica was convinced she was right. She had taken a bath yesterday. She was sure.

Like a toddler, Jessica could throw a doozy of a tantrum. "She could get violently upset," says her mother. "There were areas that just drove us crazy. She could be a real challenge to care for and raise." Once she pushed her father in the hallway upstairs after he said she couldn't leave the house, almost sending him down the stairs.

Jessica grew rapidly through adolescence, soon topping six feet two inches and 220 pounds. She wasn't necessarily fat. She was a very tall woman with a soft, voluptuous figure. She had beautiful long legs and an ample, almost maternal bosom. With her golden-brown skin, she looked a lot like how her sisters described her: a big, warm teddy bear.

In their Gladstone home, Jessica's closet was filled with expensive mail-order clothing made just for her size. At her height and weight, she had trouble finding clothes that fit her large frame, and her mom helped her pick nice clothes from catalogs. Even as a teenager, Jessica could not be trusted to buy her own clothes. If Becky gave her $20 for a new shirt at the mall, Jessica would walk away and come back later without the money or the shirt, and she wouldn't be able to remember what had happened.

As she matured, Jessica's facial anomalies looked more exotic than strange. Her wide eyes and smooth upper lip gave her an aura of innocent sensuality. On the streets, you would have noticed her for her height and size, topped with all that brown curly hair, and not necessarily for her wide-set, almost cherubic face.

In her big, warm, and diverse family, Jessica felt free to identify racially as she pleased. Though she was of mixed heritage, Caucasian and African American, she chose to call herself black because that was how many people saw her. She remained comfortable around people of all colors and counted among her friends those of all nationalities, ages, and backgrounds, from the little kids she played with down the street to the old people she met on the bus.

In her senior year, Jessica sat on the couch, carefully done up in a formal gown with a boutonniere in her lap. She was waiting for her date for the winter formal. One of the most popular boys in school had asked her out. Her sisters knew. Anyone could see it. Jessica sat on that couch for the rest of the night, refusing to believe. The boy must have forgotten. Nobody could play such a mean trick. Finally, she went to take off the fancy gown. Her mother could see how crushed she felt.

Becky tried to talk to her. Sometimes Jessica would admit to her disability and how it affected her. Most of the time, though, she refused to discuss it. She didn't want to be different. She wanted to be like everyone else.

There was no Forrest Gump romanticism for her condition. Jessica *knew* she was handicapped. She *knew* she was different. She was just smart enough to know she was handicapped and just delayed enough not to be able to change it. Becky grieved for the loss of the person God had intended Jessica to be. "She had a will that was so strong, a determination," Becky says. "Had she not been robbed before birth, I cannot imagine what kind of person she could have become. She was positive and uplifting. She could find good in anyone, no matter how rotten and scummy they were. She was so demeaned and degraded by other people. She didn't let any of that get her down."

The Williams credited Jessica's religious faith for her optimism. Jessica was remarkably devout for a teenager. The Williams belonged to a Baptist church in Oregon City, and they were heavily involved in charity work. Sam Williams often ministered to the homeless downtown in soup kitchens and shelters. That wasn't enough for Jessica, who attended two other churches as well.

At school, Jessica heard from her fellow special education classmates that eighteen was the magic number. At eighteen, she was told, your parents can no longer tell you what to do. This was exciting news to Jessica, who had begun to think her parents were too strict. Becky and Sam didn't seem to want to let her out of their sight.

Jessica celebrated her eighteenth birthday by taking off with another teenage girl down the street. The two caught the bus that afternoon and didn't come home. As afternoon waned into evening, and evening into night, the Williams panicked. Becky called the police and was told that as Jessica had turned eighteen, her parents had no legal jurisdiction over her. She was now an adult in the eyes of the law.

Jessica came home safely the next day, full of herself. The two girls had spent the night at a friend's house. Jessica had made her point: she was an adult now, and she knew it. Becky and Sam looked for safe ways to let Jessica feel grown-up. They gave her a phone line in her bedroom. Jessica loved that. She would sit and gab for hours with the other special education students. Aware that their daughter was pushing for independence, the Williams struck a deal with her. One of the bargains was that she would always call if she were going to be late or sleep over at a friend's house. For the most part, Jessica kept her end of the bargain.

It took her five years to graduate, and, still, the high school had to reduce the requirements for her, but eventually Jessica earned her diploma. She was photographed in her high school graduation cap and gown, a broad smile on her face.

But the end of high school marked a turning point for Jessica. The brighter kids went off to college, and the others had found jobs. Suddenly, Jessica had nothing to do. She qualified for developmental-disabilities services through the county, though the Williams soon discovered that there were no job programs designed specifically for those with FAS. "No one could come up with a viable career plan for her," Becky explains.

Working with caseworkers, Becky found two jobs where Jessica flourished. One was in a pet shop, the other in a plant store. Both jobs were temporary and lasted only a few weeks. After the funding dried up, the managers had to let her go, and once again, Jessica was unemployed.

Becky watched Jessica's self-esteem plummet. "She kept seeing all these people passing her by," Becky says, including her own siblings. Her older sisters got married and began careers. Her blind brother was a manager in a department store. Another brother was a successful show-business manager in California. Her parents had recently adopted an eight-year-old drug-affected boy who had been labeled unadoptable, and he was now an honor student. Jessica was the only person in the Williams household who couldn't find traction in life.

Jessica had made lots of friends over the years, and she began filling her time by visiting them. On her bus journeys, she made new friends, and some of these new friends were so weird that her parents fretted. Nothing bad happened, but the family was worried enough after Jessica brought home a few of these human strays that they changed the locks.

The summer of 2002, Jessica turned twenty-two and was determined to get a job at the zoo. She had decided this was the age at which she would become independent. Every day, she took the bus up to the Portland Zoo. The trip involved going downtown and transferring to another bus. She told her mother she had filled out four or five applications at the zoo. Becky figured it didn't hurt for Jessica to keep trying.

One day, Jessica came home and made an announcement: she had gotten the job. Everyone was so pleased for her. Jessica said the work was part-time, sweeping and cleaning up. For several weeks, she got up every weekday morning, combed her hair, and went off to work at the zoo.

After three weeks of this, Becky asked Jessica for her first pay stub. She needed to report the income to social security as Jessica received a small disability stipend from the government. Jessica hemmed and hawed and said that she had gotten hired between paychecks. She told her mother she would be on the next paycheck. She kept going to work. Another week passed, and this time Becky was firm. She needed to see the pay stub. Jessica had been working almost a month.

She had to have gotten paid. It was illegal not to report the income to social security. This time Jessica said she had lost her paycheck.

That's when Becky knew. There was no zoo job, and there never had been. Jessica had been lying. She had made up a story to make herself feel better, then got trapped in the tale. She had been unable to think her way out of the fib, so she just kept going to her pretend job. What her daughter had been doing during those weeks, Becky wasn't sure.

When confronted, Jessica cried on her mother's shoulder. "Mom, I feel like a failure," she sobbed. "My friends have apartments and jobs. I'm twenty-two, and I don't have anything."

—

Becky asked the county disability services for help. As Christmas season of 2002 arrived, they offered Jessica a temporary job at the Ross Dress for Less store in Portland. The Ross store was right on the bus mall in the heart of downtown. Jessica worked part-time, between fifteen and twenty-five hours a week. Her coworkers liked her. Her boss described her as very pleasant and always smiling.

At twenty-two, Jessica was just starting to act feminine. For the first time in her life, she wanted to look attractive. She started playing with her hair a bit, shaping it into soft, shiny curls that brushed her shoulders. She asked her sisters for makeup advice. Around her soft brown neck she wore a star-shaped pendant on a leather cord.

During her lunch breaks, Jessica explored downtown. The Williams had always lived in the suburbs, and for a sheltered young woman like Jessica, the city was a thrilling place. That Christmas, the sidewalk trees were dressed in lights, Salvation Army volunteers rang their bells in the crisp air, and the streets were crammed with shoppers with bulging bags. The Meier and Frank department store across the street from Ross opened its annual winter wonderland, which took up almost an entire floor, with a Santa and a tiny train that ran on a monorail along the ceiling for children to ride. Jessica went home talking nonstop about how much she loved downtown.

Soon enough, Jessica discovered Pioneer Courthouse Square. It was less than two blocks from her work, and it had a giant holiday tree decorated with bright lights. Just like any other working woman, Jessica could buy her lunch from one of the many food carts billowing steam into the cold air. The street families of the Square panhandled among the shoppers.

After her lunch breaks, Jessica returned to work. The Ross store was very busy at Christmas. By five o'clock it was already dark out, and Jessica caught the bus home to Gladstone. It was a long commute, the bus lumbering from stop to stop, but Jessica didn't mind. She chatted with the other commuters.

Soon after starting the Ross job, her mother says, Jessica met a street kid panhandling on the sidewalk outside the store. True to her nature, Jessica sat down next to the street kid and started a conversation. Soon she was sitting with him on her lunch breaks, the two of them chatting up a storm while he panhandled.

Within a few days of their meeting, the street youth suggested that Jessica steal some clothes from the store. He gave her a foolproof plan: he would go through the store, picking up clothes, and when he got to her line, Jessica would only pretend to ring them up. Jessica reacted with indignation. She didn't steal! She grew angry and upset. That night, she told her mother all about it. She wasn't going to be friends with someone who stole. Becky agreed that was a good idea.

Becky had begun to have some disquieting feelings about her daughter's working downtown. The job was only a week old, and already Jessica was making friends with questionable characters. Becky didn't know a lot about downtown Portland, and soon Jessica had forgiven her new friend and was sitting with him again outside the store at lunch, talking while he panhandled. Becky sighed. She wished the vocational services hadn't placed her daughter downtown.

Christmas passed; with January came 2003, and the job was over. The manager said he would have liked to hire Jessica, but he just couldn't afford it. Becky wondered why they did this to disabled people. What was the point of giving Jessica a job for just a few weeks? They couldn't have found a better way to crush her spirit if they had tried.

Having tasted independence, Jessica was upset. She wanted to work. She wasn't a lazy person; she was eager to be productive and independent. Becky soothed her daughter the best she could. They would keep trying. They typed up Jessica's résumé that night. In the morning, Jessica announced that she was going looking for a job, and she caught the bus back to downtown.

10

In February 2003, Jessica began hanging out downtown on a regular basis during the days. She told the street kids in the Square that her parents had kicked her out of the house. "I met her probably in February," recalls Joshua Brown-Lenon. "She was laying on a bench. She said, 'My mom and dad kicked me out.' She acted like any other normal twenty-year-old. She was bright and funny. I remember her in her blue jeans and baby blue sweater, all happy-go-lucky."

The street kids believed Jessica when she said her parents had kicked her out. They believed her when she said she was smart. They believed her when she said her parents were too strict. They believed anything, but Jessica didn't know that. She thought they were her friends. She was blown away by their acceptance.

For Jessica, the street kids were the first peers who were willing to pretend she was normal. They nodded as she talked, agreeing with whatever she said. Yes, she was smart. Yes, her parents were mean. She told Sara Baerlocher of her parents that they "never give me a chance to prove that I am smart." Sara, along with the rest of the Thantos Family, was willing to give her that chance. Sara was convinced that nothing was wrong with Jessica. "She was smart," Sara insists.

On second thought, Sara did notice one thing wrong with Jessica: she didn't like violence. "She refused to stay around anyone who was fighting," Sara says, with a perplexed look. She would get up and leave. To Sara, this was the only evidence of a possible mental handicap. "It was the only way she was like a child," she says firmly. Jessica's passive nature worked against her in the Square. The other kids saw it as a mark of weakness. How could you ever be old school if you hated violence?

Jessica didn't carry a weapon. Her mother said she didn't use drugs. She did smoke cigarettes, a new habit she tried to keep from her mom. Jessica loved the dramas, though. Her own mother admits she was a drama queen. "She was a drama queen to the max," Becky says.

Becky and Sam grew concerned. They sat Jessica down for a talk. They offered to remodel the garage into an apartment. That way Jessica could have a place of her own, and yet she would be safe and near the family. She could come and go as she pleased, but she'd always be welcome inside for meals. Doing the remodeling might take a couple of months, though. The family was on a tight budget. Or, they offered, they could save the money for an apartment nearby for her, someplace right down the street. They would find her a roommate, maybe someone from church. Again, it might take a little while.

Both ideas sounded okay to Jessica, but she wasn't about to wait. "She wanted it right now," Becky says. Jessica insisted she was going to get a job downtown. She told her parents a street girl had told her about the job-training program at Outside In, the homeless youth agency. Jessica said that she had signed up for their vocational services and that the agency had promised her a job.

In truth, she had lied to the agency, shaving three years off her age to make herself nineteen. At twenty-two, Jessica was too old to be using the program. That she wasn't homeless didn't seem to matter. "Jessica visited the Day Program a few times and approached the

Employment Program about assistance with a job," confirms Kathy Oliver, the same director who had run the agency in 1992 when Nelson was sixteen. The agency told Jessica they could not help her find a job until she provided identification. Jessica still hung around the agency, talking with the street kids she met. According to Becky, Jessica spent several nights in the Outside In housing unit, though she was above their age limit.

In some ways, her mother felt that it would have been better if Jessica had been just a bit more disabled. In that case, everyone would see her handicaps, and no one could deny them, including Jessica herself. She could have wished that Jessica were not disabled at all, but that was not the truth of Jessica. The truth of Jessica was that she was a handicapped person hiding in a shell of normalcy. It was a deadly place to be.

It wasn't long, however, before Jessica had found another reason to go downtown, the best reason of all. She had a boyfriend.

He was a street kid, Jessica told her mom. Becky heard his name as something beginning with an "A"—Andrew, maybe, or Adrian. It was Adrian. Becky promptly invited the young man home to have dinner with them. It was an ironclad rule in their family: the parents got to meet the boyfriend. Jessica balked. She didn't want her family to meet him. She was evasive about him. She would go downtown to see this Adrian but refused to bring him home.

Jessica said one thing about her mystery boyfriend that was jarring to her mother. She said that the mom and dad of the street family he belonged to had approved their relationship. Becky thought, what an odd thing to say. What was a street family? She pictured some older homeless man and woman watching over the youths, kind of taking care of them. She had no idea what Jessica was talking about.

James Nelson says he met Jessica in the Square soon after his release from prison. "One of the first people I met was Jessica, in the Square," he says. "We both had developmental disabilities, and we got along great. You couldn't hope to meet a nicer person." The two had a lot in common, he says. "Of course, she had a loving family, and I didn't."

His second-in-command, Carl Alsup, also recalls meeting Jessica in the Square. Carl describes Jessica as "always smiling." That was what all the street kids said about Jessica, that she was just the "sweetest" person to be around. The youths christened Jessica with a name: Giggles. It was the same street name given to one of the Family members who had helped murder Michelle Woodall in 1992.

Jessica fit right into the dramas of the Square, and yet she didn't fit. She was loud. She talked. She tattled. She got into the middle of everything. She made shows of dragging the kids to a church, unaware of how this would offend them. She was a big girl, flamboyant and yet self-conscious with her body, shy and yet overtly sexual at the same time. Adrian was her Square boyfriend, but she flirted with the other men and called them boyfriends too. She saw the other girls switching Square boyfriends with ease, so she thought she could do it too. She didn't seem to get old school rules. The code escaped her.

The street kids were confused, then angered, by her provocative behavior. She was always trying to get "everybody else's boyfriend, and it pissed everybody off," said Thomas Schreiner.

The youths didn't know that Jessica was disabled, that she was merely mimicking the behavior of other young women. Jessica wore a cloak of competency, and because it was a cloak, it never fit right. She lacked nuance. She was, frankly, a lot like Michelle Woodall. The talk of the Square grew mean and vicious. Adrian had an ex-wife. Jessica was a "whore." Sara held her head between her hands in the Square. It was all high drama, that was for sure.

Jessica stopped into the Janus Youth Access and Reception Center, whose manager Favor Ellis was under the impression that Jessica was eighteen and a bit slow for her age. Had she known Jessica's real age, Ellis says, more red flags would have been raised. But Jessica was not telling the truth about a lot of things, including her disability.

At home, Jessica dug into dinner. She loved her mom's tacos and burritos. There was always a crowd at the Williams' table, and after the clatter of passing dishes had quieted, Jessica mentioned offhandedly that her new friends downtown were teaching her how to panhandle.

Forks dropped. Mother, father, brothers, and sisters looked up at her, appalled.

"They're what?"

"Teaching me to panhandle," Jessica smiled.

Her mother tried to argue some sense into her, but Jessica just laughed. "Mom," her mother recalls her saying, "It's so much fun, like a game. And you get so much money. You wouldn't believe how much money."

"You don't need money," Becky said. "You have a family."

"The other kids have families too," Jessica replied. "They don't need the money either. It's just for fun." The Williams exchanged looks. Sometimes they just didn't know what to do.

There were many days when Jessica didn't go downtown. She visited some of her many friends in Estacada or Oregon City, or went across town to a church in southeast Portland, or went out to the mall to go shopping with friends. She stayed active in church with her family, enjoying weekend outings. Even downtown, one of Jessica's favorite places was the Liberation Street Church on the corner of Second and Burnside, directly across the street from the Harbor Light shelter.

The street life was not Jessica's whole life. She could have walked away and would not have missed it. For the youths of the Square, though, it was a different matter. The street families were their lives. They were willing to initiate Jessica into their secret society, but with the unstated assumption that she would take it as seriously as they did.

———

One April evening, Becky was at home when the phone rang. It was Jessica. "I'm staying with friends tonight."

Becky could hear laughter in the background. From the static, it sounded like Jessica was on a pay phone.

"What friends?" Becky's voice sharpened.

"Friends," Jessica replied, evasively.

Becky could hear other voices in the background. There was a girl talking in a jeering voice. "Why are you calling your mommy?" Becky heard the girl ask. There was a spat of background laughter.

Becky asked for a phone number where she could reach Jessica.

"There isn't one," Jessica said, and hung up.

Becky was furious. Jessica hadn't pulled this stunt for a long time, and there was nothing she could do. She spent a wakeful night worrying. She didn't feel like she could breathe until Jessica walked through the door the next day, and Jessica acted as if nothing had happened.

That evening, Jessica curled up in her bedroom with one of her sisters. She whispered her confession. She hadn't spent the night with friends, she said. She had actually spent the night on the streets with her boyfriend. They didn't do anything, Jessica hastened to say. He just held her in his arms all night long and said how much he loved her.

Her sister promptly told Becky, and Becky confronted Jessica. "Adrian loves me," Jessica responded. "And I love him." Becky felt that Jessica was still at a prepubescent level of sexual maturity. Jessica might act sexually provocative, but that was all it was, an act.

Obviously, Jessica shouldn't be spending the night with some man on the streets. But the Williams felt that if they gave Jessica an ultimatum, she would probably leave in a huff and maybe even move permanently onto the streets with her new boyfriend. Becky felt helpless. The harder she tried to protect her daughter, the further Jessica might run into the arms of these street friends. At the same time, she couldn't condone the lifestyle her daughter was living. "It was so hard," she says. Out loud, to Sam, she wished she could lock Jessica in the house. But that was against the law.

Sometimes, when her brain was working just right, Jessica did get it. FAS is like that. One day, out of the blue, Jessica would understand. Like a stroke victim on a good day, the damaged parts of her brain would connect, and Jessica would see things clearly. "They make fun of me, Mom," Jessica cried in her mother's arms one night. "They tell me I'm a spoiled brat because I have my own phone and I live with my mom and dad."

Becky tried, ever so patiently, to talk to her daughter about friends who love you and friends who are not really friends at all. Jessica would seem to understand. And then, the next day, she would be back to her old self. And she would go back downtown.

11

Jessica and Adrian broke up, and Jessica found a new Square boyfriend. He was Jimmy Stewart, called Neo on the streets. Jimmy bore scant resemblance to his movie-star namesake. He was small and scrawny, with short brown hair, fresh acne on his chin, and chapped lips. On the waterfront, he took off his shirt, exposing a hollow chest with tiny nipples. Jimmy and Jessica didn't look like a couple at all, the skinny white boy and the large, smiling, brown-skinned girl.

Becky understood immediately why Jessica liked this boy: Jimmy was a "little guy who needed a mom." Jessica liked playing mother hen. She rarely got to be the adult, the caretaker. For his part, Jimmy said Jessica gave him hope "to get off the streets." He described her as being filled with "peace" and "hope."

Like Jessica, Jimmy had a childlike view of relationships. He was content to hold hands, and one of his attorneys later said he didn't think the couple ever had sex. Jessica was thrilled with her new boyfriend. She asked Becky if Jimmy could move into their house. Becky demurred. She didn't want a street kid staying in their home.

Jimmy had had a truly horrible childhood. At around age four, Jimmy claimed, the abuse by his stepfather began. For years afterwards, he told a psychologist, he suffered flashbacks to "my dad killing the cat, hitting, yelling, spitting in my face." According to one source, Jimmy's mother worked, and his stepfather stayed home all day, drinking beer. He would send Jimmy out to buy more beer for him, and it was always too warm or too cold, or there was some other excuse for abuse.

Child protective services investigated the family. It was difficult for social workers to pinpoint exactly what was happening inside the home. There were allegations of drinking, drug use, and physical abuse. Jimmy learned to cover for his parents, even after being taken to the hospital with bruises. One investigator wrote that Jimmy was the "scapegoat for the family."

From a young age, Jimmy's behavior was more than a cry for help: it was a scream. In the first grade, Jimmy began setting fires. This continued in the third grade. At age ten, he was accused of inserting crayons into the anus of a three-year-old child. The doctor who evaluated Jimmy didn't think he was necessarily a sexual predator in the making but thought his behavior demanded serious intervention. He found Jimmy to be "a deeply troubled child" and "deeply damaged and disturbed."

When she was confronted with her son's deviant behavior, Jimmy's mother seemed indifferent. "He admits it, but I'm not sure if he really did it," she blithely told the doctor. The doctor was concerned. "The mother tends to minimize the seriousness and scope of her son's problems," he wrote. A year later, Jimmy was diagnosed with adjustment disorder with mixed disturbance of emotions and conduct and ADHD. The psychologist who evaluated him noted his "frequent lying" and inappropriate touching of girls.

Jimmy was a tiny boy, and self-conscious about it. At age fifteen, he was only four feet, eleven inches tall and weighed ninety pounds. When he entered an office for an evaluation with a psychologist, he announced, "Look at me! No one believes I'm fifteen!

People say I'm a midget." He was prescribed Paxil in an effort to modulate his moods.

By the time Jimmy was a teenager, the list of serious diagnoses on his chart had grown—conduct disorder, posttraumatic stress disorder, learning disorders, and the effects of neglect and abuse of a child. It seemed an empty place was growing inside of Jimmy as well. He was sent to Parrot Creek Ranch, a residential home for disturbed boys, where a staff teacher's report expressed worry about him. "He is having a very difficult time settling into the rules and expectations, although he is capable. The other students have made it clear that they do not like him. I am concerned about this boy."

The other boys in the treatment center had their reasons for not liking Jimmy. He admitted that he had eaten a cockroach and was peeing in the corners. When he felt slighted, he punched the windows out and stabbed the walls with a fork.

In October 2000, Jimmy was declared noncompliant with treatment and kicked out of the Parrot Creek treatment center. He was now sixteen and a ward of the state. He had grown only a few inches and weighed just 105 pounds. The final discharge papers indicate that the staff was troubled about this increasingly disturbed boy. "Jimmy is having difficulty connecting with peer groups. He is masturbating in public areas such as the boy's commercial toilets and bedrooms." They felt he exhibited "possible failure to thrive characteristics."

It was an intuitive diagnosis. "Failure to thrive" is most commonly associated with infants and toddlers in orphanages. Lacking proper love and touch, babies can wither and even die. It is not a lack of nourishment but of human warmth and bonding that harms them. Jimmy, with his stunted growth and inability to function, struck the staff as equally unable to thrive. Something in Jimmy made him incapable of taking a rope of rescue even when it was offered. He said he wanted to kill himself on several occasions and once stabbed himself in the hand.

Within a year, at age seventeen, Jimmy was convicted of burglary and theft after helping steal equipment worth over $10,000 from a high school. The report noted that Jimmy was with a group of boys when the crime happened, and he acted more as a follower than a leader. He was placed on probation. He met a high school substitute teacher with whom he had a sexual affair. Jimmy was accused of stealing a check from her, and this violated his probation.

Now he was a convicted teenage offender and was sent to the Tillamook Youth Authority, where he lived in a boot camp setting with other wayward boys. Son Village, as the boot camp is called, turned out to be a boon for Jimmy. For the first time, the troubled boy seemed to flourish. He liked the military-style singing in the mornings, the strict structure, and the comforting regime. He was excited about the classes he took and spoke of wanting to join the army.

Jimmy was discharged from Son Village directly onto the streets on February 18, 2003, at age eighteen. First, he went to his grandmother's home, but she lived in a crowded double-wide trailer and faced eviction if she let one more relative stay. Jimmy landed downtown, in the Square.

Before he left Son Village, one last psychological evaluation found that Jimmy exhibited "signs of emotional deprivation and undersocialization." The psychologist thought Jimmy was a needy, immature boy who was seeking the family he had never had. "Currently he seems to be looking for someone to fill the void of nurturing and guidance left by his parents," the psychologist wrote.

At age eighteen, Jimmy Stewart, still so scrawny he looked like a strong shove would knock him over, was indeed looking to fill that void. He was so scared in the Square that first day, one source says, that he was trembling. He met two street kids who introduced him to their street mother. She promised she would take care of him. And for the first time in his life, Jimmy had a mom.

———

She was Cassandra Hale, better known on the streets as Juliet. Cassandra was a big girl with long blonde hair. She had a reputation for not being afraid to use her fists. Her obedient kids called her "Mom." At her feet, Cassandra kept her Rottweiler, Chronic, his thick neck braced with a choke collar.

Across the Square, the Thantos Family watched Cassandra's family from their own benches. In the dynamics of the Square, some of the kids from different families became friends, but everyone knew the protocol. "You stick to your own," explains Joshua. Everyone respected this rule except Jessica, who bounced from bench to bench, stirring up trouble.

Cassandra was a strict disciplinarian. If her kids disobeyed, she made them bend over and hold their hands behind their backs. Then, she slapped them on the back of the head, right in the Square with everyone watching. If they cried, the beating was worse.

Like Nelson, Cassandra used the word "nigger" a lot and talked about the Ku Klux Klan and the Mafia, according to one of her followers. At the same time, she claimed a large black drug dealer called Glow Worm as her boyfriend. Her sexuality was just as unpredictable as her temper. One day she had a boyfriend. The next day she had a street wife. One day she was bisexual. The next she was lesbian.

Cassandra had the right combination of absolute entitlement and complete faith in the rules to make herself a powerful street mom. If she didn't have money, she took it from her kids. In return, she acted as if she would protect her followers. She seemed as natural to the Square as bricks, as hewn from the culture as if she had been created there. Carl Alsup called Cassandra "the boss of Pioneer Square, or at least most of the Square, anyway."

If there was one thing Cassandra didn't like, it was the oogles. She ridiculed the youths who came downtown for the day and returned home at night. "The newbies, they're like, my mom and dad made them wash the dishes." Cassandra scoffs. "They have a home. Well, I don't have a home."

———

Cassandra Hale was born on March 11, 1983, a pretty girl with blue eyes and blonde hair. She was raised in Roseburg, Oregon, a timber town a three-hour drive south of Portland. Her father was a logger named Ken, whom everyone called Kenny. When Cassandra was nine, Kenny lost an eye "in the woods," as they refer to logging accidents in the Northwest.

Robyn and Kenny Hale had two sons, Greg and Steven, when Cassandra was placed in their home. Cassandra says she didn't know she was adopted until she was nine, when she overheard her mother telling a friend about her hysterectomy after her youngest son was born. Cassandra tells a long, detailed story about this event. She says she went to school and asked a teacher what a hysterectomy was, and the teacher told her "you can't have babies after a hysterectomy." Cassandra says she went back to her mother and asked her if she was truly her birth child. "She said, 'Why do you want to know?'" Her adoptive mother, she claims, "finally told me the truth. I said, 'Then, I'm not yours.' After that, I kept pushing away."

According to Cassandra, more secrets came spilling out. "I found my records, and they said what my dad had done to me as a baby." Her birth father, she implies, had sexually molested her when she was an infant. "They took me away because of what my dad did to me," she says.

At school, she says, she was the only adopted child, and the other kids looked down on her. Her teacher brought a counselor into the class to explain, she claims, but it only made matters worse. Then, she discovered that her birth mother still lived in town. She found out a boy she had a crush on was in fact her brother through her birth mom. She was so mortified, she says, she couldn't bear to look at him for months.

All along, she felt her parents had treated her differently. "I was the only one who had to do the chores," she says. "I got up, did the dishes, came home after school and did more chores. I felt like they adopted me to be the maid."

Cassandra first ran away when she was eleven, she says. She claims she returned at twelve, pregnant. She had the baby, she says, right before her thirteenth birthday. The infant died on his father's chest. The two had fallen asleep for a nap, Cassandra says, and the baby's rapid heartbeat slowed. That year, she says, she slapped her adoptive father in a bowling alley. She had had enough, she says. Of what, she didn't say. She kept running, traveling as far away as California, then Arkansas. She never stayed in one place for long. For a time, she worked in a carnival. She says she also worked as a stripper, using a fake ID card. At fifteen, she says she got pregnant for the second time. This time the baby was stillborn.

Finally, when she was eighteen, Cassandra says, she went looking for, and found, her birth mother. She describes a reunion filled with bliss. "My adoptive parents had told me my birth mom was lazy, too young, stupid. And then, when I met her, she was the nicest person ever to me. When we met, it was like *The NeverEnding Story*. There was just so much there. . . . "

Despite her claims of having been abused by her birth father, Cassandra wishes she had never been removed from her parent's care. "My other siblings got to stay with my mom. I'm glad they got to stay together. I think sometimes what my childhood would have been like, with my mother."

At eighteen, too, Cassandra says, she had her third child, a little girl. The baby supposedly stayed with the father, who lived in California, while Cassandra kept moving. She told herself she would get her daughter back later, as soon as she settled down.

It was December 2002, according to Cassandra, when she landed in Portland. She was now nineteen and planned to get her third baby back in her life. The father was ready to send her daughter up to Portland, Cassandra says, just as soon as she was ready.

———

At least this was the long, involved story Cassandra told others, from youth shelter staff to the district attorney to other street kids. The problem is that practically none of it is true. "Cassie is a pathological liar," her mother, Robyn Hale, says sadly. "I love her and always will, because she is my daughter. But Cassie tells lies. She hears stories and takes them on for herself."

Like all adept liars, Cassandra Hale builds stories from slivers of truth. To begin with, Cassandra was adopted. That much is true. According to her parents, the adoption was never a secret. Her daughter always knew she was adopted, Robyn says. She had to have known. Robyn took her on visits to see her birth mother.

There was no record of sexual abuse according to Robyn. The birth mother, Robyn says, was homeless and had been scavenging for food in trash cans. Cassandra was removed at age two and placed in the Hale home. Immediately, the Hales noticed that their new daughter seemed neglected. "Cassie would eat until she threw up out of her nose," Robyn remembers. "She would hoard food." The Hales had been trained as foster parents and took the behavior in stride. "I just kept giving her it, until she realized she had enough to eat."

Cassandra ran away, but never as young or as often as she claims. Around the time she says she was in California at age eighteen, for instance, judicial records indicate she was arrested for theft in her hometown of Roseburg, Oregon. According to her mother, Cassandra ran away twice before the age of sixteen. The first time, she was on foot and made it as far as the local Wendy's restaurant. The second time, she barely made it out of town.

Even her name was a lie. She never was named Cassandra. It was a lie so effective, even the criminal justice system bought it. Lawyers would stand in court and argue in the name of Cassandra Hale. The newspapers would call her Cassandra Hale. But no such person exists. Her real name was actually Cassie, as it appears on her birth certificate, according to her adoptive mother. It was a small change, from Cassie to Cassandra, but significant in terms of how extensively and persuasively she lied.

The stories of her many babies were all lies as well. Cassie Hale has never been pregnant, according to her mother. There was no dead newborn, no stillborn birth, and no daughter in California.

Robyn Hale could never figure out why her daughter felt such a compulsion to lie, and at such harm to herself and to others. She remembers giving Cassie a good life. Her early years were filled with camping, fishing, and the outdoors. Her lovely bedroom had pictures of boating trips with her family. "She had so many clothes she couldn't wear them all," Robyn says. The Hales were careful never to disparage her birth parents and talked positively about adoption.

But from a young age, her mother says, Cassie made up stories and then lived inside them so completely she got lost. "She has said and done the oddest things over the years," Robyn says. Robyn remembers being sick when her young daughter came to ask if she wanted soup, only to discover later it was a ruse to go through her purse. Cassie rummaged through her brother's rooms and filled her closet to overflowing with their belongings, then pretended she had no idea how they had gotten there. When the Hales let her have a paper route, she snuck into people's houses, turning their radios on and off. She knew she wasn't supposed to, but she did it anyway. "It was like she had no boundaries," Robyn says.

Even as a young child, Robyn says, "Cassie always wanted to be a leader," but her desire to lead had a vicious streak. Robyn was alarmed one day when she got a call from her daughter's elementary school. Cassie had been taking the hand of a blind student under the pretense of leading her, only to lead her directly into walls. She would come up behind the blind girl, take her little hand, and then direct her into closed doors. "This blind girl was just devastated," Robyn says. The school asked Robyn to intervene. When Robyn confronted her, Cassie insisted she was helping the girl. She was about eight at the time.

When the Hales tried to put down limits, Cassie retaliated by telling teachers she was abused at home. "She probably told you we hit her too," Robyn says, with resignation in her voice. When the teachers realized they were being taken for a ride, they backed off. But the Hale family was torn apart by the accusations.

As she got older, Cassie threw what she claimed were "seizures." She would flip around like an epileptic having a grand mal seizure, jerking and then acting as if she were unconscious. Robyn took her daughter to the doctor several times. She says that the doctor concluded that Cassie did not have a seizure disorder. Still, Cassie insisted she had epilepsy.

Later, when she was an adult and lived on the streets, Cassandra called her mother from what she claimed was a hospital, and said that they had diagnosed her as epileptic. Robyn had no way of knowing if it were true. "When she was little, I would ask her if she was lying to me, and she would just grin and say, 'Mama, I'm lying at you right now with my eyes,'" Robyn recalls with a sigh. "But as she got older she got so good at it that even I couldn't figure it out."

The Hales kept looking for a way to help their daughter. They took her to doctors. One prescribed medication for impulse disorder. They reached out to social workers. The social workers believed Cassie when she said she was abused. "They put her in a position of authority," Robyn says. "It became all about, 'What does Cassie need?'"

Robyn thought maybe if Cassie saw her birth mother again, it might tear down the wall she had built between fantasy and fiction. As much as her daughter talked about how her birth mom had abused her, she also romanticized the woman. The Hales had kept track of the birth mother and arranged a visit. "I thought it would help her, but it didn't," Robyn says. Cassie demonstrated no real connection to her birth mother. It was just another opportunity to remake a story into her liking.

By the time Cassie was close to adulthood, Robyn felt she had to make a decision. "I had to ask myself, 'Can I let her destroy my family?'" The answer was no. Robyn stopped confronting her on every lie. She stopped trying to get Cassie to live at home as a functional part of the family. She would be there for her daughter, but she would not be her patsy.

There is no clinical diagnosis of "liar." What people call pathological or compulsive lying can be a sign of other mental illnesses, from narcissistic personality disorder (characterized by grandiose lies designed to make the person look superior) to borderline personality disorder (where lies are used to control and manipulate other people) or reactive attachment disorder (characterized by "crazy lies" intended to put others at a distance). Or it can be just plain lying.

The kind of lying Cassandra does is described by Yale psychiatrist Charles Dike as *pseudologica phantastica,* or lies woven into complex narratives. Even educated professionals have been caught making up such fabrications, such as Pulitzer Prize–winning historian Joseph J. Ellis, who was exposed for having invented his Vietnam War record.

Dr. Dike believes that such compulsive liars have little control over their fabrications. When confronted, they might admit the truth, but the compulsion to create a new narrative remains. Robyn says that when she pressed Cassie with evidence of the truth, her daughter would sometimes admit she hadn't been accurate. But as soon as she was left alone, her daughter would revert right back to telling tall tales.

Some psychologists say liars lie out of low self-esteem, but Cassie seemed to lie as a form of self-destruction. There was no way she could ever succeed in life as long as she lied to the extent that she did. Teachers gave up on her, friends abandoned her, employers fired her, and her own family distanced themselves emotionally from her. Cassie's lies were like a plastic sheet laid over her own life: they were clear enough to see through, but heavy enough to smother her.

═══

There was no dispute that by December 2002, when she was evaluated for homeless youth services, Cassie, now Cassandra, was living on the streets of Portland. She remembers it fondly as a time of belonging. "We had lots of fun times. We would kick it," she reminisces. "We'd hang out at Pioneer Square, and play Hacky Sack." On Saturdays, she and her street family would go down to the waterfront. "We'd play drums all day. There was this guy who brought us sodas."

Cassandra loved living on the streets. Searching for an analogy to life inside a street family, she says, "It's like camping—camping with rules. And I love camping." When she needed a shower or a change of clothes, she went to an agency. But she didn't use their programs. "It's a choice, you know," she remarks. "Some don't want to go in the shelters."

The agencies could argue whether street kids need a firm push or gentle persuasion to get off the streets. Cassandra didn't care. "I made the choice," she says with emphasis. "I *wanted* to live on the streets. You don't have to worry about paying a phone bill. You don't have to worry about the utilities. You don't have to worry about the house payment. It's easy. You're safe."

Safety is a theme Cassandra returns to time and again. It becomes clear, talking to her, that she is not talking about physical safety. For her, safety is protection from being confronted with her own lies. On the streets, for the first time, Cassandra was safe from the pressure of the truth.

Cassandra had found a place where her fictions were accepted, no matter how outrageous they were. Being evaluated at an agency that December 2002, the blonde-haired and blue-eyed nineteen-year-old told her intake worker that she was of "mixed" race, according to their screening records. She claimed her parents were "verbally and physically abusive." She had been pregnant, she said, though her child was not in her custody.

The shelter staff didn't appear to question Cassandra's claims. Instead, they were sympathetic. "She seems to still hold on to or be affected a lot by childhood issues involving her family. She seems to need a lot of support and attention while she begins to work on her goals," the screener wrote.

On the streets, Cassandra had found a culture where she could construct a lifelong fable. She would be nourished with sympathy by agency staff and accepted by virtually everyone she met. She took her first street name, Jewels, and then changed it to Juliet. Sometimes she changed the spelling to Juliette, or called herself Jules, or Juliet Lee. The lies got so layered and tangled, she was lost inside them:

Cassie, a.k.a. Cassandra, a.k.a. Jewels, a.k.a. Juliet, a.k.a. Jules, a.k.a. Juliet Lee.

Cassandra picked up the Rottweiler she named Chronic, a slang term for marijuana. Chronic went everywhere with her. At night, Cassandra teamed up with a street buddy to check the hot spots, Chronic trotting behind them. It was easy to have a dog. Local shelters offered free kenneling while Cassandra showered. Outside In offered a free vet-care clinic. Other cities have similar programs, such as a van in Seattle that delivers free bags of dog food to youths on the streets. Dogs are so common in the street youth culture that some cities have tried to curtail the culture by restricting their dogs. Berkeley, California, for example, passed an ordinance against dogs' sitting together on public sidewalks in an effort to reduce the large numbers of street kids.

In general, these are not pets brought from family homes. These are pets taxed from other youths, bought from pet stores, or "rescued" (stolen) from supposedly abusive owners. A common street kid story is how they found their dog being abused and liberated it from the owner. One of the most popular breeds is the pit bull, sometimes used in squats as guard dogs.

In many ways, the street kids treat their dogs with kindness. They make sure they have bowls of water and constantly pet and fuss over them. Even when drunk or high, they will remember to feed their pets, and often they will use the first money they make panhandling to buy dog food. Still, street life is tough on the animals. Tied up for hours in the sun while the youths drink or get high, fed an ever-changing diet, beset with worms, sleeping in dirty squats or hauled onto freight trains for travel, few dogs last long on the streets, even if their owners have nothing but good intentions. The street kids tax each other their pets for various indiscretions, and an accusation of being mean to a dog is cause for a beating.

The dogs are also another excuse for the youths to stay on the streets. With a dog tied to his pack, a street kid can't find an apartment or get a job—which may be the point. Cassandra tells a story, which is unconfirmed, about getting a job at the Lloyd Center Mall across the river from downtown Portland and being told she had to leash her dog. "I said, 'would you leash your child? Well, he's like my child.'" That was the end of that job.

Cassandra claims she could have afforded an apartment or even a rental house. She had enough money to get a place of her own, she says. Her own mother confirms it, and other street kids agree: Cassandra was a drug dealer.

———

Cassandra says she dealt methamphetamine. She had about twenty regular customers, she claims, and two cell phones to handle them. But Cassandra likes to embroider the truth, and others say she was just a weed dealer and never made any serious money. It was hard to get at the truth of just what Cassandra was doing.

Large or small, drug dealing has replaced prostitution as the revenue source for street kids. In their four-state study of Midwestern street youth, *Nowhere to Grow: Homeless and Runaway Adolescents and Their Families,* Les Whitbeck and Dan Hoyt found that 63 percent of the male street youth dealt drugs, compared to only 2 percent who prostituted. In Spokane, Washington, almost all the street youth in a study said they were drug dealers. In Manhattan, 42 percent of those in Marni Finkelstein's study said they were involved in the drug trade. "I would say one in five street kids is dealing," says Cassandra, and she was probably low-balling the number.

This drug dealing is not a haphazard criminal enterprise. Lee Hoffer, author of a 2006 study of street dealers in Denver, *Junkie Business: The Evolution and Operation of a Heroin Dealing Network,* says that drug dealing among street people can be "highly organized, even on the lowest levels." Even the smallest street dealers are often part of an organized system.

Street kids in New York will invest $100 in a sheet of acid, and then turn around and sell the individual hits for $5 in the East Village, clearing $400 for every sheet they sell. In Santa Cruz, street kids in San Lorenzo Park deal methamphetamine, heroin, and marijuana. In Berkeley, the street kids sell acid and hallucinogenic mushrooms. In San Francisco, they peddle heroin and methamphetamine. The one drug street kids generally do not deal is crack cocaine, which is perceived as a "black drug," as well as a subject of intense police interest.

In Portland, the street families have a lucrative, highly structured drug-dealing system. The bigger methamphetamine dealers live outside of downtown, making the drug in rental houses or importing it from Mexico. They use the street kids as low-level dealers to move the product. The kids sell the small plastic bags in specific locations: O'Bryant Square, the Keller Fountain, the stairwells of the parking garage on Tenth Avenue, and the South Park blocks. The street kids get a percentage of each bag they sell. When Cassandra wanted to make more money, she says, she would invest her percentage into buying a bunch of bags at lower cost, then "double" her money.

Marijuana dealing is also organized and largely controlled by the 420s street family. According to a thirty-two-year-old street leader called Scrappy, any street kid who wants to sell marijuana downtown has to pay $50 for dealing rights. The street family even assigns the dealers spots to stand in. The dealers are not permitted to carry harder drugs into the 420 drug-dealing territories. The idea is if the police bust the street dealers, they won't find anything harder than weed in their pockets. A street kid who broke this rule when he was caught with a meth pipe in his pocket was severely beaten and 86'd from downtown.

The 420s are known as the "hippie" street family, but they are far from pacifists. Scrappy himself was arrested in 2003 for beating an elderly man and his dog on the waterfront. The man had the temerity to turn down his offer of prime "blueberry" marijuana, so Scrappy allegedly struck him in the face with a martial arts weapon called a three-section staff. The victim suffered a perforated eardrum, permanent hearing loss, a fractured jaw, and three lost teeth. Scrappy then went after the man's golden retriever, allegedly kicking and hitting the dog in the muzzle.

"There is lots of street level dealing," Police Officer Anthony Merrill confirms. He found that street youth dealing was "pretty complex" and organized. Merrill says his unit took a zero-tolerance approach to the drug dealing, but the problem extended far beyond what two officers could possibly control. In 2003, there were dozens, if not hundreds, of street family dealers operating in downtown Portland over a wide geographical area.

There are political ramifications when police do crack down on street youth dealing. When Santa Cruz police arrested a dozen street kid dealers in San Lorenzo Park as part of a monthlong sting operation, the local alternative media labeled the street kids "drug war victims." A protest rally was held outside the city council chambers, where an advocacy group fed the protestors a "hot thick vegan soup" as they awaited the appearance of the freed street kids. The crowd applauded as the pierced and tattooed drug dealers stood in front of the city council, claiming they were victims of oppression.

None of the street kids interviewed for this book expressed any concern about the police. In months of dealing openly on the streets of downtown, Cassandra was never arrested for drug dealing.

With its emphasis on loyalty and the punishment of snitches, street families are the perfect informal organization for drug dealers. No identifying marks or colors link the dealers together. When one picks up and leaves town, there is always another street kid willing to take his or her place. The families are not organizations that lend themselves to wall charts. You have to know the culture to know the dealers.

Cassandra says she spent her earnings lavishly on restaurant meals, alcohol, cigarettes, hotel rooms, and especially drugs. "I'd go from meth house to meth house, partying, doing meth, dancing all night," she says. Cassandra drove a car, a Nissan, and loved to take her street kids on road trips out of town. Jerry Fest, author of *Street Culture: An Epistemology of Street-Dependent Youth,* confirms that between panhandling, prostitution, and drug dealing, individual street kids can make up to $500 a day. "Even with weekends off and vacations," he writes, "we're talking well over $100,000 a year, tax free."

With her cell phones, a car, and pockets full of cash, Cassandra hardly led the life most would associate with a homeless youth. She was a young adult: a criminal, actually. The city would mobilize to help her, but no one would try to change her. To the agencies, she was an abused youth needing sympathy. To the police, she was a question mark. To the public, she was just another young person hanging out downtown.

"I truly wish that being on the street were simply a matter of an environmental circumstance," Fest says, pointing out that the number of street kids has grown even as the funding for agencies has increased. "If all that was needed to help young people exit street life was the ability to provide food, clothing, and shelter, we would be demonstrating a much greater level of success with our programs."

Fest believes the problem is not always one of opportunity but of identity. "Helping a youth transition 'off the street' is about helping them make conceptual, not physical, changes," he says. The street kids have to decide for themselves to leave the streets. In other words, they have to stop romanticizing their lifestyle. They have to want to change.

Cassandra says there were times she tried to get off the streets. "When I got an apartment or a house I let it slide because I couldn't invite all my friends back," she says. Alone in an apartment, Cassandra may have been forced to confront her failings: she was almost twenty, with no real job, no real friends, and no future. On the streets, she was an important person, a leader who was respected and needed by her followers. Cassandra bagged the apartment. "There were people on the streets I was watching out for," she explains.

In March 2003, Cassandra turned twenty on the streets. Four of her street brothers tackled her down on the waterfront and gave her birthday spankings. "I blacked out, and I guess I came up punching," she says. The seizure was triggered, she explains, by the sexual abuse her biological father had forced on her when she was just an infant.

————

That spring, Cassandra created her own street family. She seemed to specialize in finding weak, needy young people to be her followers, the kind of truly homeless youth she pretended to be. Among them was a Native American drug addict who was pregnant as a result of a gang rape and a mentally ill teenager named Cory Dennison who had led a horrendous life shuttled between mental hospitals and treatment homes. But her favorite son, other kids agreed, was Jimmy Stewart. Cassandra often turned to Jimmy when she wanted spare cash.

Cassandra's followers were a world apart from Nelson's adherents. When they bent over for her rabbit punches in the Square, they did so because that was the price of being in a street family. These were teenagers so ravaged by abuse and mental illness, they could not make use of the programs available to help them. The needs of a youth like Jimmy Stewart were far deeper than any job program could fulfill.

The Thantos Family kids, on the other hand, were intelligent, articulate, and full of energy and life. They looked up to their street father, Nelson, and some worshipped him, but if they feared him, they had chosen to put themselves in that position. They could have taken a bus home at any moment.

Cassandra ran a tight ship. She boasted about the plans she had for "her" kids and talked loudly about how they were old school. She claimed taxing rights, according to other street kids. Under her leadership, Jimmy learned the art of intimidation, and another street kid complained that he was often threatening to tax and beat him.

In the evenings, two of Cassandra's street sons would head up to a park on Twenty-third and Couch, in northwest Portland. The area around the public restrooms was popular with transients and drug users. There, the two street kids would mug people passing through the park. "We would mug people all the time," one of them relates. "We wouldn't hurt them, but we'd say, 'Give us your money.' This one guy tried to argue and I said, 'Want to get hurt?'" For emphasis, the street kid carried three smiley chains, one around his neck and two at his belt.

Most of their victims, he says, had enough common sense to turn over their money. If they were on their way home from the store and carrying beer, it was all the better. The street brothers would sit down right there in the park and drink the beer. Later, buzzed on beer and high on methamphetamine, they would mosey back to the Square and find their street mom, Cassandra. This street kid recalls that they mugged people almost daily that spring. He also hotwired cars and gave them to the girls in the Square.

Cassandra's new family joined the other families at the Square: the Nihilistic Gutter Punks, the Sick Boys, the 420s, the Drunk Punks, and Thantos. On the periphery of this society was the usual motley assortment of older men, petty criminals, skinheads, addicts, and oogles, like Jessica.

And the word on the street was that Cassandra hated Jessica. According to one of her followers, a fellow drug dealer named Adam Linday, the animosity started when Jessica supposedly took a sweatshirt belonging to Cassandra from a locker at the Greenhouse agency. When Jessica showed up in the Square wearing the sweatshirt, Cassandra accused her of stealing. It was a major code violation, and Cassandra wanted to beat Jessica right then and there. The other street kids separated them.

After that, Adam claims, Cassandra had a thing against Jessica. The two tried to avoid each other in the Square. But it was hard for Cassandra to avoid the large woman called Giggles once she was dating her favorite son, Jimmy.

———

The relationship between Jessica and Jimmy quickly degenerated into dramas that April, and it looked like Jessica was the major cause. Jessica whispered to other street youths, *Jimmy is too violent. I'm afraid of him.* This caused a stir. Some of the street kids wanted to beat Jimmy up because of the allegations.

That drama passed, but Jessica then told others she was afraid to dump Jimmy because of his bad temper. This caused another drama, and there were more threats in the Square to beat him up. On April 18, Jimmy showed up at the Janus Youth Access and Reception Center and told Favor Ellis that people were threatening to kill him because of his relationship with Jessica. He was worried about getting hurt.

Others believed that Jimmy was trying to take advantage of Jessica, presumably by talking her into having sex. "He thought he could do anything to her," Sara Baerlocher says. When Jessica made it clear that wasn't happening, Jimmy retaliated, according to Sara. "He was trying to convince the other kids she was evil."

12

There was a new girl in the Thantos Family. She had an ankh, the Egyptian symbol of immortality, tattooed on her right arm. On her upper back, a fairy sat on a mushroom.

She sat near Nelson in the Square. He explained to her that he was a druid who practiced black magic. Some of his followers were warriors, called death knights, he said, and he described how the final step to becoming a death knight was to kill someone. As a new member of the family, the girl had been put on her "thirty-day newbie status." Nelson was always testing her. He would say something like, "This is your first test, go out and spange," and she would do it.

The new girl had beautiful, short, gleaming brown hair, but she wanted a Mohawk. She knew she had to fight for the right to wear a Mohawk, a warrior symbol that street kids across the country earn the right to wear by fighting. She was looking for her opportunity when she noticed someone "bothering" her new street father in the Square. According to Joshua Brown-Lenon, she punched the offender, which earned her the right to wear the hawk.

Typically, the street kids pull out their knives and take the hair off right then and there in the Square, the recipient of the new Mohawk glowing with pride as the hair is shorn from his or her head. Later, they use a razor to trim the sides. This time, though, the newbie's right to wear the Mohawk was challenged by other street kids. The girl would have to fight some more for her hawk. Thomas Schreiner watched her get into a hair-pulling match with another girl. She won, and she got the hawk.

Her name was Danielle Marie Cox, she was eighteen, and she had it all, it seemed: a loving mother, a bright and engaging mind, ambition, and opportunity. She threw it all away to live on the streets.

═══

Born July 31, 1984, Danielle was raised in Spokane, Washington. Her life story, detailed in court records, newspaper accounts, interviews, and personal letters, indicates that she had an ideal childhood. Danielle was a cherished only child. Her mother was a teacher, and her father was an engineer, and she grew up with boat rides on the lake, fresh salads eaten al fresco, and a piano that she played for her mother.

From first through sixth grades, Danielle attended a private school. At the age of eight, she began training as a classical pianist, her strong, square hands moving fluently over the keys. She was a muscular, energetic girl who seemed to be good at everything she tried: a gifted athlete, a talented musician, and an exemplary student. She played basketball and volleyball, competed at gymnastics, and still found time for her homework and piano practice. Danielle and her mother were close. Danielle programmed her mother's cell phone for her and made sure there were sliced tomatoes in the salad. She was happy to chop the firewood and took her turn rowing on the lake.

But at age thirteen, Danielle's idyllic life ended. Her father died in a plane crash. Danielle became unhinged with grief, and she lashed out, breaking curfew, running away, and arguing with her mother. She fell in with a bad crowd at the University High School in

Spokane, and in her junior year, her grades fell. She began skipping classes to drink and smoke pot with her new friends. At sixteen, she ran away, only to be picked up by the sheriff and taken back home. Despite her tailspin, she was still responsible. She took a summer job at the Rock City Grill in Spokane, where she worked for a few months as a hostess.

Her mother struggled to help Danielle. Widowed and alone, she couldn't be there after school to make sure her daughter did her homework. Together, Danielle and her mother decided a change of scenery was in order. They agreed that Danielle should go live with cousins in Helvetia, Oregon, a gently rolling countryside outside of Portland, with cows and scrubby forests. Living in the country, Danielle could finish her senior year and hopefully get back on track. Danielle agreed to her mother's rules and moved that Labor Day, September 2001, to live with her cousins.

It worked. The months in Helvetia were a balm for Danielle. She rose early every morning and took a long bus ride to attend Glencoe High School in Hillsboro, Oregon. After school, she took the bus back home, where the stay-at-home mother of the family watched over her to make sure her homework was done.

On Sundays, she attended church with her cousins. She joined the church youth group and sang in the school choir. Her best friend was Maja Radanovic. She had an "an awesome voice," Maja told Portland's *Oregonian*. "We used to make up songs together." Maja thought "Carpe Diem" was their song. Live life to the fullest, they sang.

Danielle joined the high school debate team. She was known for being an original thinker, willing to argue about animal rights in the conservative farming community. The high school principal says Danielle posed no discipline problems and earned excellent grades. Danielle later told investigators that she had maintained a 3.8 grade point average during her time at Glencoe High. Her worst sin was cigarette smoking. She'd sneak out back for a quick puff. But a lot of students did that.

That winter, Danielle and her friend Maja went stag to the school's winter formal. They dressed in long satin gowns, and the picture taken of them shows a beaming Danielle, with daring short hair and red lipstick. She looks like a confident young woman, one who has reached the other side of her grief. Her relationship with her mother had improved with the distance. For Danielle, the months in Helvetia were a good time in her life.

Danielle graduated from high school in spring 2002 at age eighteen. Everything seemed to be so right for her. She was smart, social, and assertive. She applied to several nearby colleges. She chose Pacific University in Forest Grove, Oregon, just twenty-four miles outside of Portland. Like Helvetia, Forest Grove is a rural city near Hillsboro, named for the stately white oak and Douglas fir forests of the Tualatin Valley. The city itself is small but urbane, centering on the university founded in 1849.

Danielle moved into her dorm room in June 2002, which gave her a few months to settle into campus before classes began. She wasn't idle. She accepted a position as a teaching assistant with the Autistic Children's Activity Program, or ACAP, an eight-week summer school program for autistic children in Portland.

It was a long commute from Forest Grove to the agency for autistic children, and Danielle had to take one bus into downtown Portland to transfer to another bus, which lumbered all the way out to Sellwood, a neighborhood on the edge of southeast Portland. From nine in the morning to three in the afternoon, Danielle worked with the autistic children, teaching them social skills and supervising them on field trips to farms and museums. She told her coworkers that she wanted to be a teacher, just like her mother. Full of boundless energy, Danielle continued to stay in touch with her high school friends and remained active in their debate team.

But on her own and waiting for the beginning of college, Danielle showed signs of fraying. She took the dorm room as an invitation to party, inviting her high school friends over to drink and sit up late, listening to music. Her friend Maja worried about her. "At Pacific, it was a whole new ballgame for her," Maja told the *Oregonian*. "She was on her own. No rules, no nothing. She was going to abuse that privilege. I would."

One day early that summer, Danielle was downtown waiting for her bus when she met two street kids. She says she was drawn to them because she felt sorry for them and wanted to help them. Over the following days, Danielle met more street kids, and they in turn introduced her to others, and soon she knew a bunch of street kids on the bus mall. She began taking the bus downtown on her days off, leaving her college around four in the afternoon and hanging out with the street kids until ten in the evening.

Even as her college classes began that August, Danielle was hanging out in the Square. Her first recorded appearance in a homeless youth agency was on August 30, 2002, the first week of classes. Danielle registered her street name as Phoenix. She told the screener she was eighteen and enrolled in college. She said she had a trust fund, left to her by her father, but that she had spent it all. She described her relationship with her mother as good, as long as they didn't live together. The screener noted that Danielle seemed "new" to the streets, though she claimed to have been hanging around for some time.

Danielle made new friends on campus, but these students, she admitted, liked to party. She stayed up half the night, listening to music, and then slept through her classes the next day. As the school year inched toward Christmas break, Danielle began skipping more classes and hanging out downtown. That first quarter she earned only nine college credits. As poorly as she was doing in college, though, Danielle kept in touch with her high school debate team. She helped organize their annual tournament, which was held on the Pacific University campus. She was promised an assistant coaching job for the high school team the following year.

Reinvigorated after winter break, Danielle resumed classes in January 2003. She registered for a full load of seventeen credits. She told classmates she needed extra credits to make up for the classes she had flunked. It didn't happen. "I think she was ashamed of the ways things were going," one classmate told the *Oregonian*. Danielle fell even further behind.

The streets became her refuge. That January and February 2003, Danielle began going downtown more often. She joined the ranks of street kid drug dealers and claimed she made $300 to $400 a week selling pot. On the streets that spring, Danielle met Joshua, or Scooby. He introduced her to Carl Alsup and Crystal Grace, and in April, she met their street father, Nelson.

At Pacific University, Danielle's roommate decided she had had enough and asked Danielle to move into another room. Danielle simply left. Two weeks after meeting Nelson, by her own account, Danielle quit college for good. She walked out on a scholarship, a dorm room, a phone, and a paid food plan. She took little besides the clothes on her back. She skipped her final exams. She didn't see the point of taking the tests, she said, if she would not be returning.

Nelson had invited Danielle to stay at Matt Burch's apartment, where she joined the others sleeping on the filthy mattresses strewn across the floor. Danielle quickly became indoctrinated into their lifestyle: sleep in, breakfast at New Avenues for Youth, and spend the day panhandling and hanging out in the Square.

Danielle wasn't seduced into life on the streets because of Nelson. She had been hanging out with street kids for several months before Nelson was paroled, and her life had been spinning out of control for some time before that. But the solid nature of the Thantos Family seemed to make it easier for her to abandon her plans. It wasn't like she was leaving college for parts unknown. The street family offered her a place to sleep, a group she knew would accept her, and a leader she trusted. Like the others, she called Nelson her "dad."

"While people assume most kids on the street come from abusive backgrounds," Marni Finkelstein found in her study of New York City street youth, "an equal number of kids reported that they had nonabusive relationships with their parents." Half of the street youth in Finkelstein's study came from decent homes, and one in four described their parents in glowing terms, using terms like "excellent," "a good middle-class family," "really cool," "supportive," and "the best people I have ever met in my life." Finkelstein calls these youths "adventurers." Rather than being pushed onto the streets, they are pulled toward them, drawn by the lure of excitement and thrills. Many, like Danielle, are bright, autonomous teenagers with an independent streak. "I started hanging out with squatters and I got sucked into the life," one girl told Finkelstein. "I came from a middle-class background," another explained. "I thought it would be great to be traveling and it would be interesting to learn all these new things."

These teenagers are searching for the romantic lifestyle captured in books such as Jack Kerouac's *On the Road.* Generations of young adults have acted on the same urges, from the bohemians of the 1950s to the hippies of the 1960s. One difference, though, is previous adventurers saw leaving home as a path to enlightenment and adventure, not as an end in itself. Few would have considered themselves "street kids," or even kids at all. They were young adults trying to travel a different path, and in the process, they invented new arts, music, poetry, and alternative forms of living. The street family culture, on the other hand, is creatively anaerobic. The youths squander their energies on their dramas.

Significantly, Finkelstein found that once on the streets, even teenagers raised by loving parents feel pressure to pretend they were abused. "Shared traumatic backgrounds often become bonding elements that the kids flash around in order to claim their membership on the streets," Finkelstein writes.

Once she was accepted into the family, Danielle and the street father she knew as Thantos became close, perhaps closer than Nelson was to any of the other kids. The two went for long walks together, talking about their lives. Danielle describes Nelson as her "father figure." If there was one thing she didn't like about him, she says, it was his chauvinism. Nelson talked about women in sexist ways. That bothered Danielle, but not enough to make her leave her new family.

Danielle didn't want to be a princess. She wanted to be a warrior, to be tough and strong. The life of a housewife-in-training was not for her. She was the polar opposite of the younger and more passive girls of the family, like Crystal Ivey or Sarah Caster. Danielle was destined for combat. She was built strong, with heavy shoulders and a square body. And so, almost alone out of the female members of the family, Danielle became a death knight warrior. Everyone knew Danielle would have to pass the tests of a death knight, which would include killing someone. Danielle did not seem to have a problem with this mandate.

It may have been that the Thantos Family was offering Danielle a place to act out a secret dark side, a hidden part of her character that didn't fit the image of a loving daughter and honor student. Danielle went from being a gifted student who worked with autistic children to one of the most violent members of the family, and the change occurred with startling speed and ease. According to court records,

Danielle was involved in several fights in the Square and around downtown. She got a butterfly knife, according to Joshua, and would flip it open during fights, waving the long blade threateningly. Even Thomas Schreiner, no stranger to violence himself, thought Danielle was a hard number. "Danielle was really mean," he said.

Danielle had wrestled before with her twin desires to rebel and to be good. What she didn't seem to know was how to do both at the same time. Had she been born a generation earlier, Danielle could have found a creative community on the streets, where she could have explored the urges that haunted her without hurting anybody. She might have become an artist, a singer, a street poet, or a wanderer. Her path to adulthood might not have been conventional, but it probably would have been productive. Instead, Danielle found a street culture devoid of hope and full of violence. The Thantos Family offered Danielle the opportunity to be tough, mean, dark, and ugly. It did not offer her a path to a better place.

The family christened Danielle with a street name, Shadowcat, after a female character in the X-Men comic book series. Like Danielle, the character Shadowcat had once been a bright young student, a girl with dark brown hair and hazel eyes with "no criminal record." In the comic books, Shadowcat leads a normal life, except she suffers from debilitating headaches. These headaches are her "mutant" superpowers emerging. Shadowcat adopts the X-Men as her "surrogate family," becoming particularly attached to Storm, a mother figure. Shadowcat is capable of attacks called "phasing," where she literally becomes intangible. Objects can pass right through her. Nothing can hurt her, except maybe a psychic attack.

Danielle's emerging superpower seemed to be her utter devotion to the street family, especially to her new father. Once she left college for the streets, Danielle severed her bonds with her old friends. Her loyalties were not divided; they were conquered. She seemed enthralled with her new fantasy identity. One observer commented that Danielle became so immersed in being Shadowcat that he wouldn't have been surprised if she had come to believe she was a superhero and could actually jump from buildings.

Danielle lived a sexually open life with the family, according to police interviews. Carl asserted that she had "slept with ninety percent of the Square." His girlfriend, Crystal Grace, claimed that Danielle was her "girlfriend" as well.

Nelson claims he met Danielle the night of April 27, soon after she arrived downtown. She was already running with Matt Burch, he says, and hanging around his apartment.

The next day, April 28, Nelson says his subsidized stay at Harbor Light ended. He claims the shelter terminated his occupancy because his job search had been unproductive. Nelson's parole officer referred him to other shelters. The parole board still expected that his pending transfer to California would go through. "We didn't expect him to be here for long," Steve Liday, assistant director of Multnomah County's Department of Community Justice, told the *Oregonian*.

Nelson kept showing up for his weekly appointments, and he was always clean, polite, and utterly in compliance. The parole officer noted that he had a positive attitude and seemed sober. In his records, Nelson said he was continuing his job search. When he filled out job applications, he wrote down the address of Matt Burch, on Trinity Place.

13

Cassandra was in the Square with terrible news. The three-year-old daughter she had been expecting from California was dead. She had been killed in a freak carnival accident, trapped on a Ladybug ride that had not been bolted down. It was all over the television news, she said.

Three babies dead, the last in a freak accident. The age didn't quite match: the child would have been one or two, not three, if Cassandra had been pregnant at eighteen as she claimed, but the other street kids didn't seem to notice. A check of all carnival fatalities during that period (there are relatively few in any given year, and all are recorded) came up empty, because there was no dead toddler and never had been. Cassandra's mythical baby had died at the same age that she herself had been adopted. All her pretend babies, as a matter of fact, had died before age three.

"I was going to get custody," she says, her big eyes moist.

It was her daughter's death, Cassandra says, that made her start drinking heavily and getting schwilly (drunk) more than usual. "My friend was the bottle," she says. "It's hard to admit, but though I loved my daughter, I loved the bottle more. The bottle came first. First thing when I woke up, I had to have something to drink or I would get sick."

Cassandra claims not to remember anything from that period, a blackout of epic proportions. And yet, in the next breath, she does remember events, like her version of how her street family 86'd her from drinking.

In her version of events, Cassandra drove some of her family out to the Bagby hot springs in Estacada, Oregon. Bagby is a natural hot springs, with old-fashioned wooden tubs tucked away in the woods outside Portland. In the middle of the night, you can soak in the steaming hot natural waters with the icy starlit sky above and the dark fir trees gently swaying around you. Long a favorite of naturalists, in recent years the Bagby hot springs had also become a favorite of heavy drinkers, loud partiers, and car prowlers.

Cassandra says she was driving her car up the winding hills along the Estacada River. "I was drunk and almost wrecked the car," she says. "One sister told me I'd better stop drinking. My buddies said the same thing." Whatever the real story, the word on the street was that Cassandra was officially banned from drinking by the old school street leaders. She didn't stop, she says. She just couldn't get over the fact her daughter was dead.

Not to be outdone by the all the excitement generated by Cassandra's drinking drama, Carl Alsup, known as D. K., made a pronouncement from the Thantos Family benches. From now on, his street name was Chaluchi, after what he thought was the Celtic term for Scottish deerhounds. He pronounced the name with a "ch" sound: *cha-loo-chi*. (The real spelling is "Cuchulainn," and the name refers to the famed Irish wolfhounds, not Scottish deerhounds. The correct way to pronounce the word is with a hard "k" sound: *koo-kuli-in*.) "They change their names every time they sneeze," comments Andrea Timm, who was watching the families from her security post in the Square. Sometimes the new names stuck, other times they didn't. Carl would be called Chaluchi for a short time, but soon reverted to D. K.

—

In the meantime, Sara Baerlocher had gotten a job from a young couple living in an apartment building near Matt's place. The husband often came down to the Square to score methamphetamine, Sara says, and he and his wife would hang out, talking with the street kids. "They knew everything that happened," Sara says. "They knew the scene."

The couple had two little girls, about a year apart, one a baby and the other a toddler. The couple had asked Crystal Grace to be their "nanny," but Crystal didn't show up at the Square when she was supposed to for her nanny job, and Sara was there. She offered to take the job. The couple said sure and left their two babies with Sara while they went off for a few hours.

Sara took care of the little girls after that day. She would show up at the couple's apartment, or meet them downtown, and take the girls with her. Sometimes, she says, she pushed them in their stroller to the library or down to the waterfront. The children hung out with Sara in the Square while she sat and chatted with the other youths, playing with their smiley chains and talking about killing people. They were obedient little girls, Sara says, except for the baby, who "loved to crawl." She would go crawling away, Sara says, and she would have to run after her, scooping her up.

Nelson made an announcement from his bench: he was going to create a coven of witches. He said he would make this coven out of virgins, and he nominated the pretty girl Destiny to be first virgin. Sara suspected that Destiny was not a virgin. She suspected that Nelson had other reasons for wanting to include Destiny in his coven, reasons that went back to his crush on her in the peace camp.

The Thantos Family showed off their new weapons. Carl and Joshua Brown-Lenon had matching aluminum baseball bats that they could fit under their jackets. Like everything else, the bats had to have names. "Carl named his bat Dink," Nelson says. The other bat, he says, was called the Headhunter. The names of the bats shifted just like street names. Some said the bats were Bink and Bonk, or Dink and the Little Dink, or Dink and Dink Junior. Carl liked to whack his bat against objects just to hear it sing.

———

Around what her mother recalls as May 5, Cassandra Hale went down to Roseburg for a family visit. Cassandra had asked for a spaghetti dinner, but she arrived early so it turned into a spaghetti lunch. Robyn was happy cooking for her difficult daughter. She told Cassandra not to bring her work home with her, meaning, don't bring any drugs into my house. Her daughter respected this rule, and Robyn was pleased.

Cassandra brought another street kid with her. It seemed to Robyn that the young man was concerned about her daughter. He spent the lunch trying to talk Cassandra into getting away from some group she was hanging around with. Both Cassandra and her friend had been in a fight, Robyn says. The young man showed her a shallow knife wound across his back. Cassandra shrugged off her bruises and spoke excitedly about how "her" street kids were doing. "It was all a game to her." Still, the lunch was one of the best times they had ever spent together, Robyn says.

When she got back into Portland, Cassandra says, "Everything was falling apart on the streets." Things were getting tense. Andrea Timm, the security guard for the Square, described the scene that month as a "stress pit." Something was setting the youths off and had them all on edge. Jerry Fest thought he knew why. It was all the newbies. Every spring brings a flood of new youths, but this spring was even worse. The Square was filled with new kids, it seemed. The newbies brought a spike in violence with them. The established street youths were either showing the newbies their place through beatings and taxings, or the newbies were trying to impress the old school by doing the same to each other.

The newbies made the street families feel stressed and defensive. It was harder to maintain respect. Every new kid had to be taught the code. There were so many rules to teach them. Every newbie required a breaking-in period, an adjustment to the culture. It was hard for the street families to figure out who was genuine and who was not. As part of the testing process, the families ridiculed the new youths for being soft. "They went to the store to buy Lee press-on track marks," sneered Travis Harramen, a member of the Sick Boys.

The truth was that few of the street kids had been long on the streets. In the Thantos Family, most of the kids had been on the streets for around a month or less, including Danielle Cox, Crystal Ivey, Sarah Caster, and Sara Baerlocher. While Cassandra liked to claim she had been homeless since age twelve, the truth was she had only been on the streets for a little over four months, and her son Jimmy Stewart, for about two months.

The Hale family also felt the stress. Cassandra in particular seemed upset by all the newbies. She made it clear: the streets were for the abused and homeless, like herself, and not for poseurs who wanted to play at being street kids.

Jessica showed up in this increasingly tense dynamic, as oblivious as always. After the death threats against Jimmy, their relationship had soured. Jessica, following the lead of the other girls, had made a new Square boyfriend. His name was Nicholas Saunders. A young man who had moved to the streets from his home on the Oregon coast, Nicholas was a short and heavyset man with a shaved head. On the streets, he boasted that he was a marine, according to police reports.

Nicholas says he did not have sex with Jessica. He asked her to go to bed with him, but she refused. Like Jessica and Jimmy, they were boyfriend and girlfriend in name only. Jessica might have hung all over him in the Square and made loud talk, but it was all just a game—to Jessica.

Jessica stopped in at the Janus Youth Access and Reception Center, where Favor Ellis had learned that she was not eighteen. Jessica was told she was too old for services. She was no longer welcome in the youth shelter system, but Jessica was not discouraged. She didn't need the agencies. Getting kicked out of the shelters did not dissuade her from going downtown. She only hung out more at the Square. In a sense, losing the connection to the youth agencies made Jessica even more vulnerable to the machinations of the street families and less visible to those who might have cared about her safety. Now she was on her own.

———

Jessica began hanging around the Thantos Family more often. She met Danielle Cox, the new female warrior. Danielle found her to be a sweet person. "She was very gentle and very sweet and kind and caring," Danielle said. Like others in the street family, Danielle denied noticing that Jessica was delayed in any way. "I had no idea," she told police later.

That Saturday, May 10, according to court records, Danielle was hanging around outside Matt's apartment on Burnside when two large men began arguing. It was late, around two in the morning. Danielle got involved in the fight and began pushing one of the men. Hearing the altercation, the family came boiling out of the basement-level apartment. Nelson supposedly got into the fight, and the next thing everyone knew, one of the men was choking Nelson. The fight ended, and the men supposedly shook hands. Blood was smeared everywhere, including on parked cars. The family washed the blood off the cars with bottled water.

In Thantos Family lore, this quickly became known as the fight-with-the-marines, though there was no reason to think either of the men was an actual marine. Nelson and Carl began bragging that they later tracked down one of the marines and stabbed him with the long knife they called the Death Dealer. They said they had hid the body in a construction site where it would never be found.

It was the same story Sara Baerlocher had heard a month earlier about Nelson's burying someone in a construction site. This time, however, Nelson allegedly said he had killed the marine because he had hit a woman, and Nelson just couldn't stand a man striking a woman.

Jessica playacted all day with Nicholas at being boyfriend and girl-friend; then when evening fell, she caught the bus home. After she left, everything changed. As night fell, the Square took on a different tone. The shoppers and businesspeople disappeared from the bus mall. Vendors closed their food carts, pulling canvas hoods down and locking their stainless steel cabinets. The lights inside the businesses flicked off. The Square grew dark.

Pioneer Courthouse Square was supposed to close at midnight. But as there were no gates or fences, there was no way to keep the street kids out. So the city hired security guards, such as Andrea Timm, who dealt with homeless people assaulting trash cans in their delusions and others quietly sobbing on the steps.

Larry Findling, the detective in the 1992 murders, believes that street kid culture has been nourished by the creation of town squares like Pioneer Courthouse Square. The squares serve as comfortable meeting grounds for street kids and forums where they can recruit and indoctrinate new members into the street culture. Without town squares and plazas, the street kids would be more fragmented. It is harder to organize when you are forced to stand on sidewalks.

The Thantos Family gathered at midnight at the Square. "Because that's when all the preppy people supposedly come out with lots of money," Thomas Schreiner said. He wasn't talking about panhandling.

The Thantos Family had created their own mugging group, including Thomas Schreiner (T. J.), Joshua Brown-Lenon (Scooby), and Carl Alsup (D. K.), according to police reports. They called themselves the Rolling Trolls. The term is common among street youths—*rolling* refers to mugging, and *troll* is a derogatory term for an older gay man. To "roll a troll" is to mug a gay man, usually by posing as an interested younger boy and luring the man into a secluded place where a group of friends is waiting, weapons at hand.

Joshua calmly describes how it is done: "You meet this guy who likes younger boys. You play along. You get him to where your buddies can handle that and take his money. It's a way of life." With his slim build and innocent eyes, Joshua was the perfect lure for trolling.

However, Joshua denies mugging gay men with the Thantos Family. He says he committed the crimes "back in the day," before he hooked up with the family. According to Joshua, "They asked me to, but I said no."

Nelson claims that Joshua was mugging gay men at the time. "Scooby was rolling queers in Paranoid Park [O'Bryant Square]. He mugged at least four guys," Nelson asserts. There are no police reports of gay men being mugged in O'Bryant Square at that time. Police say such crimes are often not reported because the victims are either afraid they will be prosecuted for trying to procure underage sex, or they are closeted and fear exposure.

There was a reported mugging of a gay man on May 13 during the time the Thantos Family was active downtown. The man was attacked on Burnside Avenue by the freeway overpass not far from Matt's Trinity Place apartment. The victim said he was walking home when a group of street kids came up behind him yelling "faggot." Before he could turn to see who they were, he was struck from behind. The blow was hard enough that he was knocked out, and he fell to the ground. He never saw his attackers and was unable to describe them. The youths robbed him of his cell phone.

The Thantos Family didn't target just gay men. The group was supposedly responsible for several robberies, including several ATM muggings, which Schreiner later estimated happened "five, six times a week."

Before going on their crime expeditions, according to court records, the youths would put on extra layers of clothes. "Thantos [Nelson] always made us wear two layers of clothes," Schreiner told investigators. This was so that if they committed a crime or got bloody, they could strip down to a clean layer. After a mugging, they gave Nelson the proceeds, which he kept in a special green box in Matt's apartment.

Through the dark nights of May, the Thantos Family played dark games. They marched through downtown on training missions. Nelson called these marches "urban combat training," according to court documents. He had his followers stand at attention. They practiced their fighting techniques. Nelson was passing on all of the secrets of his supposed years with the marines, as well as the secrets of the immortal dragon warriors.

———

Sara Baerlocher, or Akasha, was still babysitting the two little girls whose parents hung around the Square. The trouble started when

Matt supposedly burned their mother in a methamphetamine deal. According to Sara, the mother of the girls had arranged to buy some of the drug from Matt Burch. His apprentice Carl was supposed to deliver it to their apartment, but Carl delivered some salt instead.

Sara was irate. This was her "employer," and her street family wasn't supposed to burn her employer. Sara demanded the real drug, but salt came again. Finally, on the third try, Carl supposedly delivered real crystal. By that time, Sara was really annoyed.

Angry and sore at each other, the Thantos Family went out in the afternoon to eat at McDonald's. Sara was frustrated at how long the cashier was taking. She had been in the food business. She knew the customer was supposed to come first. Carl, she says, just had to disagree. After they got their food and sat down, she and Carl got into an argument about food service. Sara yelled at him. She told him he was starting to act like a complete know-it-all.

Nelson's knee started bouncing. When Nelson got nervous or angry, Sara says, his knee would bounce. She thought it was kind of cute, actually. He was mad at her. It was against the rules to correct your street brother in public, Nelson told Sara. Carl was a family warrior, a death knight. Sara might be Nelson's girlfriend, but that didn't mean she held rank over Carl. It wasn't okay for her to correct her street brother, especially not with people watching. It was against old school rules. It was against the code.

Sara had violated the code without even knowing it. That was when it really started, she thought. That's when the dramas began turning against her.

Within a day or two, Sara was downtown, babysitting the girls, pushing them around in their stroller. A group of excited street kids ran up to her. "Go to the Square," they told her. They kept repeating it. "Go to the Square, go to the Square."

At the Square, Sara found a girl sitting in Nelson's lap. It was Destiny, the pretty girl from the peace camp whom Nelson had said he was going to make into a virgin for his coven. He was kissing her. The kissing stopped when Sara arrived.

Nelson had an excuse. He told Sara he needed to feed off of Destiny's energy. Sara says she had heard something about this before, from the Dungeons and Dragons stuff that Nelson talked about. There were characters called Nightwalkers and Shape Changers, she had been told, and they needed to feed off the energy of others. Maybe Nelson really was a Nightwalker or a Shape Changer. Sara had heard that a Shape Changer could only feed off a few select people. Maybe this girl Destiny was one of those.

Or maybe not.

Sara was angry with Nelson. They were supposed to be girlfriend and boyfriend. She began yelling, as loud as she could. The fight became public, with the whole Square watching, and the two little girls watching as well. Nelson and Sara's breakup was official and complete. Sara was not welcome in the family any more.

Until this point, Destiny had been going out with Schreiner, the young rapist, but after Nelson broke up with Sara, he told them to stop dating. He wanted Destiny for himself, and he had gremlin rights. Schreiner obeyed, and Nelson took Destiny as his girlfriend. Destiny didn't appear to mind.

———

Right around the time of the big breakup, as this drama was called, the Thantos Family merged with Cassandra Hale's street family. Danielle Cox thought it was around the week of May 12, soon after her fight with the "marines."

There was no formal sit-down. The families just migrated together in the Square, possibly in response to the heightened stress of all the newbies. With her, Cassandra brought her followers, including Jimmy Stewart. Those who had been following Cassandra now obeyed Nelson as their "dad," and those who had been obeying Nelson now accepted Cassandra as their "mom."

With the two families combined, there were now over a dozen core members, including James Nelson (Thantos), Cassandra Hale (Juliet), Carl Alsup (D. K.), Crystal Grace (Jade), Danielle Cox (Shadowcat), Jimmy Stewart (Neo), Joshua Brown-Lenon (Scooby), Sarah Caster (Valkyrie), Crystal Dawn Ivey (Nix), Thomas Schreiner (T. J.), and Matt Burch (Leviathan).

Other members included Cory Dennison, the mentally ill boy in Cassandra's family who went by the street name Twix, and his girlfriend Heidi Keller, called the Little Twix. Cory had a soft-cheeked baby face and the stilted affect of a young man with multiple diagnoses, including bipolar disorder and schizophrenia. His girlfriend, Heidi, had long dark hair and a tiny Cupid's bow mouth. She had recently migrated down from Kelso, Washington, to escape a family she said was involved in drugs. Cory had been on the streets for around five months, and Heidi for a little over a month.

On the periphery were several other youths, including Destiny, Nelson's newly acquired girlfriend. She was a "housie," meaning she didn't sleep on the streets. Some teenagers hanging around the street kids escape the contempt appointed to oogles and are accepted, even though they return to their family homes at night. These young people are accorded a more respectful term, *housie*. Destiny's pretty looks might have helped her cause.

It is unclear if Nelson and Cassandra ever had sex. None of their followers mentioned a romantic connection. Platonic parent relationships are common in street families. Mom and dad might be friends, travel buddies, or fellow junkies. The assumption on the streets will be that they are not romantically involved unless they make it clear that they are by becoming street "wife" and "husband."

Robyn Hale recalls a call she received from Cassandra around this time. "She was on a cell phone—stolen, of course. There was this guy in the background, and he sounded a lot older. They were laughing together. I asked her about it, but she said she knew what she was doing."

The family changed with the addition of Cassandra as mother. If Nelson was all about fantasy, Cassandra was all about discipline. Nelson's lies were fantastic myths that spiraled the youths into violent games. Cassandra's lies were linear and led to one place: punishment. The kids complained that Cassandra slapped their heads, forcing them to lean over for rabbit punches in the Square. She "bossed everyone around," Carl complained. Sarah Caster, the sixteen-year-old with strawberry blonde hair, was frightened of her. Cassandra would get in their faces, using her size to bully them.

The new, extended family quickly took a rigid shape. The "kids" were expected to panhandle every day and turn the proceeds over to their street mom and dad. Sarah later told police that the youths were expected to make $5 to $20 a day panhandling and turn it all over to Nelson and Cassandra, who then decided how to spend the money.

The panhandling was their duty to their parents, the way the youths earned their keep and demonstrated their responsibility, just like chores in a regular family. As Danielle Cox later told police, her street parents were "taking care of all of our dramas . . . like they're mom and dad, basically."

Sara Baerlocher thought the drama involving her and Nelson was over, but she should have known better. The dramas never end in a street family. They just escalate. With no external checks and balances—no adults watching, willing to intervene—there is nothing to stop them from spinning out of control.

Soon after their breakup, Sara says, Nelson showed up at the apartment where she was babysitting the two little girls. He asked for his Death Dealer knife, which Sara had been holding for him. She passed him the knife through a window.

The next day, the word whipped around the Square that Sara had tried to snitch on Nelson. The accusation was serious: apparently, Sara had called the police and told them Nelson was carrying a weapon, which was a direct violation of his parole. Their street father was now in danger. If it was true, it meant Sara had violated the code. She had snitched.

It isn't clear how this story started. Sara thinks that Crystal Grace planted it. The two had never liked each other, Sara says, because one day Nelson and Carl had asked her to teach Crystal how to be a lady, which Crystal did not appreciate. Or maybe Nelson started it to get back at Sara for breaking up with him. Regardless, if the rest of the family believed the story, it meant Sara would have to be taxed or killed. "If you want to hurt someone, that's what you say, they're a snitch," Sara says.

Sara tried her own damage control. She told the other street families around the Square that she had never called the police. She told them that she had given the knife back to Nelson. She said she was innocent.

It didn't make any difference. There was an order coming down on Sara. Danielle Cox said Nelson had put the word out: Sara was 86'd.

As they had in 1992, events began to escalate rapidly. The other members of the family began passing on messages to Sara that afternoon. They followed her around downtown and stopped by the apartment where she was babysitting. They approached her with grim faces and passed on the messages with importance.

She was told that

1. She was not to appear downtown.
2. If she had to go downtown in her job as a nanny, she had to carry a melted fork upright in her hand. This would signal the family that she was on a mission for her employer and thus off-limits.
3. If she broke these rules, she would be punished.

It was the street version of the Wiccan threefold law. The street family could attack another youth but not the person who owned that kid, whether that was their street parent or someone paying them for a service. The melted fork was the family's own flourish.

Sara didn't care. She kept walking around downtown that day and the next and the day after that. As she marched boldly through the Square, the other street kids asked her why she was putting herself in danger. Nobody was going to scare her, Sara said. They were just kidding, anyhow.

Sara says Joshua quietly approached her on the street. He handed her a bus ticket to New Jersey and told her to use it. Joshua had recently been in New Jersey and was planning to return there soon. "He really was a good kid," she says. Sara didn't use the ticket. Neither did Joshua.

That evening after babysitting, Sara says she was waiting for the train when Nelson approached her. He told her that he wanted to work things out. She didn't believe him. She thought he was up to something, she says.

The next night, Sara was at the train station again, at about the same time, when Matt Burch came up the street. "He said we should talk and get it over," Sara says. Sara acquiesced, following Matt toward his apartment. It was late out, long after dark. Sara denies being afraid. She walked willingly toward danger.

They passed the Trinity Place apartment, and Matt kept walking. They crossed an empty parking lot by a church. Sara turned around and saw the family collecting behind her. The kids had materialized from the shadows.

The family surrounded her. According to court records and other sources, the following family members were present: Carl Alsup, Crystal Grace, Danielle Cox, Joshua Brown-Lenon, Sarah Caster, Cassandra Hale, and Matt Burch. Several of the street kids were new to Sara, having joined with Cassandra's family after she and Nelson had broken up.

The men of the family, Sara says, were wearing "war paint," red and black streaks across their cheeks. The family circled around her and told her to kneel on the pavement. First, she was taxed. Sara was told to take off her rings. Next came the pocket check. Sara had to empty her pockets. The youths inspected their findings. Sara told them that the library card belonged to the mother of the two girls. They handed that back.

Then, Sara claimed, one of the girls pulled out a knife and held it to her throat. She demanded to know if Sara had called the police on Nelson. Sara denied that she had ever snitched. The rest of the family stopped, confused. They didn't seem to know quite what to do. Could they punish Sara if she denied what she had done? What did old school rules say about this situation?

Matt Burch had an answer. He stood in front of Sara and told her to hold out her hands. He put his palms on top of her hands. He announced he was going to do a "truth spell" on her. He muttered something or another under his breath, very mysterious and mystical, and asked her again. Did she call the cops? Sara still denied calling the cops.

Obviously, the truth spell didn't work.

After some hurried whispers, the family decided to go ahead with the punishment. The girls pulled out knives. They were going to take her hair. Sara was forced to kneel on the pavement. She didn't think anyone was nearby to witness the assault. Even if someone walking by did look into the empty lot, all they would see was a group of street kids standing in a circle. Sara was hidden on her knees.

The girls went to work. Once again, there was trouble. Their knives were too dull for Sara's beautiful waist-length black hair. They sawed at her hair, but the knives wouldn't cut. The family stopped and had a whispered conversation. It was decided that one of the kids would go get some scissors from Matt's apartment. Sara says that Joshua was sent on the mission. He took off running, with Sara still kneeling in the circle.

He was back in a few minutes, running with the scissors carefully pointed down. Later, the image of Joshua sprinting across the parking lot with scissors to cut off her hair stuck in Sara's mind. Joshua was supposed to be her friend. But there he was, rushing to help them cut off her hair.

The girls did the work. The men watched. The girls did a tidy job, Sara says, neatly sectioning her hair and braiding it before lopping it all off. They cut the braids off right down to the skull. When they were done, her scalp showed in patches.

While they taxed her hair, Carl, his face smeared with war paint, sang a song, according to police records. It was from the Insane Clown Posse, or ICP, a punk band popular with street kids. The singers paint themselves up like clowns and rap extremely violent lyrics. The song was called "Boogie Woogie Wu," and Carl adapted the words to the moment. In the real version, the lyrics go

> *Does the Boogie Man really exist?*
> *Well, is your mother a bald-headed freak bitch? Yes*

You fall asleep and you wake up dead
With a broken broom sticking out of your forehead . . .
Tie you down and chew your fucking toes off
And then spit them out back in your face
Splat! Fuck, wash your feet bitch!

Carl later admitted to police that he sang the song, changing the words to include Sara's getting her hair taxed.

The family left Sara kneeling in the parking lot. They took her long braids of hair with them. One of the girls told Sara that her hair would be "treasured." Before they left, they gave her one more warning: "If you value your life, Akasha, you'll stay out of downtown."

Sara is adamant that she wasn't scared. She admits to being mad but not to feeling frightened. She says she had a beanie cap stuck in her pocket. She pulled it over her denuded scalp. She returned to the train station, wearing the cap. The train came, and she got on.

It wasn't until she was safe on the train that it hit her. Sara began crying. The other passengers came to comfort her, and she pulled off the cap, showing them her bald scalp and weeping uncontrollably.

═══

"Sara was so proud of her hair, always brushing it," Nelson says. Nelson claims he was in the apartment that night when the youths showed up and dropped the braids, right there, in his lap. "They laughed and said, 'We took her hair.'"

According to Nelson, the family taxed Sara her hair because Sara had tattled about the earlier plan to kill Matt. But one of his followers told investigators that before the hair tax, Nelson had been waving his big Death Dealer knife around at the apartment, demanding that the family take Sara's hair. Nelson told his followers he wanted the hair as a "souvenir."

Sarah Caster, the beautiful sixteen-year-old girl who didn't like to punch someone even in fun, was distraught. She had just helped cut off her friend's hair. She wanted to leave the family. "Sarah wanted to leave," her boyfriend Joshua says. "But she said, 'If I leave, I'll be dead.' Nelson was saying things like, 'You can't leave now.'"

The family took the braids of hair downtown to show them off. It was past midnight, and the Square was supposed to be closed, but the street families were out in force. The moon was almost full in the sky, the night crackling with energy. Matt swung Sara's long braids around his head. The street kids laughed and whooped with unbridled pleasure at the hunt and the intoxicating knowledge that they had gotten away with it.

Sara didn't report her assault to the police. She knew what happened to snitches. She says that she did take her beef to Mama and Papa Wolf, supposedly the oldest of the old school street family leaders. She says she found Mama Wolf in a hotel and took off her cap, showing Mama Wolf how the family had taken her hair. Mama Wolf was outraged at the sight of Sara's bald head, but no punishment came down. There were just too many street kids in the Thantos Family to 86 them all.

Sara still didn't take the family warnings quite to heart. She moved out of downtown, camping under the Rose Garden overpass on the east side of the river, near the Lloyd Center. She found a new boyfriend, a homeless man named Arthur who was not part of the street families. For money, Sara and Arthur panhandled around the Rose Quarter, a large stadium built above the Steel Bridge on the east side, where the Trail Blazers play basketball.

Sara still hung out around downtown at times, seemingly unable to judge the danger she was in or, perhaps, too caught up in the dramas herself to care. She decided she had better be prepared to defend herself, though. She and Arthur practiced their fighting moves outside the Multnomah County Courthouse. She was amused when the people working inside came out to check if they were really fighting. She laughed about it, seemingly pleased that people noticed.

Besides, she says, she couldn't leave downtown entirely. She had people she was taking care of in the Square, other kids she was watching over. One of them was Jessica Williams. It was one of Jessica's biggest dreams, Sara says, to ride in one of those horse-drawn carriages downtown. Sara says she was saving her babysitting money so Jessica could have her magic carriage ride.

14

There were so many dramas happening so fast during those weeks of early to mid May. Sara and Nelson had broken up, the Thantos Family had merged with Cassandra's family, and Sara was 86'd from the territories and had received a hair tax.

Now, Jessica had come downtown and was loudly and theatrically proclaiming that her new boyfriend, Nicholas Saunders, had offered her money to have sex with him. It was around May 14.

It was just like Jessica, says her mother, to tattle. At home, Jessica would yell to her siblings, "I'm going to tell mom!" even when she was twenty-two. Becky could just see Jessica going around to all these street kids saying that a boy had offered to pay her to have sex, completely unaware of the explosive situation she was creating.

Nicholas denied that he had said any such thing to Jessica. He freely admitted asking her to have sex with him, which she continued to refuse. But he was adamant that he did not offer her money in exchange for intimacy.

The new, extended Thantos Family reacted to the news as expected: appalled, angry, and eager to punish. Nicholas had broken code. It was yet another unstated old school rule: you don't insult the friend of a street family by offering money for sex. Nicholas would have to be punished. It didn't matter that he denied the allegation. The word came down. Nicholas was an SOS, a smash on sight.

The first attack occurred in Paranoid Park. An unidentified man beat Nicholas up while two family members watched. Jessica was downtown a day or so after the assault, and Nicholas gave her a computer bag filled with papers and personal belongings, telling her he had been beaten up by street kids and asking her to keep it safe. Jessica took the bag home.

The family was not satisfied with Nicholas's initial punishment. They had an entire day to think about it, hanging around the apartment and lounging on their benches in the Square. Jerry Fest, author of *Street Culture: An Epistemology of Street-Dependent Youth*, characterizes the life of street kids as containing hours of boredom punctuated with moments of extreme terror. It was boring to sit in the Square all day and panhandle. The dramas relieved the tedium. With a drama in sight, the family had something to get excited about.

The family fabricated a whole new set of accusations against Nicholas. Now the word circulated around the Square that the stocky young man had offered to pay a fourteen-year-old girl for sex. This was a serious code violation. Nicholas would have to be severely punished. The beating would be worse this time.

That Saturday, May 17, the family orchestrated another plan to punish Nicholas. Two family members were nominated for the task: Carl Alsup and Danielle Cox. For Danielle, the female warrior, this would be one more step in her training to be a death knight. Danielle accepted the assignment. The college student seemed fully immersed in her Shadowcat character, standing in the Square in heavy combat boots and her Mohawk.

Typical of Portland in spring, the mild dry weather had turned fickle. Cold rain and hail pelted the streets. But at the Square, the hardcore youths remained, including Steve Pearce, a convicted felon going by the name of Gambit. Pearce was a muscular young man with a seamed nose that looked like it had been broken and reset, a black pompadour, and absolutely cold eyes. He didn't know the Thantos street family, and he wasn't exactly clear on what Nicholas had done, but it was enough for him that the code had been broken and a taxing was about to take place.

Pearce had a violent street history in Portland. A year and a half earlier, when he was nineteen, he had been hanging outside the Greenhouse when a father had showed up looking for his runaway fourteen-year-old daughter. Unknown to her father, the girl had been telling Pearce and the Greenhouse staff that she had been abused.

She later admitted that she had made up the story. She had found a sympathetic older boyfriend in Pearce. "I told Pearce about my dad and he hinted around about hurting him," she said. "Steve asked me if I wanted him to kill him." In just two days at the Greenhouse, the girl had already been assigned a street name. The other youths called her Brat, and she was planning on moving into a squat.

The father showed up at the shelter on November 26, 2001, around seven in the evening. When he asked about his daughter, he was met with hostility by the staff. The staff "would not tell him if his daughter was inside," according to the police reports. The father left the building, frustrated. He didn't notice Pearce, who was waiting on the sidewalk, dressed in a knee-length brown trench coat over black baggy pants and a black shirt. Under his long coat Pearce held a hatchet.

The dad stayed outside a moment, watching the shelter door, and sure enough, his daughter came traipsing out. She was a slight girl, not much over a hundred pounds, and he picked her up, slung her over his shoulder, and carried her to his car. This angered the street kids loitering outside the Greenhouse, including Pearce. Several kids ran up, trying to free the girl from the car. One of the Greenhouse staff came running out of the building and "opened the car door" so the girl could run away, according to the police report.

The girl dashed off, and her father went running after her. He had no idea that Pearce was also in pursuit. Steve raised the hatchet and brought it down, sending the father crashing to the pavement. When the father rolled over, Steve was standing above him, holding the bloodied hatchet. "Leave her alone or I'm going to cut you," Steve warned him, according to the police report. The father was lucky. The hatchet had only grazed the back of his head. What could have been a fatal blow caused only a bloody lump.

A woman riding her bicycle nearby called the police. Officers soon found the girl and released her to her father. They also arrested Pearce, who ended up pleading guilty to attempted assault, but not before filling his court files with numerous pleas and petitions. Pearce wrote well and seemed to be educated on points of law, even when their application to his case was tenuous. He was given three years probation, despite an earlier felony conviction for assault with a deadly weapon in California, and was almost immediately back on the streets. His probation was transferred to California, and Pearce was told he was no longer welcome in Oregon.

Pearce says he did go to California but returned to Portland in April 2003. He was now almost twenty-one and in violation of his probation. He was not supposed to be in Oregon. He settled back around the Greenhouse and claimed alliance with the Sick Boys street family. He took a new street name, Gambit, from the X-Men comic book character. In the comic books, Gambit is an agile fighter, trained in martial arts and able to defy gravity. He is also known as a "phenomenal thief."

Though he had committed a violent assault outside their doors and was a felon in violation of his parole—a fugitive, in other words—the Greenhouse staff welcomed Pearce back home. A new assessment was positive. "Gambit says he is ready to be motivated to get his life together," the staff wrote. (It is common among agencies to refer to street youth by their street names, a practice that is supposed to build trust.)

And so, Steve Pearce, respectfully addressed as a superhero by shelter workers, twice convicted of assault and a fugitive from the law, hung around the Square and listened as the Thantos Family plotted their punishment of Nicholas Saunders. He offered to help. The family agreed, and Pearce joined Carl and Danielle in carrying out the SOS.

———

Jimmy Stewart, who had followed his street mother Cassandra into the Thantos Family, went to fetch the victim. He strolled up to the Greenhouse and told Nicholas to come with him to the Square. Nicholas may have felt he had no choice in the matter. The penalty for ignoring the order may have been worse than the planned punishment, and it was well known that the Greenhouse staff refused to call the police even when asked. Nicholas was trapped.

Nelson and Cassandra were sitting together in the Square when Nicholas was brought before them for his punishment, according to Danielle. It was Cassandra who gave the directions: Carl, Danielle, and Pearce were told to march Nicholas up to the parking garage on Tenth Avenue, three blocks above the Square, for his taxing. Inside the concrete parking garage, Nicholas was beaten from floor to floor, rammed against walls, and punched in the stomach and kidneys. "They kicked my ass for about half an hour," he later told police.

Pearce laughed as he told how they made Nicholas ram his own head into a concrete wall, just like on the show *Jackass*. When Nicholas didn't do it right, one of the street kids said, "No, no, Nick, this is how you do it," and then grabbed him by the neck and smashed his head into the concrete wall. Carl slapped him in the face. Danielle kicked him with her steel-toed boots.

When they were done, the family warriors told Nicholas to take off his shirt and wipe his bloody face. They marched him in his socks back through the rain and hail down to the Square. There he was told to kneel in front of Cassandra, apologize, and call everyone "master." Surrounded by the proud Thantos warriors, Nicholas knelt, looked up, and called Cassandra "master."

It was the middle of the afternoon, next to a popular Starbucks, and no one did a thing about the bloody-faced boy genuflecting in front of a group of street kids. Nicholas asked what he should do next, and Cassandra coldly replied, "Start running." Wet with blood, Nicholas ran. He didn't run toward the Greenhouse, New Avenues for Youth, or any of the other youth shelters. He went in the opposite direction, running in his socks in the rain toward an upscale shopping mall down the street from the Square. He went into a Discovery store and used a pay phone to call an ambulance.

At the hospital, Nicholas was treated for blackened eyes, a swollen lip, and a broken nose. The hospital called the police, who showed up to interview him. Nicholas refused to talk. He told the police that he had no idea who had attacked him and declined to say what they looked like. "Complainant told me that he had no idea who the 'street kids' were and didn't know why they assaulted him," the police officer wrote. "He also told me he didn't know what they looked like or what they were wearing." Like every other street kid, Nicholas knew the penalty for snitching was death. "I was scared," he later admitted.

Nicholas called his grandmother who lived on the Oregon coast. He told her that he was afraid. He was worried he was going to be killed. He asked his grandmother to wire him $25 for a Greyhound bus ticket. While he waited for the money, he laid low, hiding as best as he could from the Thantos Family.

Though witnesses placed him in the Square at the time, Nelson claims to have no knowledge of the beating. When he came home to Matt's apartment that night, he says, he was real tired, and he plopped down on the couch. "I told Sarah [Caster] to get her butt off the couch." Only then, he claims, did he learn from the family that they had assaulted Nicholas. They told him about the blood and the parking garage. He also says that was when he met Steve Pearce, who was apparently at the apartment.

Nelson and Pearce became fast friends. They had a lot in common. They were both convicted felons, both from California, and both firm believers in the street family culture. Like Nelson, Pearce had no intention of leaving the streets. He told shelter staff that he was afraid of turning twenty-one because then he wouldn't be able to live in the youth shelters anymore. Pearce joined the Thantos Family and took part in their mugging expeditions and night prowls.

With the beating of Nicholas Saunders, Nelson's power was established. As one attorney associated with the case describes, there was a sense that Nelson had tentacles. He could reach anywhere in downtown Portland, even into a shelter, and find his victims. Nothing would happen in recourse: no one would be caught, and no one would be punished. There was no escape for a street kid who aroused his anger.

According to one of his attorneys, Jimmy Stewart tried to escape the family at around this time. He went out to a truck stop in Troutdale and tried to hitch a ride out of town, but he was unsuccessful. He went back downtown to his street mom, Cassandra, and his new father, Nelson.

Nelson says that Jessica Williams was in the Square that day. She did not participate in or witness the assault on Nicholas, but she knew it was going to happen. According to one street kid, Jessica was going around the Square before the assault, begging others to stop the beating. "She was saying, 'They're going to beat Nick. Do something about it,'" he claims. The other street kids did nothing. One kid explains why: "Twelve against one, I wasn't going to go against them."

Jessica was upset enough that she went home and stayed there for three days. Becky was relieved to have her daughter home. She thought that Jessica was finally through with her rebellion, that she could move on to other things.

Jessica always liked working in the garden. Her mother got her a nice set of plants, and Jessica decided to make a flower bed out front. The next day warmed up, and Jessica puttered in the shifting sun and clouds, lining a flowerbed with river rocks. Her mother joined her, helping Jessica lift the plants from their containers, set them into the soil, water lightly, and pat the dirt around their stems. The bed was right by the front door, so anyone who walked up the path would pass the waving flowers.

On the night after the beating of Nicholas Saunders, May 18, the family was out in force. The rain had been swept away by the winds, and the night was chilly, with a sharp bite to the air. Joshua Brown-Lenon says he was doing speedballs that day, an injected combination of heroin, cocaine, and methamphetamine, and had smoked "a bunch of weed. I had a good buzz going on."

On Burnside Avenue, Carl found a likely victim for a mugging. Eugene was thirty-two and a tattoo artist. He had been at a bachelor party for a friend held in an exotic dance club on Fourth Avenue called Magic Gardens. The club is small and seedy, with a small square stage and stained handwritten cardboard signs admonishing that the dancers only work for tips. The drinks at the Magic Garden are potent, and Eugene, who admitted to having more than a few, was weaving his way up Burnside, looking for an ATM machine to get some cash. It was almost two in the morning, he says.

Eugene had just moved up from San Francisco. If he thought a smaller city would be safer, he was wrong. He was a big guy, five feet, eleven inches and close to two hundred pounds, with a congenial, broad, smiling face and heavy shoulders covered with tattoos. He wasn't a naïf, but he was loaded.

At a gas station on Burnside Avenue four blocks from the club, Eugene met two street kids, a young man who introduced himself as Chaluchi and a girl. It was Carl and an unidentified woman who was never arrested. Eugene asked the two if they knew of a Wells Fargo cash machine nearby. They told him there was a cash machine right up the street, near Pioneer Square, and since they were heading that way, they offered to accompany him.

As the three walked, Carl bragged to Eugene that he had been in prison. When Eugene said he was from San Francisco, Carl said he didn't like the city since there were too many Irish there and pot smokers as well. Eugene, who is Irish with reddish hair, wondered drunkenly if the street kid was trying to insult him.

At the bank machine, Eugene wanted to deposit a check. He couldn't find a pen, and Carl offered to get one from his friends across the street. It was then that Eugene noticed a group of seven to ten street kids standing in the Square. They just stood there, watching Eugene at the bank machine. Eugene suddenly became aware of how deserted the streets were. It may have been the middle of downtown, but it sure was empty.

Eugene deposited the check and took out $40. He began to walk back to the club, and Carl and the girl walked along with him, saying they wanted to guide him just in case he got lost. About this time, he says, "My gut told me this was bad."

After a few blocks, Eugene became aware of other youths materializing behind him. One he described as tall and thin with wide eyes and a hippie-sort of look. It was Joshua, known as Scooby. He had his baseball bat Little Dink along for the crime, tucked under his jacket. Thomas Schreiner, or T. J., was along for the crime as well, as was at least one other family member. Behind Eugene, Carl loped in his uniform of black shirt, black jeans, work boots, and jacket. The girl kept up a happy chatter at Eugene's side.

As the group got closer to Burnside Avenue, Eugene figured he was just a few blocks from the club. He tried to tell the street kids he was cool, that he knew his way back. No, they insisted, he might get lost. They crossed Burnside. About a block away, on a dark stretch, the girl asked Eugene if he missed San Francisco. He turned his head to answer, and as he turned, an object came swinging out of the dark.

It was Little Dink, swung by Joshua. The baseball bat cracked Eugene in the head. At first, he thought, "I must have been hit by a car. A car jumped the curb," he thought irrationally, "and hit me in the head." He felt his body literally rise up off the sidewalk and fly through the air. He landed, hard, on his knees. Befuddled, he turned his head to see Carl running straight at him.

Eugene scrambled to his feet and took off for his life. He made it about twenty feet, he estimates, when the bat came swinging again, this time striking him hard in the side of his ribs, then across his back. He might have been hit many times in the head, he thought later.

Eugene fell across the sidewalk, and Carl climbed on his back and began "strangling" him. As he began to lose consciousness, Eugene felt someone—he thought it was Carl—reaching into his front pocket for his wallet. The hand took his money and his wallet and his identification. The street kids went running down the street.

On the sidewalk, Eugene slowly came to and staggered the rest of the way to the club. His head was swollen and bleeding, and he felt like his ribs were cracked. At the club, a doorman took him to the bathroom and helped him wash the blood off his face. He found his friends, and the group went back up to the Square.

They found the security guard Andrea Timm, who according to police reports told Eugene that she knew the street kids involved, that "they did this all the time and that nothing would happen to them, so chalk it up to experience." As a matter of fact, she had just treated a scrape on the arm of one of his assailants. When the youth heard an ambulance siren in the distance, he said, "Oh shit," and ran off. Timm did not call the police.

Eugene didn't want to chalk it up to experience. He had been attacked in an assault that could qualify as attempted murder. Not everyone gets struck in the head with a baseball bat and lives to tell about it. From his recovery bed the next day, Eugene called the Wells Fargo bank and asked if there was a videotape of his ATM transaction. The bank said there was, and the video might have captured images of some of the perpetrators. Wells Fargo told Eugene they would release this tape to the police if requested.

The following evening, on May 20, Eugene went to Portland Police and filed an armed robbery report. The officer who took the report noted that Eugene was injured. "I noticed Mr. [name removed] had trouble moving the right side of his torso," he wrote. "He kept his right arm against his ribs. I saw an abrasion to his right forehead and his right eye was swollen and bruised. In addition, he showed me a lump on the right occipital area of his skull." Like other street kid crimes, the baseball bat assault on Eugene was not reported in the local paper.

Only a few hours after the robbery of Eugene, Sara Baerlocher woke up in her squat across the river. She and her new boyfriend, Arthur, followed their usual morning routine. They woke up in a leisurely fashion, tidied themselves the best they could in squat, then moseyed up to the Lloyd Center mall for a cup of coffee at Starbucks. Sara took her smiley chain, the Equalizer, with her.

Sara knew the street families went to the mall on the east side of the river as well. They would go to the food court on the third floor, where there was an arcade, or take in a movie at the indoor theater.

The Thantos Family had not forgotten about Sara, and when they spotted her walking through the underground parking lot, an echo-ing cavern with old concrete partitions and shadowed corners, they decided now was the perfect time to teach her a lesson. Sara began running and tried to hide behind a partition, but the family found her. Sara claims that Crystal Grace, Sarah Caster, and Steve Pearce, the newest member of the family, were among those present. Nelson claims that Danielle was also there.

Sara pulled out her smiley chain and swung it in defense, but she says one of the youths took it away from her. Someone jumped on her. She says she rolled the youth over on a bike, and then claims to have made a short speech. "I said, 'I'm not going to run from you anymore. I'm tired of running from a group of little kids.'" Whether or not this artificial-sounding speech occurred, the family did run away.

After the assault, Sara claims she ran into Nelson in the food court on the third floor of the mall. He inquired about how she was doing. "He acted very innocent," she says. He asked why her hair was so short, and this made her mad because she had heard he knew all about the taxing.

Nelson admits he was in the mall that day, saying he had gone to Barnes and Noble to look for the latest Harry Potter book. He was a big Harry Potter fan, he says. Once again, he claims he had no idea the attack had occurred. He says that the family members later told him Sara was the one who had started the fight by swinging her smiley chain at them.

The Thantos Family was on a spree, having committing three serious assaults in three days: the beating of Nicholas Saunders, the baseball-bat mugging of Eugene, and the latest attack on Sara. But Joshua shrugged it off, explaining that's how it is on the streets, with life condensed into violent dramas that can unfold with frightening speed. "Everything is fast-paced on the streets. Everybody is trying to get everything over. You've got to come up quick."

Matt Burch, the alleged methamphetamine dealer with the apartment, was the street kids' next target. After squatting at his place for several weeks, the family turned on him. According to his account, the family 86'd Matt because he had been involved with a runaway girl. This, they said, endangered them by possibly attracting the police.

Matt said that he came home and found his apartment door open. His couch was sliced up, and his possessions had been stolen. Frightened, he called his mother, who came and helped him move. He never returned. He left the syringe-littered mess for the apartment manager to clean up.

Schreiner admitted that the family stole from Matt, taking his X-Box game and his DVDs. Nelson has a much different story. "I wanted to get away from Matt. He had ripped me off for five hundred eighty dollars," he claims.

Around May 20, the day after the parking-lot assault on Sara, Nelson says, the family left Matt's apartment and pushed shopping carts piled with their belongings down to the Square. They stopped there, over a dozen of them, milling around, trying to figure out where to go next. It was cool that day, with gusts of wind blowing food wrappers across the bricks.

Pearce was hanging out in the Square. He had just been kicked out of the Greenhouse, he said, and had no place to sleep that night. He asked the Thantos Family if he could "move in with them." Nelson said yes, and Pearce fell in with the group as they pushed the shopping carts out of the Square. Pearce said he helped push their carts, which earned him credit with the group.

Nelson knew where to go. He led his large family back to the lower Lair Hill neighborhood, which he remembered from his days with the 1992 Family. Up the street from where Checkpoint Charlie had been, the Front Avenue squat was still open and looked very much the same as it had eleven years before. There was the same 7-11 store across the street and the same LaGrande warehouse next door.

Thirteen family members made the move to the Front Avenue squat, including James Nelson (Thantos), Cassandra Hale (Juliet), Carl Alsup (D. K.), Crystal Grace (Jade), Danielle Cox (Shadowcat), Jimmy Stewart (Neo), Joshua Brown-Lenon (Scooby), Sarah Caster (Valkyrie), Crystal Ivey (Nix), Thomas Schreiner (T. J.), Steve Pearce (Gambit), and the mentally ill Cory Dennison (Twix) and his girlfriend Heidi Keller (Little Twix).

The family cut a large hole in the chain-link fence and set up camp. They organized their clothes and set up what cardboard they could find, laying the squat out in military fashion.

They established rules for the squat.

1. No female was to leave without the protection of a male.
2. Everyone had to panhandle at least $10 a day and turn the earnings over to Nelson and Cassandra.

3. If you didn't make money panhandling, you couldn't come back to the squat that night to sleep.

4. Two members would be assigned the job of staying in the squat to watch over the family possessions every day.

5. Everybody was to be armed, preferably with a knife. In the back of the squat was a bag of cheap steak knives called the "throwaway" knives. If one of the family members didn't have a personal knife, he or she was to take one of these knives.

On the wall of the warehouse, Nelson drew a Wiccan star and went into a trance. The family became concerned about their father and wanted to wake him. Cassandra intervened and told the others to leave Nelson alone "because he was possessed by the spirits of the people who had died under the bridge," Pearce later told police.

In the smooth dirt in the middle of the squat, Nelson and Jimmy Stewart drew a magic Circle of Seven where the warriors would practice their martial arts training for the day they would become death knights. Danielle, the female warrior, joined the men throwing karate-style kicks and making dramatic poses. Now that Cassandra was part of the family, she was said to be a warrior too.

The housewives-in-training tidied and cleaned, and when they weren't busy with those chores, their job was to sit around, looking pretty, according to court reports. In the morning, Nelson took his shaving kit into downtown and used one of the bathrooms in a department store to trim his beard and mustache. He liked to stay neat and clean.

About the time the extended family began camping in the Front Avenue squat, Cassandra took a new street wife. Her name was Crystal Elliott, and she had been a ward of the state since she was nine. Crystal Elliott was the third and final Crystal to join the family, along with Crystal Grace (Carl's girlfriend) and Crystal Dawn

Ivey (the diminutive housewife-in-training). Crystal Elliott made number fourteen in the squat.

Crystal Elliott was only sixteen, four years younger than her street wife. She was short and round and pregnant, with a heavy face and blonde, blunt-cut hair. She went by the name Spitfire because "she would fight anyone and never loses a fight," according to police interviews.

Cassandra was still the mother of the family, and Nelson was still the father, but with the addition of Crystal Elliott as a street wife, the power dynamic shifted once more. Spitfire seemed to think she was next in command under Cassandra. When Cassandra wasn't in the squat, she bossed the other youths around, which they didn't like at all. She was too new to the family to take on such a powerful position, the other kids grumbled. Even Nelson seemed irritated by Crystal Elliott. "I didn't like Spitfire," Nelson says.

15

At the Williams home, Becky was so angry she felt tears of frustration. She had thought that Jessica was getting over these so-called friends, and here she had hoofed off to downtown again. "I really thought she was about over this phase," Becky recalls.

Jessica had gotten bored. That was all it took. She was dressed in nice clothes: new blue jeans, a fresh sweatshirt, and brand new Lugz shoes. Her hair was freshly shampooed, and her skin gleamed with good health. She went downtown unaware of all that had transpired in the three days she was gone: the baseball-bat attack on Eugene, the parking-lot assault of Sara, and the trashing of Matt's apartment. In the Square, three days were forever. Jessica didn't know that. She came downtown rested, happy to see her street friends, and ready to have fun.

That day, Jessica connected with her old boyfriend, Jimmy Stewart and the two fell right back into their dramatic, explosive relationship. Jimmy had gone through a lot to be Jessica's boyfriend. He had been threatened because of her, he had been called evil and accused of abusing her, but, still, he was happy to have her back. Having followed Cassandra into the Thantos Family, Jimmy was now under the guidance of Nelson as well. When the street family invited Jessica to their new squat, she was more than willing to tag along.

Jessica called her mother that evening. She told Becky she was spending the night with friends. Becky begged Jessica to come home. "Jessica, I don't like this," she pleaded. "Who are these people? If you could give us a number at least."

Jessica laughed it off. "I know what I'm doing. I can take care of myself," she told her mother.

"No, you don't. You can't," Becky replied.

Their words were heated, acrimonious. "I got really upset with her on the phone," Becky says. "She had done things, and we always forgave her. That's what we say in our family: chances never end." The last thing Becky heard before Jessica hung up was laughter in the background.

That night, Jessica slept with the family in their new squat without incident. The next day, Wednesday, May 21, she stopped in at a friend's house in southeast Portland. Jessica told the friend that her parents had kicked her out. She claimed she was staying under a bridge with a bunch of street friends. These friends, she said, needed a bike to collect food and go panhandling.

Jessica took a shower while her friend's father fixed up an old bike for her to use. The father says he had a long talk with Jessica. He claims he made her promise she would visit her pastor and then go back home. He says he warned her. Two things are going to happen to you on the streets: you'll get raped, and you'll get killed. Despite these concerns, he did not call the police or Jessica's parents. Instead, he watched Jessica pedal off. "She was in a good mood, happy about going on a bike ride with all these kids," the father says.

Either that night or the next day, depending on the account, Jessica broke up, this time for good, with Jimmy Stewart. "I was there when she broke up with him," Nelson relates with a laugh. "She said, 'Jimmy, I love you, but I can't go out with you.' Jimmy was all crying.

He asked how come? She said, 'Because you're lame, that's why, and I don't go out with lame guys.'"

Jimmy's reaction, a number of people agreed, was not funny. He seemed genuinely wounded. Jimmy Stewart would later tell police he honestly cared for Jessica and was hurt when she broke up with him. In terms of the street culture, it was just another mock relationship ending in drama, but to Jimmy, a boy who had never had anyone love him, his relationship with Jessica may have seemed different. Jimmy went to his street mother, Cassandra, and told her what had happened. "He told Juliet and she got pissed," Nelson says.

Cassandra seemed primed to be angry with Jessica, perhaps because of the drama over the stolen sweatshirt or perhaps because Jessica was the sort of oogle she despised. And when Cassandra got mad, the whole street family culture sat up and listened.

Jessica was oblivious. She had no idea what she had just done. And what she had done was serious. By breaking up with Jimmy, Jessica had injured the favorite son of a protective street mother in a powerful family. Then, the badmouthing began. Cassandra told others that Jessica was treating Jimmy with "disrespect."

The street kids of the Square were already annoyed with Jessica for so many reasons. They were tired of her religious talk, her flamboyance, her simple-minded loudness, and her refusal to mind their arcane, shifting, and frequently unstated rules. They had put up with Jessica, this oogle, this summer bunny who went home to mommy and daddy at night while they crashed hardcore in squats, for over three months, an eternity in their world. Jessica didn't slam eighty units or drink herself sick. She didn't carry a weapon or attack strangers with baseball bats. She was useless in their world. Jessica would never be old school. In the unspoken shift that accompanies such moments, Jessica's fate was decided. Her dissing of Jimmy would not go unpunished.

That night, probably unaware of the escalating animosity toward her, Jessica slept again with the family in their squat. She hadn't called home before bed. In Gladstone, Becky was watching the phone and worrying late into the night.

The next morning, Thursday, May 22, the street family woke up, crawled from their blankets in the squat, and set about their daily panhandling around town. Two of the kids were assigned to stay at the squat and guard the family belongings.

According to police reports, Nelson told the youths they had to bring in extra money that day because he wanted to buy a present for his girlfriend, Destiny, and surprise her. (It was just one of those weird things their street father did, one family member recalled.) The family made plans to meet at the Square that evening at eight o'clock, where everyone was expected to hand over money to Nelson.

Jessica went spanging that day with Steve Pearce, who later told police that he took Jessica along because no one else would. Their first stop was outside a gourmet food store. The panhandling was dry, and after making $4, they moved to the sidewalk outside Ross Dress for Less, where Jessica had first encountered street kids. The quarters began to flow. Jessica's old boss stepped outside to find Jessica sitting on the sidewalk with a street kid. Jessica told him she was helping her friend panhandle, and she asked him for a few cigarettes. He noticed that Jessica was wearing clean new jeans and a nice sweatshirt. She didn't look homeless. Pearce, on the other hand, looked like a street person, with his seamed face and dirty clothes.

Pearce said they made about $10 at the Ross store, then moved on to a Rite Aid, where they took in $20. After that, he said, they spent some of their earnings on pizza and stopped by the Greenhouse shelter, where Jessica was told again that she was too old for services. Jes-

sica may have been pleading for some sanitary products. Her period
had started.

———

At four o'clock that warm and pleasant afternoon, Danielle Cox
walked into a youth shelter and was reevaluated for services. According to their records, she told the shelter staff she had been living in a squat under an overpass with twelve street kids. She had
dreams and aspirations. She said she wanted to study Holocaust
history. "She says she can't go back home and wants to try to make
things work out so she can go back to school in the fall," the evaluator wrote.

Danielle had chosen the streets a month before when she had left
college for downtown. At the time, she could have said she didn't
truly know what she was getting into. But by the time she walked
into the shelter on May 22, 2003, Danielle knew full well what she
had done. She had joined a street family. She had been assigned a
street name and the role of a warrior. She had taken part in several
assaults and beatings. More than any other member of the family,
Danielle, who had been raised with sensibility and caring, was aware
of the depravity around her.

Danielle was offered a menu of programs, including emergency
housing in the Porch Light shelter and longer-term housing through
agencies like New Avenues for Youth and Outside In. She was offered job training, medical care, drug and alcohol treatment, and
short-term or long-term employment—anything to help her leave
the streets. She could have asked for help right then and there, and
she would have been given a bed and a locker. She could have called
her mother and said those simple, humbling words: I want to come
home. But she didn't.

Instead, Danielle did what she had done virtually every day on the streets of Portland: she made a choice. She left the agency and walked back out the door onto a street bathed with late afternoon sunlight. It was a glorious spring day.

———

Jessica and Pearce were back in the Square by that evening. Both gave Nelson $10. Pearce kept the extra money they had made. Jessica apparently kept nothing.

According to a street kid hanging around the Square that night, the family had "six or seven" bags of groceries with them. The street kid asked them where they got all the food. "An old guy felt sorry for us and gave us all this food," they chortled. When Jessica showed up, the street kid says, Nelson started heckling her, saying, "you're going to carry all these groceries whether you like it or not." The street kid said it was obvious that Jessica had been targeted as a weak link. "Every single one of them knew it was going to be Jessica," he says.

The family trickled back to the squat that evening. Accounts vary on who came in at what time, but eventually thirteen people would be present. One core family member went missing. Thomas Schreiner felt sick, so he checked into the Greenhouse. Their records show he had contracted pneumonia. Two others were also not present at first. Joshua Brown-Lenon, or Scooby, and his girlfriend, Sarah Caster, or Valkyrie, had decided to take in a movie that night. They were watching *The Matrix Reloaded* at the Regal, a new cinema two blocks from the Square. Sarah says the movie began around ten or eleven, and she fell asleep during the show.

By the time Jessica crawled through the hole in the cyclone fence with Pearce that evening, many of the family were present, including Danielle, Jimmy Stewart, and Cassandra's new street wife, Crystal Elliott. Jimmy had been sleeping off a drinking binge in the back of the squat. When he saw Jessica, he got angry. He didn't want Jessica around the family anymore. He was mad at her for breaking up with him. He wanted her gone. "I said, 'What the fuck are you doing here?'" he later told police.

The situation immediately escalated into an argument. Everyone began yelling. Crystal Elliott tried to take charge. She told everyone they were on bed restriction. Jessica sassed back to the new street wife, asking "Who left you in charge?" This made Spitfire very angry.

Cassandra showed up with Carl Alsup, and she immediately took control of the situation. Jessica had just insulted her new street wife, and she had already disrespected her son Jimmy. Cassandra was not in a forgiving mood.

In the back of the squat, Cassandra began interrogating Jessica. First, she accused Jessica of making up the whole story about Nicholas Saunders offering her money for sex. Jessica, she claimed, had exposed family members to arrest by causing the assault. She had put them all in danger with her lies.

With the mood growing even more heated, Cassandra then announced that a small amount of money was missing from the family coffers. She accused Jessica of stealing. In case that wasn't enough, Cassandra leveled one more accusation: Jessica, she said, had been "keeping book" on her weed sales, or secretly writing down information so she could snitch to the cops.

That was it. Jessica was an informant, a snitch. A line had been crossed. Old school rules. Jessica would be punished. It took only minutes to decide her fate. It was a smash on sight, or SOS.

The family ordered Jessica to go stand in the magic Circle of Seven. Danielle told police the family used their feet to redraw the circle around Jessica. Then, Jessica was told to kneel. She did this, lowering herself carefully to her knees. It was hard for Jessica to sit on her knees. She was a big girl, and her disabilities made her awkward and inflexible. At home, she could only kneel for a short period of time.

Jessica was ordered to not make a sound or cry out. According to Crystal Elliott, Jessica was told that if she flinched, she would be hit with a baseball bat. The family gathered around the circle, surrounding their victim.

The energy in the squat was intense. Carl began capering, "dancing and prancing" around the squat, according to other kids, swinging his baseball bat against the pillars, singing the words to the Insane Clown Posse song "Boogie Woogie Wu," once again changing the words to suit the moment. "Somebody's going to *die* tonight," he sang. "Somebody's going to suck my *dick* tonight." Each time he hit a pillar, the squat rang.

First, Jessica was taxed her property. According to police interviews with the youths, they took Jessica's cell phone, wallet, identification, jewelry, and sweatshirt. They left her in only her jeans, shoes, and T-shirt.

Carl came into the circle and teased Jessica with a cigarette, holding it close to her lips and then jerking it away. "Does somebody want a cigarette? Oh, too bad!" he sang, returning to whack the pillars with his beloved Dink, still crusted with Eugene's blood. "Run and tell mommy!" he sang.

They were all laughing. At one point, the men came into the circle and cut Jessica's hair. Carl kept swinging his bat against the pillars, singing, "A snip here, a snip there!"

The family sobered. It was time for the beating. They organized themselves. One of the kids was given orders to keep Chronic, the Rottweiler, in the back of the squat. The dog had become excited with all the noise. Other street kids were told to take turns at the pillars, watching for passing cars.

Cassandra announced, "Jessica needs to feel what Nick felt." Jessica was told to stay kneeling, to keep her hands behind her back, and not to move. "You're a worthless piece of shit," Cassandra told Jessica, according to Danielle. Then, Cassandra told everyone to take a turn hitting Jessica. The idea was that all of the women would punch her, one at a time.

Danielle, the warrior called Shadowcat, was the first to hit Jessica, according to police interviews. She walked up and slapped Jessica across the face, then kicked her in the ribs anywhere from fifteen to twenty times, according to Jimmy, who was watching from the sidelines.

Cassandra went next, becoming so savage in her assault, screaming and kicking and punching, that the men had to pull her off Jessica. This happened "many times," according to one street kid, who told police, "She probably would have beaten Jessica to death right there."

Cassandra's street wife, sixteen-year-old Crystal Elliott, took the next turn. She estimated she struck Jessica between "forty to fifty times with her hands and fists, and approximately forty to fifty times with her feet," according to her police interviews. She hit Jessica until her hands started to hurt, she said, and then moved on to kicking her. She was angry with Jessica, she told police, because Jessica had sassed her.

During her turn, Crystal Grace, Carl's girlfriend, admitted to kicking Jessica at least three times, while others said it was more. Danielle got the impression that Crystal Grace was enjoying the violence. Around the circle, the men offered advice and encouragement as the women attacked Jessica.

Around this time, Nelson claims, he arrived, crawling through the hole in the fence, and was filled in on what was going on. "When I first got to the squat, everyone was in the back, you know, in the dark back there, and they had Jessica," he says. "They are all excited and arguing. They came up to me and said, 'She lied about Nick, and we almost went to jail.'" The street kids had already been beating Jessica, Nelson claims. To show how bloody she was, he swishes his hand across his face.

But other family members say that Nelson had been there all along. Pearce later told police that Nelson came in at the same time as Cassandra and Carl. Others familiar with the case believe that Nelson was instrumental in directing the beating and that he had decided that only the women would strike Jessica. The idea was that the women would be the only perpetrators and therefore too afraid to report the crime.

Soon after the beating started, the family realized they were missing two members: Sarah and Joshua were still at the movies. Nelson dispatched Pearce and Crystal Ivey to go find them, according to police interviews. On the way back to the squat, Crystal informed Sarah what was going on. "She told me Jessica was way lying and she was a snitch," Sarah said.

Sarah didn't want to go back to the squat to beat Jessica, but she was worried that if she didn't, the family would put an SOS out on her next. She obediently followed the other family members back to the overpass.

Once back in the squat. Joshua confronted Jessica. The two had been friendly since their first meeting at the Square benches three months before. Now Joshua told Jessica he was upset about her lying. Jessica told him she was "sorry." Joshua took his place in the circle surrounding Jessica.

Sarah pled that she had never been in a fight before. She appeared to be trying to avoid hitting Jessica, but Nelson was not going to allow any of the women to evade their role in the SOS. He told her that she had to hit Jessica to prove her loyalty. "Thantos [Nelson] told me exactly what Crystal said, that she [Jessica] snitched and she lied about Nick and that this was my trial to prove my loyalty," Sarah later related to police.

The men coached Sarah, giving her advice on how to punch. Pearce gave her a bowling glove with a metal bar inserted in the back and told her how to swing her fist. Sarah, the product of loving parents, stepped into the circle and struck Jessica with the weighted glove, knocking her head back. Sarah said she talked to Jessica during her assault. "Why did you lie to them?" Sarah asked. Jessica responded, "Oh, well, I'm a stupid girl." Sarah recalled to police that she told Jessica that no, she was a nice person. The others began to grouse. It was time for hitting, not for talking. They told Sarah to get back to punching Jessica. "I was trying to delay it," she said. "I hit her a few times in the face, along the jaw line," and then she told Jessica she was sorry.

Crystal Ivey, the housewife-in-training, also claims she didn't want to strike Jessica. She ran around the squat, trying to find other things to do. Finally, she says, she went into the circle, where she slapped Jessica. Detective Barry Renna demurs. "The women struck her more than once or twice," he says. He describes a beating that went on for up to several hours, with "slapping, closed fist hitting, and kicking."

After all the girls had taken a turn hitting Jessica, Cassandra declared that Jessica was a "human ashtray" and that everyone should put cigarettes out on her, according to police reports. One girl stepped in and put her cigarette out on Jessica, but Jessica's hair caught fire. The girl claimed she put the fire out quickly. Others followed her lead, grinding their cigarettes out on Jessica's body.

Carl stepped into the circle to use a lighter to burn one of Jessica's eyebrows and some of her hair. "This is what happens to liars," he announced, according to court records. Crystal Grace and

Cassandra ordered Jessica to hold out her hand, palm down, according to interviews. They used a lighter to burn her palm, moving it back and forth.

By this time Jessica was a mass of injuries, her blood dripping down onto the dirt of the circle. Her face was cut and bleeding, her head was hurt, her eyes were swollen and black, and her lips were twice their normal size. "She was bleeding from her ears and her mouth," Danielle later told police, crying as she spoke. "We hit her pretty fucking hard. We burned her face with cigarettes and burned her arms with cigarettes."

As painful as her injuries must have been, Jessica was quiet during the beating, minding the family's instructions not to make a sound. At most, she sniffled, according to Jimmy. She made a little "squeak" every time someone hit or kicked her, he later admitted to police.

Those who knew Jessica, and about her disability, would understand exactly what was going on in her broken mind. She was probably thinking that it would be over soon, that the family would forgive her, and they would all go back to being friends. With her four-year-old's thinking process, she would be thinking that this was the same as being trapped by the man next door who had molested her as a child: if she closed her eyes and kept quiet, it would be over soon.

The family members took turns by the support posts and called out when they saw car lights approaching. Everyone was told to duck, including Jessica, who obeyed, lowering her head to the bloody dirt even as she was being beaten.

It was dark in the squat. The wall of the warehouse looked on blankly, the Wiccan star of chaos Nelson had drawn now invisible in the dark. The only light that crept through the weed-covered chain-link fence came from the flashing of car lights. Across the street, the clerk at the 7-11 sold hotdogs and beer and wine and the other things people pick up at midnight. The occasional car pulled in and out, its lights sweeping through the squat. It bothered Detective Renna later how alone Jessica was in this, for so long, surrounded by thirteen young people she had thought were her friends, and how alone she would be in the end.

After at least two hours, it looked like the beating might finally be ending. The family seemed fatigued. But one of the warriors did not want to stop. Carl claimed that Jessica had spit at Cassandra. "D. K. said, 'Mom, she just spit at you,'" Cassandra told police. The beating resumed in earnest. Jessica was kicked and punched "hundreds of times," according to the district attorney's office, many times with objects. Crystal Grace estimated to police that Jessica was punched and kicked between three and four hundred times.

The most violent of all the family members, by all accounts, was Cassandra. She simply would not stop beating Jessica. At one point, she allegedly picked up a leather belt and whipped Jessica repeatedly. The street kids said they had to stop her, pulling her off Jessica's kneeling form. "Let me kill her, let me kill her, I want her dead," Cassandra yelled, according to several kids present. The others held her back as she screamed. According to Nelson, Cassandra begged to use one of the baseball bats on Jessica. But the men told her no.

In the back of the squat, one of the street kids held Chronic in his arms, the big dog trembling with excitement at the smell of blood. The street kid thought the "SOS had turned into a DOS," and now Jessica was being destroyed on sight.

Toward the end of the assault, Cassandra had one of her fits, jerking and flailing around. The family dragged her off to the side. Jimmy held her head in his lap, stroking his mother's hair and face. Jessica was left in the circle, silently kneeling, almost frozen in the posture after hours of beating. Cassandra came out of her fit. She got on her hands and knees and vomited in the black dirt.

While Cassandra was having her seizure, Crystal Elliott was told to go buy lighter fluid, which she claims she believed was to help Cassandra snap out of the fit. The video camera at the 7-11 across the street recorded Crystal Elliott purchasing the lighter fluid at 12:57 in the morning.

A half hour later, at 1:25, the camera recorded Joshua and Steve buying another container of lighter fluid. Joshua says Nelson gave him $5 for the lighter fluid. They soon returned to the squat, paper bag in hand.

On her side of the squat, Cassandra thought she saw a police car pass, according to several of the youths. She announced that Jessica needed to be escorted to the Steel Bridge "NOW." Nelson agreed. According to several youths interviewed, he said something along the lines of "Get her out of here" or "She needs to leave." In the back of the squat, Crystal Grace watched as Carl began rummaging for an extra pair of pants.

Jessica was told to stand. She staggered to her feet, leaning against one of the dirty white pillars. Her jeans and shirt were stained with blood. Her eyes were blackened, and blood trickled from her ears. Danielle said Jessica's face was "unrecognizable." Pearce commented that she looked just like the Elephant Man.

When Danielle first told her story, she said that Carl approached her at the end of the assault. "He said, 'You want to have some fun?' I shrugged my shoulders, and I said, 'I guess, yeah.'" Later, after discussions with the district attorney, Danielle changed her account, claiming Nelson had pulled her aside and gave her orders to kill Jessica. He told her, "Every death knight needs to kill someone. This is your time to prove yourself. This is your final test." Joshua would confirm seeing them talk, telling a grand jury that "Thantos pulled Shadowcat, D. K., and Jimmy aside before the killing."

Jimmy said Nelson commanded him, "Listen to D. K., what he tells you to do, do." His attorney believes that Jimmy was ordered to commit the killing because he was the only family member not implicated in the violence thus far. Jimmy had not been rolling trolls or mugging people at ATM machines, and he was not involved in the robbery of Eugene. If there was one person in that squat who could have gone to the police with relatively clean hands, it was Jimmy.

The three designated warriors pulled on an additional set of clothes. Carl wore dark jeans and a black sweatshirt with a hood. Danielle wore dark coveralls over a long-sleeved shirt and pulled a dark stocking cap over her Mohawk. Jimmy wore an extra T-shirt and baggy jeans. He wore brand-new shoes he was proud of: Shaquille O'Neal basketball shoes.

Danielle had a knife in her pocket. She described it later in court records as a switchblade, four to six inches long, with a single-edged, serrated blade. Carl called this a Confederate knife. Danielle harbored no illusions about what was going to happen. "I knew I was going to kill her," Danielle said.

According to Crystal Grace, Carl told her "he was going to finish it that night" because he didn't want Jessica to snitch. Crystal promised they were going to have sex when he got back. "She said, 'We are going to have sex,'" Carl said. He assumed Crystal was turned on by all the violence.

Crystal Ivey, the diminutive housewife-in-training, said she was the next member dispatched to the 7-11 to get some water so she could clean up the area where they had been beating Jessica. When she returned, Jessica was gone, and so were three family warriors: Carl Alsup, Jimmy Stewart, and Danielle Cox. It was between 1:30 and 1:45 in the morning.

After the three warriors left with Jessica, Nelson and Pearce went to the 7-11, where the video camera recorded them buying two cases of Pabst beer at 1:48 in the morning. At the squat, many of the youths drank themselves into sleepiness. A few of the kids were on drinking restriction, according to police records, including Sarah. In the back of the squat, Sarah stripped off her bloody pants, according to Crystal Grace, and changed into fresh ones. The girls cleaned up the Circle of Seven. "I was told by Thantos to go get some water to clean the area just in case there was blood lying around," one of the girls said. She poured the water in the circle and kicked the dirt around.

While the family drank their beer, Crystal Grace said Nelson took the hair they had taxed from Jessica and did a magic spell on it. He then told her to walk down to the river and throw the hank of hair in the water. "And since he was my street dad, and still is," Crystal Grace said, "I was to obey him. So I did." She didn't walk down to the river alone. The family rule was no woman was to leave the squat without a male companion, and Crystal Grace obeyed all the family rules. She took Joshua with her.

Crystal and Joshua walked through the dark down to the river and came to a place not far from where Nelson had murdered Leon Stanton over ten years earlier, where the wild fennel still grows. They threw the magic hair in the water. It floated downstream, toward another bridge, where Jessica was now heading.

═══

The three family warriors walked Jessica across the freshly mowed grass of the waterfront park that ran along the river. The lawn clippings, night-damp, clung to Jessica's new shoes.

Cherry trees had been planted along the waterfront, and the air along the river was fragrant with their blossoms. The city was preparing for the upcoming Rose Festival, and construction pieces for the rides were piled around the lawns. In another week, the waterfront would be blocked off for the carnival. For now, though, the walkway was clear. According to one account, the four youths passed a security guard. No one intervened. Danielle wasn't worried that Jessica would run away. "We would have caught her," she said later to the police. "We would have run to catch her if she tried to run."

Jimmy talked to Danielle as they walked. "I told Shadowcat I was scared," he recalled in court records. "She said she didn't want to do it." Walking between them, Jessica cried softly.

They passed under three bridges: the Morrison, the Hawthorne, and, finally, the Burnside. After the Burnside Bridge, they passed Pothead Hill, deserted at this time of night except for the few homeless tucked into their bags in the dark recesses along the ramps. The esplanade ended at the Steel Bridge, and the group turned to follow a footbridge over the water.

Their shoes echoed over the poured concrete footbridge, worn bare in places and lined on one side with a metal mesh fence. They were only feet above the river, close enough to smell the water and feel the liquid heave of the waves. In the dark, the river underneath the footbridge is more a sensation than a reality. Bridge lights send little arcs shining out over the waves. A single light hangs over the walkway, and the bridge trembles every time a truck passes overhead.

Unknown to the street kids, a company called ComNet had been hired by the city to install two security cameras on the walkway to ensure that no pedestrians arc on the walkway when the drawbridge is being lifted. There is one small camera on each side of the bridge, about twelve to fifteen feet above the walkway, filming foot traffic.

In the ComNet offices across the river, a camera silently recorded the progress of the four young people crossing the footbridge. The tallest was in the middle: Jessica. Three others flanked her, one in the front and two guarding the back. Carl led the way, swaggering in an almost grotesque manner, his arms akimbo. He kept tugging at the black sweatshirt hood he wore self-consciously low over his face, gangster style. In her dark coveralls, Danielle walked somewhat stiffly behind Jessica. With the stocking cap and no makeup, she looked all of fourteen. Jimmy strolled next to her, with one hand casually jammed into his pocket. Danielle and Jimmy chatted as they walked. At one point Jimmy turned to look over the river. Surrounded by the family warriors, Jessica tried to pat and fix her unruly hair, which was a mess from the beating. For a moment, her swollen face turned up toward the camera.

At the end of the bridge, the street warriors came to where the walkway meets the concrete walking path of the esplanade. They passed under the eye of the camera and disappeared from view. Here, the path turns south. If the family members had kept walking they would eventually have reached the McLoughlin Caves. Instead, they turned to a low, gray fence that blocked off an area of railroad tracks under the Steel Bridge. This was where Nelson had allegedly bit into a pigeon some eleven years before.

The family warriors told Jessica to climb over the fence. This she did, awkwardly. They led her behind the retaining wall of the staircase to the Rose Quarter where no one could see them. Only the train tracks ran nearby, and at this time of night, few trains moved out of the Albina yards.

The youths instructed Jessica to kneel in the gravel behind the wall. The gray rocks were sharp and would have bit into her knees. Obedient to the end, Jessica knelt. She had been beaten for hours, and now she was here, preparing to die, and she didn't try to run away. It is possible that the ordeal simply didn't compute with Jessica, that she lacked the ability to comprehend this madness. "I don't know if I would say Jessica was compliant," Detective Renna says slowly, with a pained look in his eyes. "I think, with her disability, she was frozen." Jessica was paralyzed, and the others were in free fall.

Danielle pulled out the knife. Opening the switchblade, she showed Jessica the blade. At that moment, Danielle could have been miles away, tucked into bed in a warm dorm room, a debating trophy in the window. Instead, she was here, under a cold bridge by a railroad track, brandishing a switchblade at a scared, disabled girl. The college student who had worked with autistic children was now facing a mentally handicapped woman she herself considered sweet and kind, and she was planning to kill her in order to impress a street father who was a murderer himself.

According to Danielle, Jessica began pleading, there on her knees. "What are you doing?" Jessica begged. "Please don't do this to me. What are you doing? Please don't kill me."

Danielle, holding the knife, talked lovingly to Jessica. "I just told her, 'Don't worry, sweetheart,'" Danielle said. "And I said, 'Don't worry.'"

That was when Jessica understood she was going to die. She looked up at the street kids. According to an investigator involved in the case, Jessica spoke directly to her killers. "It's okay," she said. "I won't hold this against you."

Carl was jittery and excited. He told Danielle to cut her already. Instead, Danielle handed the knife to Jimmy. Jimmy told his exgirlfriend he was sorry and gave her a kiss on her forehead. He took the knife and stood behind the kneeling Jessica. He said he sliced at her throat, but the blade wouldn't cut. It made only a small laceration. Jimmy handed the knife to Carl, he claimed, and said, "I can't do it."

Carl was more than willing to take the job. He stood behind Jessica and kicked at her knees, according to police reports. Jessica fell forward and rolled on her back. Carl put his knee on her chest, forcing the knife into her throat. He stabbed at her throat four or five times. Jessica's confused voice rose, pleading, "What are you doing?

What are you doing?" Danielle described it as a "gurgling" voice. It was the sound of blood filling Jessica's throat.

Carl passed the knife to Danielle, who went next, leaning over and pressing the blade deeper in Jessica's throat. Blood poured out of Jessica's neck, bathing her shirt and the rocks underneath her.

Danielle yanked the knife out and handed the blade to Jimmy. He stabbed Jessica in the throat at least twice. Jessica was still making the gurgling sounds, trying to breathe. They rolled her over onto her stomach, exposing her back. Jimmy stabbed her in the back at least twice. Carl took another turn, and according to Danielle, kept "stabbing and stabbing because she would not stop gurgling."

Carl, according to numerous accounts, began dancing around once more, singing the Insane Clown Posse "Boogie Woogie Wu" song again, changing the lyrics to suit his mood, as he slashed and stabbed. Danielle described this as a "monkey dance." The Insane Clown Posse song lyrics go,

> *I don't beat women, fuck that, I'm above it*
> *But I'll cut her fucking neck and think nothing of it. . . .*
> *And the cops do the best they can*
> *They pull the axe out of your face and say,*
> *"Was it the Boogie Man?"*

Jessica was still alive, struggling to breathe, and the street kids had begun to panic. Carl announced that they had to get the air out of her lungs, Danielle claims, so they took turns stomping on her chest. Jimmy stomped on her seven or eight times, by his own estimate. Blood splattered all over his pants. He looked down and saw the blood covering his new Shaquille O'Neal sneakers. Blood splashed on his shirt.

Carl used both feet to jump on Jessica's chest. "Why don't you die? Why don't you die?" he yelled. Carl, the others say, did most of the jumping, especially on Jessica's head. Jimmy said he watched the skin above Jessica's eyes split open. The bones of her face broke, and her teeth fractured in her mouth.

At last, Jessica lay still. Jimmy took out the lighter fluid. They sprayed the body with the liquid, passing the bottle around. The heavy smell of lighter fluid filled the air. Using a lighter, the three warriors lit Jessica on fire. The flames quickly climbed over her jeans, burning brightly, but the fire didn't catch on her shirt, which may have been too wet with blood.

But then, Jessica either said something or took one more breath. The street kids thought she was still alive. "The first time we lit her on fire she still made sounds, so we put it out," Danielle told police. The street kids jumped on her body to put out the fire. Finally, there was a "big, rattling sigh," as Danielle described it, a sigh that "went out of her."

Jessica Kate Williams was dead.

One last time, they lit her body on fire. Danielle sprayed Jessica with the lighter fluid, and then they covered her with a gray blanket they found nearby, and sprayed the blanket with fluid too, until the bottle was empty and the blanket was saturated. They lit the soaked blanket with their lighter and took off running. In the background, Danielle said, they could see the flames rising off of Jessica's body. The fire reflected off the retaining wall, casting shadows over the railroad tracks.

The night was so quiet. The river made little chopping sounds against the shore. The warriors stripped off the extra layer of clothes they had worn, now soaked with blood. They threw their bloody shoes and clothes into the river. Jimmy said he threw his extra pants in a trash can. Carl hid the empty container of lighter fluid in a tire tube along the riverbank. The group walked back to the squat in their socks. Carl was elated, Danielle said. He wouldn't stop talking.

"We got that bitch. We stabbed her good," he boasted. Danielle told him to shut up, but he just kept talking.

At the squat, much of the family was asleep. Cassandra was sleeping, drained from her "anger seizure," as the kids called it, curled up next to her street wife, Crystal Elliott. Danielle took a beer from the case of Pabst. She sat down and began drinking the beer next to her street father. "He just asked if I was okay," Danielle said. Danielle told Nelson she was *not* okay. "It'll get easier," Nelson assured her.

Nelson had killed too, and if Danielle hadn't realized the implications of that before, she did now. Her street father had crossed to the other side a long time ago. He was comfortable with what he had done. The question now was how comfortable Danielle would be. It was one thing to imagine murder, to brag about murder, and to plan murder. It was another to actually kill someone. Danielle gulped down her beer and lay down.

When Carl came into the squat, Nelson asked him, "Is it done?'"

It was done. Carl curled up with Crystal Grace. He said they had sex because Crystal was so turned on by the beating of Jessica. And then, the family slept.

16

Dr. Karen Gunson of the medical examiner's office examined the body. It was 1:10 in the afternoon on the day the victim was found. Observing the autopsy was Detective Barry Renna.

The autopsy took several hours. Dr. Gunson described the victim as a well-nourished, healthy, young woman who had suffered severe head trauma. The body tested negative for all drugs, and there was no alcohol in its system. The internal organs were healthy. The skin of the left forehead was split in four places. Two teeth were fractured in the jaw. Dr. Gunson removed a menstrual-blood-soaked tampon and sent it to be frozen as evidence.

It was not the stab wounds that had killed her, Dr. Gunson concluded. It was the blows to the head. The cause of death was "blunt force head trauma, subdural hemorrhage of the brain, [and] cerebral edema." The burns appeared to have happened either after death or close to it. The lungs were pink and healthy, and they did not show signs of smoke inhalation. If the victim was alive when she was burned, it was close to her last moments.

The next morning, Becky sat at her kitchen table. The sunlight filtered through the window. She was reading her morning paper. The *Oregonian* had a small article in the local metro section, "Woman Found Slain Near Eastbank Esplanade." The article said the body had been found near the Steel Bridge. The victim was described as African American or possibly Pacific Islander. "I saw the story in the newspaper, and I just knew," Becky says.

Becky and Sam left a message that morning for detectives, and almost immediately Detective Renna and a crime team arrived at their home in Gladstone. The Williams gave the police a photograph of Jessica, which one of the officers took down to the medical examiner's office. There was too much trauma to the body to allow for identification. The police asked to dust for fingerprints, so Becky took them into Jessica's room. Crime specialist John Courtney used ninhydrin to get prints off a library card call slip Jessica had used. The slip had been folded, and the print inside was nearly pristine. Police also found Nicholas Saunders's bag, and he immediately became a person of interest. Becky explained to the police that her daughter had taken to going downtown to hang out with street kids.

Detective Renna waited with the Williams while the fingerprints were taken down to the medical examiner's office. It was 3:15 in the afternoon when the medical examiner called to say they were a match. The fingerprint on the library slip matched the left index finger of the body.

"We told the family it was Jessica," Detective Renna says in his quiet voice. He sat with them until more family members arrived. He didn't want to leave Becky and Sam alone in their grief.

Becky Williams demanded to view Jessica's body. For twenty-two years she had loved and cared for Jessica, and now she needed to say goodbye. She and Sam went to the medical examiner's office, where Jessica was waiting for them, stretched on a table. Her body was wrapped in clear plastic because her charred skin was peeling off in chunks. Her skull—her mother describes it with a gesture of her hand—was smashed in the back. Becky held Jessica's body and cried.

Back at Central Precinct, the phones wouldn't stop ringing. "There was public alarm" about the murder, says Detective Renna. A lot of the calls were from concerned citizens wanting to express their outrage. Some of the calls were more fruitful, including several from street kids who seemed to want to deflect interest from their community. With those calls and Saunders's bag, Detective Renna had a place to start.

In the days after the murder, detectives canvassed the downtown streets, passing out their business cards and asking street kids about Jessica. Detective Renna worked morning to night tracking down leads, returning calls, and driving to the coast, where he found Saunders and cleared him. He discovered that the ComNet security company had been videotaping the Steel Bridge walkway and ordered copies of those tapes.

Word swept through the Square that police had identified the body found under the Steel Bridge. It was Jessica, Giggles to some. When reporters showed up in the Square, the street kids were eager to share their theories. It was a gang murder, one street youth told reporter Jennifer Anderson of the *Portland Tribune*. No, another said, it was a race killing because Jessica was a "mulatto." It was skinheads who called themselves the Eastside Killers. They beat Jessica in the back of the head with a baseball bat after chasing another street family away from Candy's Market. No, another street kid argued, the murder was drug related. He told the reporter he had known Jessica in California where she was doing her thing with a trucker, and she was into methamphetamine, pot, and alcohol. No, yet another youth said, claiming that Jessica had joined a gang in 1996, when she would have been sixteen. Jessica, he said, was the second leader and told people what to do. "When you get that high up in the rank, there's no way out except death," he said. He claimed Jessica was called Baby J on the streets, but Baby Blue was her gang name because she always wore blue clothes. Anyhow, he was her best friend, and she lived under the Steel Bridge.

They were all her best friends, and they all vowed justice. "If we find out who it is before the cops do, someone's going to disappear," a street youth promised the *Tribune* reporter. They were going to find out by the end of the week, he promised. All of 425 street kids were gathering for justice.

Yet, even as they wove complicated conspiracy theories and promised retribution, some of the street kids seemed to know exactly who had killed Jessica. "Jessica was labeled as a liar and a snitch," one youth commented. "They were going to finish the job. Why not kill her?" Jessica deserved to die, some said, because she was stupid. The streets "aren't dangerous if you're not stupid," a twenty-one-year-old who had recently arrived in town told a reporter. The problem with Jessica, as she saw it, was Jessica was naïve, and "being naïve is dangerous."

Down on the waterfront, a shrine appeared, hung with balloons. White butcher paper was taped along a fence, and street youths wrote on it with marker pens: *Jessica, RIP. We Love You Jessica,* with a peace sign. The paper quickly became tattered, then blew away.

＝

Just as his mentor had done eleven years before, Carl Alsup immediately began bragging about his first murder. He told one girl that he had stabbed Jessica thirty-seven times, then lit her on fire so the burns would "seal up the scars and make them look old." He told Thomas Schreiner that he had "pulled out her teeth and stabbed her and slit her throat and set her on fire with lighter fluid to get rid of all the DNA evidence." He boasted to Steve Pearce that he got an erection while he was killing Jessica.

While Carl bragged his way around the Square, Danielle Cox appeared stricken. "Shadowcat keeps getting drunk and walking in the middle of roads hoping somebody would hit her," Sarah Caster later told police. Danielle struggled to tell her street father how she felt. "I told him it was eating me up. Thantos shrugged and said it would be okay."

Others in the family made fun of the murder. "They were joking about it," Carl's girlfriend, Crystal Grace, later told police, saying things like "we burned her body real bad." Carl wanted to save a newspaper article about Jessica, a memento of what he had done.

Nelson proposed that the family have a beer toast to Jessica. The family drank to her, and then everyone "poured out a sip of beer" in her memory. Steve Pearce, one of the newer members, was impressed that Nelson had such control over his family. Over breakfast one morning, he asked Nelson, "How do you keep D. K. [Carl] so wrapped around your finger?" Nelson didn't reply.

That Sunday, two days after the murder, Nelson called a family meeting at a bus terminal. Nelson told the others to cover for him when they talked to detectives. If they didn't cover for him, he allegedly warned, they would get 86'd and STD, or smashed to death.

The family talked about cover stories. They agreed that they would say that they last saw Jessica on May 11. Nelson told them to tell others that Jessica had gotten into a fight and left downtown, according to Crystal Grace. There was talk of pinning it on Saunders, who the family knew had left town. He made a convenient scapegoat. They would tell police that Jessica had been in a fight with Saunders.

Meanwhile, romantic relationships inside the family shifted once more. Danielle began dating Jimmy Stewart. They didn't talk about what they had done that night. Crystal Elliott broke up with Cassandra Hale so that she could go out with men. Nelson used his gremlin rights to order Carl to break up with his long-time girlfriend Crystal Grace, according to court records. Carl was told to go out with a new girl, while Crystal Grace was told to go out with Schreiner, whom she had been accused of flirting with before. "Thantos ordered me to date" Crystal Grace, Schreiner said.

But Crystal Grace didn't want to date the young rapist called T. J. She was still in love with Carl. She began cutting her own arms to cope. She was so stressed by everything that was happening, she said. The family kept hitting her in the head. They were turning against her. "Jade [Crystal Grace] always had some form of drama going," Nelson complained. "She was always making trouble."

Even as Detective Renna roamed downtown, interviewing reluctant and deceptive street kids, the family was putting out more SOS orders. Within a day or so of the murder, according to investigation reports, Carl, Schreiner, and Pearce took a black drug dealer called Glow Worm, who had been Cassandra's boyfriend, to the top of a parking garage and assaulted him. They were going to throw him off the top of the garage when a security guard intervened and told them to leave.

Then, the family targeted Sarah Caster, the beautiful sixteen-year-old called Valkyrie, a weak link by street family standards. Sarah was accused of using family money to buy her own food and cigarettes. The family went to fetch her from the Porch Light shelter above the Greenhouse for her SOS, but she was sleeping, and the staff there had a policy not to wake anyone up. Sarah missed her beating by pure luck.

In another incident, Pearce says the family went to a squat to kill a street kid because he had supposedly made threats against a girl they knew. According to Pearce, Carl was all pumped up to kill another victim, but this murder never came off. Meanwhile, Schreiner took a new street name. He didn't want to be T. J. anymore. From now on, he was to be called Malice. Joshua Brown-Lenon, once Scooby, also took a new name. He wanted be called Stifler.

The family also attacked Sara Baerlocher's boyfriend, Arthur, who was unable to say exactly what day it occurred. It may have been shortly before the murder, but some facts suggest the assault occurred after Jessica's death. Arthur said he woke up one night in his squat near the Rose Quarter to feel a metal pipe dropping onto his leg. He opened his eyes to see the family standing over him. He identified Danielle, Carl, Crystal Grace, Joshua, and Nelson, according to court records. The men were wearing war paint across their faces, he said. The group allegedly told him to stay away from Sara because they were going to slit her throat.

Back at the family squat, another dog was supposedly killed after it bit one of the family members. The story went around that Carl had killed the dog in the squat, and blood and hair went everywhere.

———

Only four days had passed since the murder, when on May 27, Crystal Elliott went shoplifting at the Clackamas Town Center, a large mall in Oregon City outside of Portland. With her was a new street kid hanging around called Booster. The flow of newbies had not abated since the murder of Jessica, and already new youths were trying to get into the family.

It was Booster's idea. He wanted to go "jack some shit," according to Crystal. The two had a baby with them, the infant of a street kid who went by the name Pimpaducky. Crystal Elliott and Booster were babysitting for the day, stealing, and hiding the stolen merchandise in the baby stroller. They weren't careful enough. The two were arrested, and police grew concerned about the infant in their care. They threatened to call child protective services, but first they located the child's mother, Pimpaducky, and she came to retrieve her child. Crystal Elliott was released from the Oregon City Jail and returned downtown.

When this story got back to the Thantos Family, they were outraged. Crystal Elliott had endangered them by getting arrested for shoplifting, and by getting child protective services involved. It was the same charge that had been leveled against Jessica; Crystal Elliott was bringing the heat down on them. An order went down: SOS on the girl called Spitfire. Crystal was ordered to appear in the Square at 9:30 the next morning, May 28, for her beating. The fact that she was pregnant didn't seem to impact the family's decision to beat her.

The next morning, a family member caught Crystal and began escorting her to her SOS beating at the Square. Terrified, Crystal mouthed, "Help me," at a passerby, but nothing happened. Her escort left Crystal momentarily at a Borders bookstore not far from the Square to go locate the rest of the family. According to the police report filed on the incident, Crystal used a pay phone to call the police. She told the police she "knew the people who killed the girl on the Steel Bridge, Jessica Williams."

When a police officer arrived, Crystal requested that she be handcuffed "so it looked like she wasn't being an informant," he wrote. The officer cuffed her and radioed detectives: he had a girl willing to talk about the murder. "Bring her down," the detectives replied, and soon they had Crystal Elliott in a room with them.

Crystal told Detective Renna that the family had already taxed her wallet, necklaces, bra, underwear, and two skirts and now they were going to stomp her. She talked about the assault of Jessica in the squat that night. She consented to a polygraph examination, which confirmed she was telling the truth.

That day, Detective Renna and a crime team took Crystal Elliott down to the squat under Front Avenue, where again the warehouse worker cranked open the loading dock doors. The worker says Crystal stopped to talk to him, exclaiming, "I'm homeless, but I don't kill people." The police shushed her.

Crystal pointed out to the detectives and crime specialists where the family had camped, and where the Circle of Seven had been drawn in the dirt. In the days since the murder, the highway department had cleaned out the squat and inadvertently removed much of the evidence. Near where Jessica was beaten, however, a clump of hair was found, which would be tested as "similar" to her hair in texture, color, and other traits. Across the street, police obtained video from the 7-11 showing the youths purchasing the lighter fluid, water, and beer. These videos offered some of the first photographs of the family members.

Back at Central Precinct, the detectives arranged for Crystal Elliott to stay in a group home for foster youth. They wanted the Thantos Family to assume she had been picked up as a runaway foster ward. They did not want to return her to the streets where she would most certainly be in danger.

The next day, May 29, police showed up to photograph and videotape the Square discretely. Unknown to the street kids, they hid a video camera near the Starbucks. They took photographs of Danielle, Schreiner, and a few others. The next morning, Detective Renna got a court order to force the Porch Light shelter to turn over their shelter intake forms for the suspects known as Shadowcat, Neo, D. K., and the others.

———

It had only been a week since the murder, and Portland's annual Rose Festival was ready to open. The beautifully manicured lawns of the waterfront along the Willamette River had been turned into an expansive carnival scene. A Ferris wheel rose high over the Hawthorne

Bridge, the wind rocking its cars. The sky was a clear blue, with perfect white clouds scooting across it.

Evicted from the Front Avenue squat by the police, the Thantos Family had relocated to the east side of the Burnside Bridge, where a cyclone fence enclosed a dry, rocky area in which the homeless camped. The camp was a short walk up the railroad tracks from where Jessica Williams had been murdered.

On the night of Friday, May 30, the family was squatting at their new camp when Portland police officer Gregory Pashley arrived to move them along. Officer Pashley noted that a dozen or so youths were sleeping under the bridge. He also noted what a tidy camp it was, with everything organized just so.

The next morning, Officer Pashley returned to patrol the area. Like other officers, he had been working almost around the clock, canvassing downtown to collect evidence to help in the investigation. Under the west side of the Burnside Bridge, near the stairwell that led up to the bridge, Officer Pashley and his partner found Cassandra Hale, the mother of the Thantos Family, along with a street daughter. The two were lounging under the bridge with other street kids.

Cassandra, her eyes red, was wearing a blue bandana tied over her blonde hair. She had on loose dark pants and a blue shirt. She happily posed for a photograph for the officers, standing with her arms out, looking fierce. A close-up of her hand showed bitten nails rimmed with dirt.

Officer Pashley chatted with Cassandra. "Among other things she told us was that she considers herself the 'mother of the group,'" he wrote in his report. "She told us there are twelve or more members of this 'family,' not all of whom sleep in the same camp each night." Cassandra had a terrible background story. She said her father had tried to rape her when she was a teenager, and "he is looking for me." She claimed her father had spent time in jail for raping her.

Cassandra and one of her street daughters were surrounded by what looked like trash: a shopping cart with clothes in it and blankets and belongings spread over the ground. Leaning against the shopping cart were two aluminum baseball bats. These bats perked the interest of the officers, and they took photographs of them. One of the aluminum bats had green lettering; the other had red. In their report, the officers wrote, the "heavily dented bat with green lettering had an orangish substance which did not appear to look like rust or paint but I could not be sure it was blood."

Lying on the ground was a braided leather belt, which also interested the officers. They took a picture of this as well. When they were done chatting with Cassandra and her street daughter, they left and drove around downtown, asking more street kids to pose for pictures.

Officer Pashley was headed back across the Burnside Bridge when he saw some more familiar faces. It was most of rest of the Thantos Family, including their street father. Officer Pashley pulled his car over. The youths stood around, chatting, while Pashley leaned against his car. Down below was the sparkle of the carnival tents, and the hot, sugary smell of elephant ears drifted over the bridge.

The family seemed relaxed with Officer Pashley. Some of them smiled. Their street father wasn't so friendly. Nelson wore a clean dark shirt with oriental patterns on the sleeves, and his long brown hair was tied neatly off his neck. The sun flashed off his wire-rimmed glasses. His brown goatee was trimmed, and his short brown beard brushed. He did not smile.

When Officer Pashley asked him for his identification, Nelson was belligerent. "I don't have to show you my ID," he said. Officer Pashley agreed. "I told him it was no big deal." Nelson stormed off across the bridge, according to Officer Pashley's testimony. The rest of the family hung around, still chatting with the officer. Nelson soon came back. He seemed unable to stay away with all of his followers right there, talking to a cop.

Once again, Officer Pashley says he asked Nelson for identification. This time Nelson held out his wallet, his identification showing through the plastic window. Officer Pashley wrote down the information. Now the police had the real name of the man called Thantos.

Still chatting, Officer Pashley complimented the youths on doing such a nice job of keeping their squat clean the night before. Nelson took credit for this, bragging about how he kept his street family in order. He claimed to be a person who "watches out" for the younger street kids. Now that he was talking, Nelson couldn't seem to stop. He told Officer Pashley about how his "sister" Misty Largo was raped and murdered under the Marquam Bridge in 1992.

Officer Pashley asked to take photographs of the family. The street kids consented. Pashley snapped several pictures with his digital camera, showing the youths against the backdrop of the Willamette River. The day was so clear, and the sky so bright, that the street kids had to squint against the sunlight off the river. In the photographs, some of the youths wear befuddled expressions, their eyes smudged with lost sleep. Joshua makes a pseudo gang sign for his picture. Crystal Grace looks trashed.

Before they left, Nelson asked Officer Pashley about good places to squat. The officer seemed a bit taken aback by the request. Street families don't usually ask police where to squat. "I said the spot under the freeway was as good as any," Pashley wrote in a report, because it was out of the way and the family was less likely to disturb anyone there. The street family took off, heading across the bridge.

That night was the Starlight parade. As dusk fell, downtown grew choked with locals who set up plastic lawn chairs behind makeshift, temporary metal fences, opened coolers full of fried chicken, and unwrapped sandwiches. Parents perched their children on their shoulders to watch the parade. Even the street kids were excited about the parade, though they were inclined not to show it. Some boasted loudly they had the best seats, right there on their dirty benches in the Square.

Maja Radanovic had come downtown from the outlying city of Hillsboro for the parade. Maja ducked into the Square, passing by the benches with their crowd of pierced and pointedly angry youths. Suddenly, there was her high school friend Danielle, sitting with a bunch of kids. Danielle looked awful. Her once clear skin was blotchy and dotted with acne sores. Her Mohawk was untidy and dyed the sorry blue-black color of shoe polish.

Maja wasn't sure what to say to her best friend. "I heard you got adopted into a street gang," Maja said, according to an account in the *Oregonian*. "No, it's a street family," Danielle replied. "We just kinda go together and take care of each other."

═══

But the family was falling apart. Two days later, on June 2, Carl snuck into a local hospital, where he attempted to steal medical tape, towels, alcohol prep pads, hospital masks, and other supplies. A hospital staff member caught him, and Carl was given a no-trespass order. If he appeared in the hospital again, he would be arrested.

That same day, Nelson's application for transfer of parole was rejected. The California authorities didn't want him back. They said his stepfather was not a blood relative, and too many years had passed for Nelson to claim residency.

On June 4, Sarah Caster crept back into a shelter. The screener seemed alarmed at what had become of the beautiful girl in just a month on the streets. They urgently suggested the agency "work on reunification if at all possible before creating a dependency situation here." Crystal Grace was also reevaluated that day. She told the staff she had been "squatting outside with various friends and groups," and they expressed concern. "Jade seems like she is struggling with creating and maintaining some stability in her current situation. She seems like she could use some emotional support."

Crystal Grace had plenty to worry about. She had just learned that the family had put a death order out on her for cutting her arms and for supposedly kissing another family member. The warrior assigned to kill her was Danielle, but Danielle didn't want to kill her street sister. She liked Crystal. It was Nelson who had ordered her to kill Crystal, she later told police. First, he told her, take her money. Then kill her.

Hearing about the order, Crystal Grace decided it was too dangerous to return to the streets. She approached another street kid and confided in him, sobbing that she had a secret she could not keep. She asked him to call the police, and within hours she was in custody. Detective Rich Austria, who had solved the 2000 street family murder of Richard Crosby, sat down to interview Crystal Grace on June 5. "She confirmed what had happened that night in the squat," Detective Renna says, "and who had left with Jessica."

Meanwhile, other members were trying to creep away from the family. Danielle began staying in shelters and storing her belongings at New Avenues for Youth, but she continued to take part in the family's assaults. Jimmy was also staying in local shelters.

There was talk of splitting the family into two groups and moving to California. Cassandra would head one group, Nelson would take the other, and they would all meet up in California. That was the plan, at least. But Pearce said Nelson took him aside and told him, "Juliet [Cassandra] knew too much to be allowed to leave to California." Danielle had heard the same thing: Cassandra knew too much to live.

The family was turning on yet another member, this time its own mother. Cassandra's own stories had finally backfired. The word on the streets was that the street mother was going to get 86'd because she had had three children and had not taken good care of them. Cassandra was a bad mother and would be punished for failing her own children. As tough as she appeared, Cassandra showed that not even the old school street kids were immune to the dangers of a drama.

———

Detective Renna walked along the rocky shore of the east side of the river looking for an empty lighter fluid bottle. He was hoping to find the fingerprints of the murder suspects. He walked up and down the rough shore, climbing over the broken concrete lining the river, looking inside tires, but he found nothing.

Next, Detective Renna waded through hours of ComNet's grainy footage of the Steel Bridge. A few moments of video that crossed the screen made him pause. He rewound the tape and watched as Jessica, whom he described as "distinctive," walked across the bridge, surrounded by two males and one female. He thought Jessica was walking normally, despite the heavy beating she had taken. The family warriors walked in formation around her. "It was apparent to me that she wasn't going freely," Detective Renna says.

That same day, the Porch Light shelter turned over its records of the suspects. It had been a week since the subpoena. With these in hand, the police could learn the real names of the street kids in the Thantos Family. Detective Renna compiled a list of ten names, including James Nelson (Thantos), Cassandra Hale (Juliet), Carl Alsup (D. K.) Danielle Cox (Shadowcat), Jimmy Stewart (Neo), Joshua Brown-Lenon (Scooby), Sarah Caster (Valkyrie), Steven Pearce (Gambit), Cory Dennison (Twix), and Heidi Keller (Little Twix). Two suspects were already in custody: Crystal Elliott (Spitfire) and Crystal Grace (Jade).

The police knew they would have to orchestrate the arrests carefully. It would take a wide net to capture so many suspects without all of them scattering. If they handled the arrests badly, they could find themselves with a few street kids in jail and the rest on the lam.

In the early hours of June 9, everything was prepared. A roll call at the Southeast Precinct announced the massive search, and a sergeant passed out photographs and names. Nelson's parole officer was informed of what was happening. She was expecting Nelson that day for a visit and promised to call the police when he arrived. Officer Anthony Merrill was called back downtown to help.

That morning, dozens of police quietly fanned out along the river. "We set them loose," recalls Sergeant George Burke, "and they searched from the Steel Bridge all the way down past the Fremont Bridge into the Oaks Park wetlands." The search went on for grueling hours, with police canvassing both sides of the river, checking out every squat and every spot the street kids might hide. In the meantime, Nelson showed up for his scheduled meeting with his parole officer and was arrested without incident. In a holding room at the Central Precinct, he told Detective Renna he wanted an attorney, then spontaneously said he wanted to tell his version of events. He kept quiet after that.

In the Square, Officer Merrill found Steve Pearce hanging out in a "large congregation of street youth" in the Square. While he was taking Pearce into custody, Carl Alsup appeared nearby, saw what was happening, and ran. He would be the only family member to escape arrest at the time. For several days, Carl hid in local squats, and then headed to Seattle, Washington.

Early the next morning, police swept the Porch Light shelter. They took several family members into custody, including Jimmy

Stewart, Joshua Brown-Lenon, Sarah Caster, and Danielle Cox. In her booking photograph, Danielle has tears in her eyes. Sarah has cigarette burns and a dog bite on one hand.

That same morning at 9:34, Officer Merrill caught Cassandra Hale in the south park blocks, where the street family drug dealers hung out. "She was there with her big dog, just hanging out with her friends having a good old time in the sun," Officer Merrill says. "I asked her about her dog, and she said it was okay, her friends could take care of it." When Merrill went to cuff her, Cassandra complained of a hurt wrist and asked him to be gentle. In one of her pockets, he found three plastic bags filled with what looked like marijuana.

There was one more remaining family member to be arrested. Crystal Ivey, the housewife-in-training known as Nix, was arrested when she came in to talk to detectives for a scheduled interview. She was so unimportant that other family members had forgotten to mention her.

There were so many youths sitting in holding cells the day of the arrests that the homicide unit had to bring in extra detectives to help with the interviews. Detective Renna wanted to interview the principal murder suspects himself.

At nine in the morning, Renna and another detective, Shirley Parsons, started with Danielle Cox. "Shirley did a very good job of connecting with her," Renna says. "Danielle was crying. It was brutal. It's hard to be professional and make that connection." He pauses. "It's hard when someone is describing to you the sounds another person makes while dying. Shirley had to take a break at one point, and she had been around a long time. She went upstairs for a few minutes."

Danielle told the police in rending detail how she had killed Jessica. The detectives passed her tissues as Danielle sobbed. "I can't take this back . . . it just eats me up inside," Danielle cried. When she described the gurgling sounds Jessica made, she was sobbing so hard she could barely get the words out. "I'm so sorry. I never meant for it to go that far," she sobbed. "Didn't even want to hurt her." And yet, Danielle was protective of her street father, refusing to implicate Nelson. She said it was Carl who had made the decision to kill Jessica, not Nelson, "in this case."

Next, it was Jimmy Stewart's turn. Jimmy also wept during his interview, and yet he seemed fatigued, as if he just wanted to get it over with. He told Detective Renna he didn't want to tell any more lies. "I don't really want to live anymore. And I'm hungry. I need a cigarette." Detective Renna didn't believe Jimmy was a suicide risk at the moment. He sent out for hamburgers. After Jimmy ate, Detective Renna turned on the tape, and they began again.

Next came Cassandra Hale. For the first time, anger laced the voice of Detective Renna. Cassandra told him she wanted to cooperate, but she just kept lying. She claimed she was having a seizure while the others beat Jessica and only came out of it when Jessica was leaving the squat. She claimed she had blacked out during the assault in the squat and couldn't remember a thing. All of this was contrary to what the other street kids had said, and Detective Renna let Cassandra know it.

Finally, after changing her story a couple times, Cassandra told the truth, or the closest she would ever come to the truth. She admitted she had beaten Jessica, that she held the lighter under Jessica's palm and burned her hand, and that she had hit and kicked her numerous times. Yet, Cassandra still refused to take full accountability for many of her acts, saying, for instance, that the palm burning was "how I was raised."

There was no remorse in her statement, no tears. Cassandra explained the rules of the street with flat pride. "When the kids know they've done wrong, they bow their head and you barely have to smack them on the back of the head," she said.

———

While the detectives spent a long day interviewing most of the accused, the Outside In youth agency held a memorial for Jessica Williams, as well as other "homeless" youths who die on the streets. A year before, the agency had commissioned an artist to make a metal tree sculpture for the courtyard after another young street woman was murdered. The tree was now ready for dedication. The copper-colored leaves on the tree were blank. Every time a street youth died, his or her name would be inscribed on a leaf. The tree was expectant. There were at least a dozen leaves waiting for names. Jessica's was one of the first names inscribed.

The service was held in the courtyard of the agency's large building. Street kids and agency staff gathered around the death tree. It was exactly the sort of dramatic gesture that appealed to the street kids. For them, Jessica was now immortalized as a tragic symbol of how tough and dangerous their lifestyle was.

The Williams were not invited to the service. Becky says they were not asked for permission to have Jessica's death used in a shrine to murdered homeless youth. She felt it was their daughter they had lost, and yet the youth agencies had claimed her as one of their own, another Portland street kid thrown cruelly to the wolves.

"The streets are not a safe place for homeless youth, but, by far, the majority of homeless youth are good kids," Outside In director Kathy Oliver told a reporter. "This is a tragedy and shouldn't be reflective of the homeless youth." She went on to claim such violence is "very rare."

It was a perspective repeated by other service providers. They all appeared to believe the murder of Jessica Williams was an aberration.

In truth, they seemed more concerned with protecting the image of homeless youth than addressing the reality of street family violence, though the street families prey on genuinely homeless youths time and again.

Multnomah County district attorney Norm Frink had a different perspective. "The citizens are subsidizing an environment for these kids to take drugs and playact," he says. "We've enabled them to behave these ways." Frink believes the agencies make it too easy for young people to live on the streets, allowing teenagers who have homes and parents to immerse themselves in a criminal subculture. The result, he says, is a society of teenagers "playing cowboys and Indians on the street," only these youths are not supervised, and their games are bloody and real. "Some of these people could have been functional members of society," Frink says. "Danielle Cox, for example. She could have been a successful person. Crystal Grace was working in a jewelry store. And then, on the other hand, you've got . . . Joshua [Brown-Lenon]. I don't know what you do with people like that."

In the weeks after the murder, a remarkable number of people blamed Becky and Sam Williams for what happened. "Where were you when your child was wandering the streets with her murderers?" asked one particularly vicious blogger. The writer stated that the murder was "yet one more example of our 'nobody's home' syndrome at work." Other writers were equally condemning. "I blame this girl's death in large part on those parents," one wrote. "Since she was so like a child why weren't they protecting her like a child?"

Articles in the media mentioned Jessica's fetal alcohol syndrome without mentioning that she was adopted, leading readers to assume Becky was the alcoholic mother who drank while pregnant. Angry readers called the Williams house to yell at Becky, blaming her for Jessica's disability and murder.

Chuck Currie, an advocate who served on the board of the National Coalition for the Homeless, wrote an article titled "Jessica Williams Did Not Have to Die," which implied Jessica had been forced out on the streets by her family. "The only way to truly bring justice to the death of Jessica Kate Williams would be to make sure that no young person be forced out onto the streets where she can be killed," Currie concluded. An opinion piece in the *Oregonian* claimed Jessica's murder was the result of a lack of funding for youth shelters and suggested donations.

Everyone had a finger to point. The agencies blamed the parents. The district attorney blamed the agencies. Some of the parents blamed each other. And everyone together blamed James Daniel Nelson, who was portrayed as a charismatic Manson-like leader who turned a dozen street kids into his mind-zombies and then ordered them to kill a developmentally disabled woman, all in less than two months since his release from prison. No one examined the culture of street families.

―――

While the Williams grieved, other parents grieved too. Robyn Hale visited Portland and walked the streets her daughter Cassandra— really Cassie—had walked. She walked across the Steel Bridge and looked at the spot of rocky gravel where Jessica had died, where tattered crime scene tape was still snagged on the rocks. She stopped in the Square and talked to the street kids, who called her daughter by her street name, Juliet. They shrugged and told Robyn that they had tried to warn Juliet. It was all the fault of Thantos. It was a bad family.

Robyn wasn't comforted by any of this. Maybe her daughter would find a safe place now in prison, a place where her lies couldn't do any more harm to herself or others. She grieved for the Williams.

They would never see their precious, difficult daughter again. "I tell myself the pain I am feeling is nothing compared to what they are going through," Robyn says.

The Hales dodged the media. The articles about throwaways stung. "She always had a home to go to," Robyn says, confusion in her voice. Robyn wanted to attend the hearings, but she was afraid to confront the Williams, especially Becky. She saw Becky's face in her mind every time she thought of what Cassie had done. She felt so guilty, she says. She just couldn't do it. How do you say sorry for a thing like that? "You know, you are taught that your children are gifts from God," Robyn says. "You want to raise them to be trustworthy and good. You are told you are responsible for how they turn out. And then . . ." Her voice trails off. "I'll always wonder if I could have done something different."

Kelly White, the mother of Carl Alsup, wept outside the court-house. "I feel two ways, as a mom and someone who knows right from wrong. My son has to take responsibility for what he did," she says, shaking hard. "I feel empathy for the Williams. I want to say sorry to her parents, but there is no place."

Danielle Cox's mother wrote to her daughter in jail. Her letters reflect a woman coming to terms with something beyond belief. Her writing is small, careful, and crammed with details and fond memories, as if skirting a truth too horrible to contemplate. The memories retrace a childhood filled with love and privilege and caring, and they all seem to ask the same question: why, Danielle?

Danielle didn't answer the unstated question apparent in those letters. Instead, she pressured her mother to come up with the $50,000 bail. Her mother wrote Danielle that she loved her and always would, but Danielle stayed in jail.

According to Becky Williams, only one parent of the accused took the step of contacting her to apologize. It was the father of sixteen-year-old Sarah Caster, the girl who had never hit anyone. He called to say he was sorry for what his daughter had done.

———

In the Square, the street families were done with sadness. It was time for anger. "The media needs to be put in check," one street kid told *Street Roots*, a newspaper for the homeless. "Every time something like a murder happens on the streets its like all street kids are murderers." It was the fault, the youth said, of "corporate whore media centers."

There was a more immediate reason they were mad. Panhandling had dried up. "People don't even look at me when I ask them for change," complained a twenty-one-year-old who had recently arrived from the East Coast.

A few family members were still on the loose. Despite his role in several family crimes, including the mugging of Eugene, as well as his own crimes, including the rape of the minor girl, Thomas Schreiner was still running free that summer. Of course, he hadn't participated in the murder of Jessica Williams, but had he not been sick that night and left the squat to go to the Greenhouse shelter, he later told an investigator, he probably would have taken part in the assault. "I don't know. I probably would have gone along with it," he said.

When Schreiner heard that another street youth had been cooperating with Detective Renna in the investigation of the murder, he grew angry at the snitch. "I was going to kick his ass for being an informant," he later admitted to the police. Schreiner and another street kid caught the snitch and assaulted him. They punched him several times in his face, taxed him his backpack, and used a knife to threaten him not to testify in court. "A lot of people get killed for lying," Schreiner growled at the youth.

After an extensive manhunt that included scouring woods along the Oregon coast, Carl Alsup was finally caught in Seattle that August. In a bizarre move, he left a message for Norm Frink, the Multnomah County district attorney prosecuting the case. "Hello, Mr. Frink," he told the machine. "Um, I'm calling about, a, um, girl that was killed about a month ago. . . . I was a witness." Carl claimed to have not participated in the murder but was willing to help with the investigation. He insisted he had to remain "completely anonymous." He left a voice mailbox number he had set up specifically for Mr. Frink. Seattle police traced Carl to a Seattle home and arrested him.

Detective Renna drove up to Seattle as soon as he heard about the arrest, arriving at two in the morning. He found Carl sleeping in a holding room at the Seattle jail. At first, Carl denied taking any part in the murder. Detective Renna confronted him with what he already knew. Finally, Carl admitted his role, but he claimed Nelson had forced him into the murder, showing Detective Renna a scratch on his shoulder that he said came from where Nelson had poked him with a knife in the squat. Detective Renna told Carl he had experience with knife wounds, and that sure didn't look like one.

Carl ended up confessing not only to the murder of Jessica Williams but to his role in the beating of Nicholas Saunders, and he told the detectives about the baseball bat assault of Eugene. Back in Portland, detectives located the robbery report Eugene had filed. That September, four months after the murder of Jessica Williams, the case was forwarded to the district attorney.

When Kelly White heard that her son had been caught, she wanted to visit him at the county jail. But she was so repulsed by what he had done, she could not bear the thought of touching him. So, she asked the investigator on his case, Sandra Gillman, to touch him instead. Every jail visit, Sandra hugged Carl for his mother.

Sara Baerlocher, the young woman whose hair was taxed by the family, went back home that summer to live with her father. She still couldn't find decent work, so she filled her time with babysitting chores. She remained connected to the street culture. She found excuses to go downtown. She spoke of a street friend trapped in an abusive relationship. Sara believed she now knew a lot about abusive relationships.

Sara didn't seem to notice that only days separated her from the murder of Jessica Williams. She could have just as easily been the one killed or one of those doing the killing. If she and Nelson hadn't broken up, she may have been in the squat that night, administering the same brand of misbegotten justice to Jessica that she herself had received.

Instead, Sara appeared cavalier about the entire affair, from start to finish. She laughed and giggled, wondering out loud if she would be called to the stand against Nelson and giving a little shiver at the thought. One got the feeling Sara didn't want the dramas to end.

The murder did change her mind about James Nelson, sort of. "I'm beginning to wonder if he was a habitual liar," she muses, as if this idea has just occurred to her. Then, she remembers his muscles when he took off his shirt. "He was perfect," she sighs.

———

In the months after Jessica's murder, the Sick Boys took over much of the power in the culture, with the Nihilistic Gutter Punks waning in influence. As proof of this new allegiance, a member of the Nihilistic Gutter Punks tattooed a Sick Boys logo over his old NGP tattoo and, underneath, a flying banner with the proclamation *Sick Boys for Life*.

Street family crime continued. In October 2004, a street family called the Portland Riders went on a crime spree downtown, stabbing and assaulting people. The Portland Riders ranged in age from sixteen to twenty. Their father figure was an older homeless man who was the cofounder and former leader of the lauded homeless tent city Dignity Village. The family was unusual in that many of the members were African American, as was their alleged street father.

The Southeast Precinct police followed the family for some time, but the Riders mostly targeted the homeless, who were generally unwilling to identify themselves as victims. For weapons, the Riders carried knives and smiley chains with padlocks attached. At night they roamed, looking for victims. A man bicycling across a bridge was stabbed, seemingly out of the blue. He was just riding across the Steel Bridge esplanade, he told a grand jury, when the group of street kids jumped out at him. They kicked him so savagely he was convinced he would have been killed if he didn't protect his face with his hands. Two other victims were robbed and forced to jump into the river. A homeless man was stabbed through the lung in another assault that could have easily resulted in murder charges. A tourist from London was mugged and beaten severely with a smiley chain. "They just attacked me for no bloody reason," he told the *Oregonian*.

"They're all part of this weird street kid culture," says Kristen Snowden, the deputy district attorney handling their case. The mayor at the time, Vera Katz, told the press she would consider redefining street families as gangs, but this did not happen. Inside Central Precinct, her announcement caused some snorts and chuckles, as the police said they had made exactly the same suggestion to the mayor some two years before, and she had shot it down. The Riders quickly vanished from the news. The media moved on.

Detective Renna visited the McLoughlin Caves, where Nick Moore, the paranoid schizophrenic young man, had been murdered in 2001 by the street kids led by Valerie Derscheid. Police had recently swept the caves of campers, and the department of transportation had covered their graffiti with gray industrial paint. But new graffiti was up, including a version of the Nihilistic Gutter Punks' tag with the chaos star underneath.

Detective Renna stood in the cave where Nick had died, and pointed. "There was a pool of blood here," he says. Down the sandy slope where Nick's body had been dumped, there was a small white cross with *NICK* in plain letters. "I think his family put that there," he says. It was obvious that Renna had visited here before.

Climbing through the caves, Detective Renna kicked at the red dirt that had been carved into platforms and steps. "I was thinking about this the other week," he says in his soft voice. "Here these kids say they are rebelling against the rules, and then they go create a society that is all about rules, a place where you get beaten if you do the slightest thing wrong." He pauses. "I wonder sometimes what Nick was thinking, his last thoughts, when he realized that this wasn't simply going to be a street beating."

Down the river, at the Steel Bridge where Jessica was killed, a fresh tag appeared, marking the spot on the retaining wall behind where she died. *Government Is Violence*, it said in black spray paint.

In the weeks and months after their arrests, a flurry of jailhouse letters passed among the family members. Inmates in the county jail are allowed to write to whomever they please, but their communications are opened and recorded. Nelson appeared to know this, and he passed a note to Danielle Cox through underhanded means. Danielle wrote back and sent her reply through the same means.

When the sheriffs saw the notes being passed, they tried to confiscate them. Nelson quickly tore the notes to pieces and tried to flush them down his toilet. Pieced together, Nelson's note warned Danielle that he knew she had testified before the grand jury. "I don't know what you said," he wrote. "I am going to need you [missing section] they will revoke my parole and give me [missing section] write back and let me know what's up." It was signed *Thantos*.

Danielle's return note was in a feminine, back-rounded script. "Didn't say ANYTHING against you [missing section]. Don't believe them." It was signed *Shadowcat*.

A private investigator working for a defense team heard about the prison papers that Nelson had carried and went to a family squat to look for them. The investigator discovered dozens of water-stained papers and took them into evidence. There were certificates for classes Nelson had passed in prison and library checkout records: *The Anarchist Cookbook, Be Your Own Detective, The Criminal Law Handbook,* and *The Complete Idiot's Guide to Writing*. There was an application for housing in which Nelson disclosed his history as he saw it: "I went to prison at 16 for murder for killing a rapist." There were pages of hardcore pornography, an application for an Honored Citizen bus pass, which had been filled out by Nelson, and the articles on Hitler. There were pages of detailed Dungeons and Dragons characters, written in a neat hand. You can tell, reading the tightly woven paragraphs, how much Nelson enjoyed the fantasy game. There were cartoon drawings of men with spectacular muscles and wings and women with spectacular breasts. There were panhandling signs, including one that said *Homeless Please Help*, and there were drawings for homemade grenades and bombs, including a detailed diagram of an alarm-clock bomb.

———

Through the minefield, the Williams picked their way. They wanted to adopt more special-needs children. Their adoption caseworker was concerned. It wasn't their fitness for parenting that worried her because the Williams had shown themselves to be capable of handling anything. It was the loss of Jessica. The worker knew that after the murder of a child, many parents divorce. Sam and Becky, however, were determined to weather their loss together.

They had room, Becky says, meaning they still had room in their hearts. Two years after Jessica's death, the Williams adopted a special-needs sibling set from foster care, this time a toddler boy and his six-year-old sister. Both of the children are African American. The girl bears a resemblance to Jessica with her wide-set eyes. Becky found happiness in once more chasing a two-year-old, though she jokes that she had forgotten how tiring it is. It was soon discovered that the boy had serious medical problems. The state asked the Williams if they still wanted to finalize the adoption. Becky said yes. "Things can happen to birth children too," Becky says.

The Williams family, at this writing, remains whole, though missing a crucial piece. Jessica's sisters remember their boisterous, laughing sister. They wish they had gone to the concert that Jessica wanted to go to. They wish they had spent more time together. One placed Jessica's photograph at the altar when she married. They cry when they remember her.

Becky Williams grapples with grief on a daily basis. She and Sam had Jessica's remains cremated, and now her ashes stay in their house. Becky cannot let them go.

17

James Nelson asked to have his trial moved to the Netherlands, where apparently he thought his Aryan peers would give him a better shake. His motion was denied, and Nelson agreed to plead no contest to murder, thus, to a life sentence with no chance of parole. After two years of waiting, the case had withered in the media. Inch by inch, the circle of concern had shrunk, until only the Williams and a few others showed up in the courtroom. Detective Barry Renna sat in the back row.

Nelson pled no contest, wearing a blue jail smock over a pink jail shirt. His hair had been cut short, and there were angry red slashes on his neck. He had been getting into fights again. During his exercise time, guards watched as Nelson practiced karate kicks, writhing on the ground as if fighting off attackers while handcuffed. They ordered him to stop.

Asked if he had a statement to make at the plea, Nelson said nothing. The Williams were also quiet. Becky says the district attorneys had asked them not to make a victim statement out of concern that Nelson would grow angry and refuse to sign the deal. Although he was pleading no contest, Nelson insisted he was innocent. He seemed convinced that he would win his freedom on appeal.

In a jail visiting room shortly after his plea, Nelson seemed calm. Two years in a county jail had thickened him, and he moved slowly, but that could have been because he was accustomed to being transferred in cuffs. His hair was plastered down with water. Behind his glasses, his dark blue eyes were direct. The skin on his face was tan, but the skin on his arms was white under wiry black hair.

In person, Nelson is not frightening. Rather, he is polite and appears reasonably intelligent. He is articulate and processes information in a coherent fashion. He is able to use analytical thought and keep up with a fast conversation, sensing where it is going. But there is something disconcerting about a grown man who talks about gremlin rights and taxing and death knights. It's as if Nelson is frozen at fifteen, an immature, fantasy-oriented teenager who doesn't grasp the gravity of the world, even when it comes and grabs him by the ankles.

Nelson's entire adult life has been spent in two milieus: prison and the streets. They could be mirror institutions, both with rigid codes of behavior, harsh punishments, and gangs masquerading as families. If there is one factor that is seldom discussed about crime and violence, it is the fictive kin elements of the networks that support them.

The street family culture didn't just define Nelson in terms of his relationships. It defined his language, his morals, his choice in friends, his place in the world, and his direction in life. This was his culture, his gestalt. He knows this, in his own way. "You can't help being on the streets and not be involved in the culture," he says.

Nelson speaks freely and frankly, yet to say he plays Stalin with his own history would be generous. He acknowledges no fault. He says the sexual-battery conviction when he was fifteen resulted from an "orgy" he had with the other students in his special education class. "There were eight of us," he says, "four guys and four girls, and we were all in the same special education class at school." He retells the murder of Leon Stanton in 1992 with a gloss that would impress Jerry Spence. His new story is that he killed Leon because he "snapped" after what Leon did to his good friend Michelle Woodall. "I can't stand a man hitting a woman," he says repeatedly. "Leon bragged about how they had raped and killed her, and I just snapped."

During every bad thing that happened in 2003, Nelson wasn't there. He played no part in any of the family crimes. It was all the fault of the other youths. He claims he had no idea Jessica was being taken from the squat to be killed. He says that Carl said they were taking her to another squat where she would be safe. No one else confirms this account.

And yet, sometimes Nelson's stories are the truth. His version of Cassandra's role in the squat, for example, is largely consistent with other witnesses. While Nelson is eager to incriminate his followers for the murder and frequently disparages many of them, he avoids speaking about one member of the family, Danielle Cox, his beloved street daughter. Nelson does not say anything negative about Danielle. When her name comes up, he pauses, and a reluctant, almost pained look creeps into his eyes. It is the only time he looks human.

Nelson was sent to serve his life sentence at the Snake River Correctional Institution, a barbed wire fortress of a prison in the arid deserts of eastern Oregon. There, he lives with other incarcerated street family members, including Sick Boy Travis Harramen. Travis claims Nelson has joined the European Kindred, or the EK, the white supremacist pagan prison gang. Nelson, he says, "got all the Nazi thugs on me Irish ass." Even in prison, the dramas continue.

———

Most of the Thantos Family youths quickly pled out under cooperation deals with the district attorney's office. Crystal Grace, Carl's girlfriend, received a sentence of five years for her role in the beating and burning of Jessica Williams. She did not respond to requests for an interview. Other girls and women of the family did write or speak, and many did express remorse, including Crystal Elliott, the sixteen-year-old called Spitfire. Crystal had her baby in juvenile prison, a girl she named Annalessia. She wrote from the juvenile home saying she felt badly about what had happened to Jessica. She will be released in 2008.

Crystal Ivey, the seventeen-year-old "housewife-in-training," was given three years in a juvenile facility in exchange for her testimony against the others. Crystal appeared to try to make the most of her opportunity to change. "Since I've been in jail I've rebuilt me and my dad's relationship," she wrote from Hillcrest, a juvenile home that declined to approve a nonfamily visit. Crystal wrote that she went through a drug-and-alcohol group and a violent-offender group. She made an effort to get her high school equivalency, taking the necessary classes, though she said she struggled with math. Crystal Ivey was paroled in late 2005 and is now free.

Steve Pearce, called Gambit, received almost six years for his role in Jessica's kidnapping and assault, as well as the assault on Nicholas Saunders. From prison, he filled his court file with motions and petitions, including the claim that his defense attorney allowed the district attorney to "lie, trick, deceive and threaten me with charges they couldn't even indict me on."

Thomas Schreiner was eventually convicted for his rape of the minor girl that spring, the robbery of Eugene, and other assaults. All told, Schreiner received over seven years in prison.

Joshua Brown-Lenon, or Scooby—the self-proclaimed gutterpunk who helped cut off Sara Baerlocher's hair, smashed Eugene in the head with a baseball bat, trolled for gay men to mug, took part in other family crimes, watched Jessica get beaten, and bought the lighter fluid that was used to burn her—was treated sympathetically in the press. He was reported as saying he had wanted to stop the assault on Jessica but was afraid he would be "stabbed to death" if he didn't cooperate. He told the judge he had crept up to Jessica and whispered he was sorry. He maintained that he had absolutely no idea the lighter fluid was intended to burn Jessica. Joshua was given almost six years in prison for the robbery of Eugene, which he is serving with the two-year sentence for being present at the assault on Jessica. He was sent to Snake River Correctional Institution, the same prison as James Nelson, Travis Harramen, and other street family members.

Inside the prison, Joshua communicates with other street kids, helping to keep the culture alive. He can tell you where the killers of Nick Moore are being held, as well as the location of street kids convicted in other crimes. The incarcerated street kids inside Snake River prison produce their own punk fanzine, *Solitary Existence*, in which they extol street culture. The fanzine, which is protected as free speech, is decorated with violent and pornographic images, such as a naked woman holding a gun with an anarchy symbol and the banner "Fuck the Man." Its pages are filled with proud stories of the times the street youths taxed, beat, and assaulted their victims.

When they are paroled, many of these young criminals will take their old school credits—and prison experiences—back to the streets, where they will become the street fathers and mothers of new families, just as James Nelson did. The street family culture will continue, becoming ever more violent and criminal.

Joshua himself plans to return downtown as soon as he is released in 2010. "Downtown life to me is my life," he says. He has no other plans. When he is paroled, Joshua will be in his late twenties, close to the age that his street father Nelson was at his parole. Joshua will be ready to take on the role of a street father. He seems excited by the prospect.

———

Cassandra Hale reached a deal with the district attorney's office, giving her nineteen years for the assault on Jessica. She has remained a persuasive liar, even to those trained to be skeptical: some associated with the case seemed convinced that Cassandra was having an epileptic seizure during the assault.

While she awaited sentencing, Cassandra was held at Inverness Jail, a large white cinderblock building on the outskirts of North Portland in a maze of sloughs. Meetings at Inverness are held in a sort of cattle pen, with a row of little booths and spit-spotted windows behind which the inmates gather. Each woman gets her own little booth, with a thick shield of safety glass and the obligatory greasy phone.

Cassandra had lost weight during her first year of incarceration, but she was still a large woman with quick reflexes. Her long blonde hair had been cut into a short, boyish haircut, and she had spiked it with gel off her pale forehead. Her blue eyes were glassy with new contacts that she claimed a street mom had brought to her. She had made a new family in jail and talked about her jail sisters and her jail wife like they had been her family for her entire life. She now identifies herself as a lesbian and complains that the jail guards discriminate against her for being homosexual. She appears comfortable in prison, as native to the environment as she once was to the streets. She acts as if she has spent her entire life behind bars.

Cassandra remains connected to the street culture through visitors and the inmates entering the jail, and she enjoys sharing the stories of their dramas. When she talks about the street culture, it is like she never left. She plans to get her dog Chronic back. She is adamant that her birth family abused her and insists she has dead biological children. She discusses her adoptive parents with hostility. It is her street family Cassandra talks about warmly. One national magazine article appeared on the case in *Jane* magazine. Cassandra didn't like the article at all. It "compared us to Manson," she says.

At her sentencing in 2006, Cassandra wept and apologized to the Williams. Robyn watched her daughter and felt a glimmer of hope. But Cassandra's father, Kenny, was not convinced. He thought her performance was missing a few beats. Later, after talking with her daughter, Robyn came to the conclusion that indeed she hadn't really taken responsibility for her acts. "It was like a television show she was watching," Robyn says. Cassie had already made up a new version of the assault: strangers had killed Jessica. It is possible that what conscience Cassandra has resides in her baffling seizures. Perhaps that was her way of getting herself to stop that night.

For Cassandra, the night with Jessica was much like the time as a child when she took the hand of the blind girl and led her directly into walls. Afterwards, she insisted to her mother that she was watching out for the blind girl. She said the girl was really her sister. Robyn never could figure out where she got such a strange idea. It was the same with Jessica. Cassandra now says she was watching over Jessica on the streets.

———

While waiting for trial, Carl Alsup continued to imitate his hero Nelson, becoming the king of grievances and complaints. He complained so often about other inmates who "annoyed" him, and asked so many times to be moved to different units, that a sheriff finally told him to "get over it." At the same time, the tall, blond-headed boy with the stick-out ears seemed vulnerable. A concerned jail guard noticed that Carl appeared to be getting a "sexual grooming" from a recently arrested sexual predator named Edward Stokes. Carl was quickly separated from Stokes, who had admitted to molesting 212 boys.

Carl kept looking for a place to belong. First, he became a Muslim. He took to being a Muslim the same way he took to being a street family warrior, becoming so immersed in the religion that he had rug burns on his forehead from all the praying. Then, one day, out of the blue, he decided he didn't want to be a Muslim after all. He abandoned that faith and became a Christian. Then, he wouldn't stop reading his Bible. As a Christian, Carl was docile and preached nonviolence. Even his voice was softer.

Soon enough, he dropped Christianity and hooked up with a gang of skinheads being held for assault in the county jail. It was the gang fronted by the same notorious skinhead, Dennis Mothersbaugh, who had been hanging out with street kids in the Square. In the two years since Jessica's murder, Mothersbaugh had been arrested for numerous crimes, including stabbing a black man, intimidation, menacing, and assault. In August 2005, his skinhead gang was arrested for attacking another black man at a convenience store. According to reports, the group had threatened the man with a machete while giving him white-power salutes. One of the girls had a swastika tattooed by her left eye.

Thrown together in county jail, Carl and Mothersbaugh apparently hit it off. According to reports, Carl joined his skinhead gang. Another inmate, Rob Taylor, recalls sitting at the cafeteria table while the two talked about Jessica Williams. "That's one less nigger to worry about," Mothersbaugh allegedly crowed. Carl, he said, "just sort of dropped his head and didn't say anything."

A month later, on September 12, 2005, Carl pled guilty to the murder of Jessica Williams and no contest to the robbery of Eugene. He was sentenced to forty-one years in prison. He will be fifty-eight when he is released.

At his sentencing, Carl appeared contrite, weeping and saying he was sorry to the Williams. He sobbed, saying he deserved to go to hell. "I was evil, probably the most evil person in that group," he cried. "In 2043, when I come up for parole, you'll see the sincerity."

One of Jessica's sisters stood to address Carl, saying she was willing to forgive him if he was truly repentant. "I can see from your family's faces that they love you," she said, looking directly into the eyes of Carl's mother, Kelly, who sobbed. She then turned to Carl. "Please look for God while you are away."

Shortly after his sentencing, Carl called the investigator on his case and told her he had joined the European Kindred, the white supremacist prison gang. The investigator, who had hoped greatly that Carl would find true remorse, told him she could no longer take his calls. Carl was transferred to Oregon State Prison, where several of the killers from the 1992 Family are presently housed, including Grant Charboneau. On his first day in the state prison, he found a way to land himself in segregation for a six-month term, the maximum. His mother cried over what her son had become.

Several of those interviewed believe that Carl is a frightening young man, even more bloodthirsty than Nelson was at his age. "He is a dangerous young man," Detective Renna says with quiet emphasis. "He will do what he can to impress people."

Jimmy Stewart's attorneys fought feverishly on his behalf. They wanted to show that Jimmy was a damaged young man who was less culpable than others in the family. Their primary argument was that Jessica's fatal brain injury occurred during the beating at the squat, not during the final assault across the river. They were prepared to call a neurologist who disagreed with the autopsy report and would testify that Jessica was, in fact, already "walking dead" when she crossed the bridge. The jurors never had to decide whether they found this argument convincing enough to reduce the charge from murder, as the attorneys hoped, because Jimmy accepted a deal that gave him the chance of parole after twenty-five years.

Jimmy remains a cipher. To his attorneys, he was a salvable victim. To the police, he was a turncoat, first kissing his girlfriend on the forehead, then killing her. To the Williams, he was a major reason Jessica stayed linked to the street culture. But to the rest of the world, he was no one, and this anonymity seems to define Jimmy best. Even when he is in the midst of a serious conversation about the murder, Jimmy will suddenly change the subject to something trivial that interests him, like Pokemon. He doesn't seem to grasp the severity of what he did. Or else he doesn't care.

At his sentencing on November 10, 2005, Jimmy did make an apology of sorts to the Williams, saying he was sorry he "failed to stop" the murder. "I'm sorry for everything I've done, and I hope you can forgive me someday," he added. When he spoke, it was with a deep tiredness of spirit. He didn't appear mentally ill, or suicidal, or heartless. He just seemed . . . empty.

———

Danielle Cox, the college student called Shadowcat, agreed to plead guilty in a deal that gave her twenty-five years for murder in exchange for her testimony against the other family members. She will be eligible for parole when she is forty-three.

Danielle cooperated with the police, and to those associated with the case, she consistently expressed poignant and seemingly sincere remorse. But to those on the outside, she showed a different side of her personality. In a letter to a person called Gee over a year after Jessica's murder, Danielle wrote she was upset that he was judging her "personally" for the murder of Jessica. She said she didn't know Jessica was mentally challenged. "I thought she was around 18, maybe a little immature for her age," she wrote. "Plus, where's the psych doctor to test her now?"

Danielle wrote she had been "ordered" to kill Jessica. Besides, she wrote, Jessica "died of brain swelling, not the stabbing. So I didn't outright kill her." She did admit, however, to watching Jessica die.

"You don't know how hard it is to live with this *pain*. I suffer every day. Jessica's *lucky*." The newspapers, she wrote, were "bullshit."

Two years after the murder, Danielle wrote from the Coffee Creek Prison in Wilsonville, Oregon. She expressed no regret for what she had done. It was possible she kept her horror to herself. But now her allegiance was to Jimmy Stewart, who was still facing trial at the time. "I cannot see myself standing up at trial and testifying against someone who is no more guilty than myself," she wrote about Jimmy with perfect penmanship. "He is a good person, and if I have to go back to trial because of him, then in my eyes, it is worth it."

The tone of Danielle's letters, the language, and even the handwriting appear to change depending on the person she is communicating with. When writing to professionals, Danielle writes with a delicate hand and a restrained vocabulary. When she is writing to her street friends, her cursive rounds into childlike curls, and she becomes foul-mouthed. Writing Crystal Ivey from prison, Danielle referred to another street kid as a "bitch fucking talking to the cameras against me."

Danielle may have bought her attorney's theory of the case a little too closely. Her attorney proposed that Danielle had fallen prey to group dynamics and the power of authority. His defense leaned heavily on Stanley Milgram's famous experiment in which college students administered electric shocks to each other after being told to do so by a man presenting himself as an authority figure. Despite their victim's escalating cries of pretend pain, the college students continued to give what they thought were stronger and stronger shocks. Only a few challenged the authority of the leader and refused to continue. Danielle, the attorney argued, exhibited the same blind obedience to Nelson. It was a theory he admitted probably wouldn't go over well with a jury. No one likes to believe people murder just because they are told to do so.

Danielle's own lack of insight seems to disprove the theory. Had it been valid, it seems that once away from Nelson, Danielle would have woken up, shaken her head, and asked herself who she had become. She did not. Perhaps this is because the higher power Danielle had adopted was not Nelson but the criminal street culture he espoused. And part of Danielle still believed in it.

On October 26, 2005, two and a half years after the murder, Danielle Cox called a local radio humor show from prison. "We always get calls from the women's prison late at night," host Cort Webber joked. He asked Danielle why she was incarcerated. "I'm in for thirty years for aggravated murder," Danielle replied in a girlish voice. The host seemed taken aback. "What did you do, stab someone a hundred and twenty times?" he asked. Danielle laughed nervously and replied, "Once."

The various talk show hosts continued to ask Danielle about her crime, and Danielle continued to laugh nervously, going along with their questions. She agreed her victim had "screwed her over," and she had "twisted the knife." She said she had "three bitches" under her in the prison, meaning prison sex slaves. It is hard to tell if Danielle really intended to sound so callous or if the nervous laughter signaled a young woman unable to say, "Stop." The hosts suddenly realized they were talking to one of the street family members who had murdered Jessica Williams. "Wow," one of them said. "Way to pick on the retards."

After Danielle hung up, the hosts replayed her call and commented on how cold she sounded. Danielle called them back, this time crying on the air. "All I want to say is Jessica didn't deserve what she got," she cried. "I'm sorry for what happened to her." Like Jimmy Stewart, Danielle apologized for what had "happened" to Jessica, not what she had done.

Four months after that radio show call, on February 15, 2006, Danielle sat down in a private meeting with Becky and Sam Williams. Almost three years had passed since the murder, and Danielle was about to be the final family member fully sentenced for her acts. Danielle apologized more directly this time. "I know what I did was really wrong," she sobbed later in court. "If I could trade places with Jessica, I would." She portrayed herself as a caring person who had been seduced into the street family life. She did not appear to take full accountability for her own aggressive pursuit of violence. It is possible that what Danielle did that night was so horrific, she could not face it. Maybe the guilt would destroy her.

Forensic psychiatrist Dr. Keith Ablow warns that teenagers who are detached from their true selves cannot stay that way for their entire lives. Reality, he writes, "will not be frustrated forever." Sooner or later, the disconnected will connect, and the truth will come crashing down on their psyches. "You have to pay back emotional debt," Ablow warns. The longer you wait, the heavier the debt.

When and if Danielle fully wakes up, she may find hers is a reality with a staggering debt, perhaps one that cannot be paid.

———

James Daniel Nelson cannot be blamed for everything that happened in the spring of 2003. He certainly played an instrumental role, and this role was probably an incendiary one: the youths were the powder, and Nelson was the fuse.

But when Nelson ordered the murder of Jessica, it was in the context of a world where such orders can happen, where punishments extend to death. *Snitches get stitches and wind up in ditches.* Had that code not been there, Nelson's orders would have been meaningless. Nelson was not the one who invented the code, and he was not the only one to use it. He was a representative of a world, not an isolated occurrence.

One can go to any American city and find street families talking about smiley chains and taxing, anarchy, dramas, and punishments. They will be squatting in similar squats and calling each other brother and sister, mother and father. They will be enforcing the same brand of ruthless street justice on each other and resisting all efforts to dislodge them from the streets, as scared and confused as they may be.

Not all will murder, just as not all gang members kill. But the groundwork is there. The dramas, the fantasy games these youths play outside the law, spiral all too easily into violence, and the codes they have created act like steps on a ladder leading them into further alienation from society. They are buffered from the consequences of their own violence until it is too late.

The outside world doesn't exist to these teenagers and young adults. With each taxing or assault, they become more entrenched in the fantasy life they have created. When Nelson took the name Thantos, he wasn't just pretending to be a god of death. In his world, he was a god of death. And in his world, this was more than acceptable. It was respected.

"Inside this world, this is normal," says Randy Blazak, an assistant professor of sociology and criminology at Portland State University and the coauthor of the 2001 book *Renegade Kids, Suburban Outlaws*. Blazak has observed street families and the powerful psychological effect they can have on their followers. "Take the kids out of this situation and they'll say it was wrong, what was I doing? It's the same as sports riots. You talk to someone and say, 'How come yesterday you were overturning cars?' And they will say they got caught up in it."

Some of the teenagers in the Thantos Family, especially the minor members like Sarah Caster and Crystal Ivey, were relatively normal teenagers going through a rocky time. If they had not encountered the street family culture, they would probably have had survived adolescence and arrived at adulthood intact. Instead, they were sucked into a world that dismantled their morals and principles, forever altering their futures and the future of the Williams family.

Others in the family were fundamentally disturbed, including Carl Alsup and Cassandra Hale. In the street family society, they found a home that nourished their malignancies and extinguished any hope they had of intervention. Shelter staff reinforced their fantasy identities by calling them by their made-up names. On the streets, their crimes went ignored by the media and the outside world. And so, they thought they could get away with anything.

Still others were damaged and vulnerable, such as Jimmy Stewart. Their vulnerabilities were exploited by the more cunning and violent in the street family society. For a genuinely homeless youth, the street family offers a powerful lure of protection and guidance. And one youth, Danielle Cox, remains an enigma, a child of middle-class privilege driven by motivations perhaps even she could not fathom. Together, these young people descended into group violence if for no other reason than that they could, and no one stopped them.

Regardless of their backgrounds, most of the street kids in the Thantos Family seemed disconnected from themselves and representative of a society where young adults are encouraged to immerse themselves in fantasy games. The result is young people who are allowed to divorce themselves fully from reality and pretend to be magical characters. For teenagers still developing a sense of moral obligation and ethics, these fantasy identities play a frightening trick: no longer themselves, they are severed from their consciences and the consequences of their actions. Everything becomes a mirage: it is all only kidding, only pretend, and even when someone is brutally murdered, the drama only continues in new and exciting forms.

James Nelson was as responsible for Jessica's murder as any of the others involved, and probably much more so. But the assault could have happened under the sole direction of Cassandra Hale, who in her frenzied attack seemed intent on killing Jessica in the squat that night. Jimmy Stewart could have passively followed his street mom into another murder. Carl Alsup could have found another street father he wanted to impress or another victim on whom to take out his internal rage. Danielle Cox could have joined another street family. Maybe she wouldn't have murdered if she had, but then, Danielle wasn't looking for protection from that sort of thing.

The Thantos Family could have found another target: a Richard Crosby to stomp, a Nick Moore to stab to death. Another street family could have murdered Jessica because she failed to understand the nuances of their barbed and dangerous society. And all of this could have happened if James Nelson had never been released from prison. "It's a world within a world," one former street kid says. "They have their own judge, their own jury, and their own executioners. And you better hope you aren't the target."

The street family culture had been created with James Daniel Nelson, it had grown with James Daniel Nelson, and it would continue to grow without James Daniel Nelson. Locking Nelson up would do nothing to stop it. It did, however, make a lot of sense. In four months of freedom in a dozen years, Nelson had managed to kill twice.

Asked why he didn't just leave the streets, Nelson looks momentarily blank. He doesn't seem capable of imagining life outside a street family.

"Where would I go?" he asked.

Notes

PROLOGUE

xxiv *There are an estimated 1.5 million street kids* This is a commonly cited estimate. See Dilip R. Patel, Donald E. Greydanus, "Homeless Adolescents in the United States: An Overview for Pediatricians," *International Pediatrics* 17 (2002). Estimates of the number of street youth are based on shelter statistics, street counts, and runaway reports. Some believe that the estimates are artificially low and miss many youth who do not use shelters or are not reported as runaways. According to some accounts, as many as 2.8 million youths experience a homeless episode over the course of a year. See "Issue Brief: Runaway and Homeless Youth Reauthorization," Child Welfare League of America, 2002.

xxiv *Asheville, North Carolina* Cliff Bostock, "Haight-Asheville?" *Creative Loafing,* September 25, 2002.

xxiv *In San Francisco street kids are said to be the "fastest-growing" homeless population* Fact sheet, Larkin Street Youth Services, 2002.

xxiv *Street family in Spokane called the Rat Pak* Jeanette White, "Dead-End Streets," *Spokesman Review,* July 9, 2000. This article was part of an excellent series on Spokane street kids.

xxiv *In Sacramento, California* Darragh Johnson, "Dead-End Dreams: Gritty Streets of an Illusion of Home," *Sacramento Bee,* October 31, 1999.

xxiv *Berkeley street kids* Jan Sturmann, "Child Left Behind: The Lost Kids of Telegraph Avenue?" *Albinocrow* (December 2004).

xxiv *In Austin, Texas, over seven thousand street kids were counted* "Street Outreach," Lifeworks Street Outreach, 2004.

xxiv *Ashland, Oregon* Chris Honore, "Here Be Dragons," *Ashland Daily Tidings,* October 26, 2004.

xxiv *Arcata, California* Arno Holschuh, "Who Are the Plaza People?" *North Coast Journal,* February 15, 2001.

xxv *Thirty-seven thousand in Australia* See "Youth Homelessness Fact Sheet," Salvation Army Australia Eastern Territory, 2005. There are an estimated 8,000 to 11,000 street youth in Canada. See "Facts and Stats about Youth Homelessness," Covenant House, Toronto, 2005.

xxv *Tokyo* Ryann Connell, "Enterprising Street Kids Scrub Up to Play Lover," *Mainichi News,* October 12, 2004.

xxv– *John Hagan and Bill McCarthy* John Hagan and Bill McCarthy, *Mean Streets:*
xxvi *Youth Crime and Homelessness* (Cambridge, UK: Cambridge University Press, 1999).

xxvi *Street family in Des Moines, Iowa* Kathy Slobogin, "On the Run: Young and Homeless," CNN.com, October 4, 2004.

CHAPTER ONE

4 *Nelson could learn how to cast "binding spells"* No author listed, *Necronomicon* (New York: Avon Books, 1977).

4 *A 1998 grand jury investigating the Hall found filthy kitchens* "Final Report: B. T. Collins Juvenile Hall," Sacramento Grand Jury, June 30, 1999.

5 *A study by the Vera Institute* Marni Finkelstein, Mark Wamsley, Dan Currie, and Doreen Miranda, "Youth Who Chronically AWOL from Foster Care: Why They Run, Where They Go, and What Can Be Done," Vera Institute of Justice, August 2004.

5 *Two thousand homeless youth in Portland at the time* Mike Magrath, "Death on the River's Edge," *PDXS,* January 3, 1993. In the interest of disclosure, I worked for this newspaper at the time of the 1992 murders.

5 *A 1985 study found* Jennifer James, "Kids on the Streets: Whose Responsibility Are They?" City Club of Portland, July 19, 1985.

6 *Boy prostitutes as young as ten were recorded* "Report on Adult Prostitution in Portland," City Club of Portland, August 31, 1984. This report has a section on child prostitution.

14 *Rick Van Savage* Anders Corr, "Squatting the Lower East Side, an Interview with Rick Van Savage," *Kick It Over* 35 (1995).

CHAPTER TWO

18 *Pearl Stewart* Pearl E. Stewart, "Afrocentric Approaches to Working with African American Families," *Families in Society: The Journal of Contemporary Social Services* 85, no. 2 (2004).

24   *Only 6 percent of street youth are African American* Office of School and Community Partnerships and Homeless Youth Oversight Committee, Portland, Oregon, October 31, 2002.

CHAPTER THREE

29   *With him was a friend* Joel Seaquist, also age fifteen, helped murder Hal Charboneau. Joel and Leon were friends from high school, and Joel became briefly enmeshed with the street kids through Leon. He was found guilty in the murder of Hal Charboneau and is presently incarcerated.

CHAPTER FOUR

41   *Dr. Keith Ablow* Keith Ablow, "Speaking in the Third Person, Removed from Reality," *New York Times,* November 1, 2005.

CHAPTER FIVE

57   *Greenhouse supporter* Mike Magrath, "Death on the River's Edge," *PDXS,* January 3, 1993.

CHAPTER SIX

62   *Sean Otero writing about Minneapolis* "Stories by Frhate," *Vinylexchange.com,* August 28, 2005.

62   *Scum Fucks encouraging ganglike atmosphere* Anonymous posting, "Street Society," *Roaddawg.org,* March 24, 2003.

62–63 *Tempe Dank Krew* David Holthouse, "Meet the Crusties: Spanging, Squatting and Looking for Hot Dog Jesus with Tempe's Street Kids," *Phoenix New Times,* February 26, 1998.

63   *Bart W. Miles spent time with another Tempe street family* Bart W. Miles, "The Role of Social Establishment in Defining a Stigmatized Social Identity," (Under Review) Qualitative Social Work, 2006.

65   *"There's that bitch,"* Sue Lindsay, "Guilty Pleas in Homeless Death," *Denver Rocky Mountain News,* March 14, 2000. For more on the Denver street culture, see John C. Ensslin, "Violence Part of Everyday Routine for Those Police Call 'Mall Rats,'" *Rocky Mountain News,* September 9, 1999.

65   *One of the Denver family send a threatening letter* Sue Lindsay, "Teen Guilty in Homeless Man's Death," *Rocky Mountain News,* March 23, 2000.

65   *An outreach worker said the youth were unfairly accused* Sean Kelly, "'Mall Rats' Unfairly Accused, Many Say," *Denver Post*, November 18, 1999.

65   *New York Times characterized slaying as hate crime against homeless* Evelyn Nieves, "Violence Is Becoming a Threat for Homeless," *New York Times*, December 23, 1999.

65   *Bridge Over Troubled Waters reported* "Homeless Persons," Crime Fact Sheet, Cambridge Police, 2003.

65   *Cambridge police* "Homeless Persons," Crime Fact Sheet, Cambridge Police, 2003. Also see Sarah Andrews, "Closing Pit No Longer a Priority," *Cambridge Chronicle*, March 10, 2005.

65–66 *Hate crimes by Pit street kids* "Police Call Beating of Harvard Student a Hate Crime," *Harvard University Gazette*, September 21, 2000.

66   *An opinion piece accused the students of intolerance* Meredith B. Osborn, "Strangers in Our Midst," *Harvard Crimson*, October 6, 2000.

66   *"Bam. Eliminated from the gene pool"* Stan Grossfeld, "The 'New Homeless': Harvard Square Street People Increasing," *Boston Globe*, May 17, 1999.

66   *David Clark* "Teens at the Pit," broadcast, Greater Boston Radio, December 5, 2001.

66–67 *Io Nachtwey's childhood* Kathleen Burge and Farah Stockman, "Murder Shatters a Street 'Family,'" *Boston Globe*, November 18, 2001. Also see Gary T. Kubota, "Murdered near Boston," *Honolulu Star Bulletin*, November 15, 2001.

68   *According to news reports* Kathleen Burge, "5 Held in Woman's Riverside Slaying," *Boston Globe*, November 10, 2001; Sarah Andrews, "2001 Murder Trial to Begin March 7," *Cambridge Chronicle*, March 3, 2005; Associated Press, "Admitted Accomplice Testifies in Harvard Square Murder Trial," *Boston Herald*, March 28, 2005; Associated Press, "Prosecutor Describes Night of Woman's Murder," *Boston Herald*, March 9, 2005.

68   *1999 sample of Pit Rats* Ryan Kearney, "The Pit Problem," *Cambridge Chronicle*, April 9, 2003.

69   *"There are bad things that happen. . . . "* Anthony Flint, "Slaying of Street Kid Draws Critics' Eye to 'Pit,'" *Boston Globe*, November 23, 2001.

69   *There was a stabbing* Jenifer L. Steinhardt, "Three Teens Arrested after Square Stabbing," *Harvard Crimson*, June 2, 2003.

71   *Street kid crimes* Several studies have shown that street youth are highly criminal. See Michele D. Kipke, et al., "Homeless Youth and Their Exposure to and Involvement in Violence While Living on the Streets," *Society for Adolescent Medicine* 20 (1997), and Stephen W. Baron, "Street Youth Violence and Victimization," *Trauma, Violence and Abuse* 4, no. 1 (January 2003), for a good review of the literature. Baron concludes that street kid crime is often not motivated by economic need but by revenge and showboating. "In fact, street

youth work to build reputations by engaging in violence in front of their peers," he writes.

72 *Very few of these crimes were reported* Seven months after the beating of the blind man, one article on street kid crime did appear. See Maxine Bernstein, "Thug-Style Justice among Portland's Street Kids Reaches Extremes," *Oregonian,* November 10, 2002.

75–76 *The Richard Crosby murder* Details of the Crosby murder are from police reports, interviews with the suspects, and an interview with Detective Rich Austria.

76 *A brief article characterized Crosby's death as a street dispute* Maxine Bernstein, "Nine Portlanders Charged in Fatal Beating of Man," *Oregonian,* August 19, 2000.

76–79 *The Nick Moore case* Details of this homicide are from police records, investigation reports, and personal interviews with Connie Moore and Detective Barry Renna. Also see the reporting of Maxine Bernstein, including "Details Emerge of Street Killing," *Oregonian,* November 5, 2003.

CHAPTER SEVEN

87 *Oregon Prison manual on Wiccan services Handbook of Religious Beliefs,* Oregon Department of Corrections, 2001.

88 *Mattias Gardell* Mattias Gardell, *Gods of the Blood: The Pagan Revival and White Separatism* (Durham, NC: Duke University Press, 2003). Also see "Dangerous Convictions: An Introduction to Extremist Activities in Prisons," Anti-Defamation League, 2002. For a pro-pagan position, see the National Prison Kindred Alliance, a propagan organization advocating on behalf of prisoner's rights.

88 *David Lane and Wotanism* "David Lane," Anti-Defamation League, 2004. David Lane explains his views in his essay "Wotanism (Odinism)," available online http://www.mourningtheancient.com/dl-2.html, (accessed May 19, 2006).

88 *Richard Scutari's kindred* Mattias Gardell, *Gods of the Blood: The Pagan Revival and White Separatism* (Durham, NC: Duke University Press, 2003).

89 *Prisons are surprisingly porous institutions* Randy Blazak, "Prison Odinism and Hate Crimes: Using Religion to Do Gender," draft copy, permission for use granted by author.

89 *In Oregon skinhead group Volksfront is largely pagan* For example, see the Volksfront Web site Volksfrontinternational.com.

89 *E. K. graffiti tags have appeared in southeast Portland* Personal interview with Randy Blazak. There have been hate crimes committed by paroled racist pagans. Jack Sullivan, "Suspect May Have Joined Racist Group in Prison," *Boston Herald,* June 21, 2001.

91   *The Portland Peace Encampment* "Camping for Peace: How Justin Elder Spent His Spring Break," *Willamette Week,* April 2, 2003.

91   *There was some grumbling about freeloaders* Amy Roe, "Scroungers Swell Protest Ranks," *Willamette Week,* April 16, 2003.

91   *Nelson talking about "niggers"* Thantos family member Thomas Schreiner recounted how Nelson talked about "niggers" and boasted that he had never done cell time with an African American.

92   *Skinhead Dennis Mothersbaugh* A records check shows that Mothersbaugh had a long record of charges, from methamphetamine possession to racial attacks. Antiracist groups have documented his crimes. See "Admitted Skinhead Gets Prison in Racial Attacks," *Hate Crime News,* Coalition Against Hate Crimes, 2005.

93   *Jerry Fest* Personal interview with Jerry Fest. Also see Jerry Fest, *Street Culture: An Epistemology of Street-Dependent Youth* (Portland, OR: Jerry Fest, 1998).

100   *Sara's overnight transition to the streets* Research suggests that youth become rapidly indoctrinated into the street kid culture, often within a day or two, and successful intervention requires accessing these youth before they become entrenched in the culture. See Colette Auerswald and Stephen Eyre, "Youth Homelessness in San Francisco: A Life Cycle Approach," *Social Science Medicine* (May 2002).

100   *Sara was twenty* The average age of street youth has risen over the past decade, and the majority now identifying as "street kids" are actually adults. See the Office of School and Community Partnerships and Homeless Youth Oversight Committee, Portland, Oregon, October 31, 2002, documenting an ongoing rise in the age of street youth to over age eighteen. The reason for this rise is unclear. In interviews, street youth say the streets are too dangerous for younger teens.

102   *Territories of street kids* In San Francisco, reporter Kevin Fagan found similar territories. See Kevin Fagan, "Shame of the City: The 'Territories' of the Homeless," *San Francisco Chronicle,* December 3, 2003.

103   *The squatter's symbol* Raven, "Squat or Rot! The Movement and Brief History of the Squatterz Movement," *Roaddawgz.org,* February 2003. Interviews with street kids confirm they see the symbol as Runic in nature.

103   *Some cities are raising the age of street youth served in shelters* There is a push among some providers to serve older adults who identify as street kids. For example, the Tumbleweed Center in Tempe, Arizona, serves children as young as nine and adults as old as twenty-two.

105   *Easy eating while traveling* Matt Bastard, "Reno and San Francisco," *digihitch.com,* December 15, 2003. Marni Finkelstein found that when street kids go without eating, it is usually because they are stoned, drunk, or simply disinterested, not from a lack of available food. See Marni Finkelstein, *With No*

Direction Home: Homeless Youth on the Road and in the Streets (Belmont, CA: Wadsworth, 2005).

106 *Ken Cowdery* Phil Busse, "The Truth about Hobo Teens," *Mercury*, June 24, 2004. Ken Cowdery did not respond to repeated interview requests for this book.

109 *He tried to run it like a cult* There has been virtually no examination of the similarities between street families and cults, though the two share several aspects in common: alienation from extended families and nonbelievers, a rigid hierarchy with leaders, and an endorsement of violence when used to enforce allegiance to the group. Perhaps the most compelling similarity is how both street families and cults encourage their members to adopt new names and identities, often mythical or religious in nature, which cement bonds within the group, as well as distance followers from the rest of society.

CHAPTER EIGHT

113 *Preference for sleeping in squats* Christine Barber, "Homeless in Santa Fe: 'You've Been Out Riding Fences,'" *The New Mexican,* November 17, 2004. The problem is not a lack of shelter beds. A number of studies show that only half of youth shelter beds are used. For example, a Seattle survey found that only 40 to 50 percent of youth shelter beds were occupied. When asked why they reject shelter beds, the street kids complained about rules against drugs, alcohol, sex, and cell phones. See "Barriers to Shelter Study Pilot Project Needs Assessment," Street Youth Taskforce, City of Seattle, March 31, 2002. This study cites other studies on low shelter-occupancy rates, from an Alaskan study to a national survey.

113 *Portland Police raided the Peace Camp* Andy Seaton, "Police Raid Portland Peace Encampment," *Portland Independent Media Center,* April 15, 2003.

114 *The dramas on the streets* Researchers have documented the fascination with drama among street kids. See, for instance, Natasha Slesnick, *Our Runaway and Homeless Youth: A Guide to Understanding* (Westport, CT: Praeger, 2004).

117 *Study on runaways in the Midwest* Les B. Whitbeck and Dan R. Hoyt, *Nowhere to Grow: Homeless and Runaway Adolescents and Their Families* (New York: Aldine de Gruyter, 1999).

122 *Heroin and methamphetamine* Michael Kamber, "Heroin (and Heartache)," *The Village Voice,* July 10, 2002, is an excellent glimpse inside the junkie life of New York City street youth, while Adam Richter, "Young and Homeless in Seattle," *Seattle Press,* November 21, 2001, discusses the use of methamphetamine in Seattle. Agency providers interviewed for this book confirm that methamphetamine is popular along the Pacific Coast and in the Midwest and less popular on the East Coast.

123 *New York City street youth* Marni Finkelstein, *With No Direction Home: Homeless Youth on the Road and in the Streets* (Belmont, CA: Wadsworth, 2005).

123– *Smiley attack in Spokane* John Craig, "Ruling Shaves Years off Killer's Prison
124 Sentence," *The Spokesman Review,* January 22, 2005.

125 *The knife drawer* Ilan Brat, "A Safe Haven: After a Year of Helping Homeless Youth, Tempe's Tumbleweed Center Is Going Strong," *ASU Web Devil,* June 24, 2003.

CHAPTER NINE

129 *The term fetal alcohol syndrome* Rachel Greenbaum, "Fetal Alcohol Spectrum Disorder: New Diagnostic Initiatives," *Paediatrics and Child Health* 7, no. 3 (March 2002).

129 *Facial anomalies* FASCETS presentation by Diane Malbin, Portland, Oregon, 2004; also, Resource Sheet, Fetal Alcohol Syndrome (FAS), *Crossroads,* May 2001.

130 *Forty thousand babies born with fetal alcohol syndrome* "Fetal Alcohol Spectrum Disorders," Florida Resource Guide, Florida Department of Children and Families, May 2004.

132 *60 percent of children with fetal alcohol syndrome end up getting expelled* Resource Sheet, Fetal Alcohol Syndrome (FAS), *Crossroads,* May 2001. For more on fetal alcohol spectrum disorder, see Judith Kleinfeld and Siobhan Wescott, eds., *Fantastic Antone Succeeds: Experiences in Educating Children with Fetal Alcohol Syndrome* (Fairbanks, AK: University of Alaska Press, 1993), Diane Malbin, *Trying Differently Rather than Trying Harder: Fetal Alcohol Syndrome and Fetal Alcohol Effects* (Portland, OR: State Office for Services for Children and Families, 1999). FASlink is an excellent networking and educational resource for parents and professionals. See www.acbr.com/fas/faslink.htm.

CHAPTER ELEVEN

154– *Cassandra's lack of attachment* The link between neglect in infancy and later dif-
155 ficulties forming attachments has been well documented in studies, especially those on reactive attachment disorder in adopted children. See, for example, Mary Hopkins-Best, *Toddler Adoption: The Weaver's Craft* (Indianapolis: Perspectives Press, 1997). Hopkins-Best discusses the effects of early neglect, loss, and grieving on the adopted toddler, which can lead to lifelong difficulties forming attachments.

156– *Compulsive lying* Ken Hausman, "Does Pathological Lying Warrant Inclusion
157 in the DSM?" *Psychiatric News,* January 3, 2003.

161 *The shelter staff didn't appear to question Cassandra's claims* Many of the high abuse rates cited for street youth come from unverified shelter interviews. For example, the Outside In agency reports that 90 percent of their clients experienced violence in their family homes, but this figure comes from street kid claims such as Cassandra's screening, which may or may not be true. Only a few studies have ever attempted to confirm the abuse claims of street kids. In their study of Midwestern runaways, Whitbeck and Hoyt interviewed both parents and their runaway teenagers. They found sharp disagreements among parents and their teenagers when it came to serious accusations of abuse. See Les B. Whitbeck and Dan R. Hoyt, *Nowhere to Grow: Homeless and Runaway Adolescents and Their Families* (New York: Aldine de Gruyter, 1999).

162 *Berkeley ordinance against dogs* Chuck Squatriglia, "Berkeley's Telegraph Avenue Takes a Profit Turn," *Contra Costa Times,* December 11, 1998.

163 *Four-state study of Midwest street youth* Les B. Whitbeck and Dan R. Hoyt, *Nowhere to Grow: Homeless and Runaway Adolescents and Their Families* (New York: Aldine de Gruyter, 1999).

163 *Spokane drug dealing* Cited in Marni Finkelstein, *With No Direction Home: Homeless Youth on the Road and in the Streets* (Belmont, CA: Wadsworth, 2005).

163– *Denver drug dealing* Lee D. Hoffer, *Junkie Business: The Evolution and Operation*
164 *of a Heroin Dealing Network* (Belmont, CA: Wadsworth, 2006), as well as correspondence with author Lee Hoffer.

165 *Political ramifications of arrested street youth dealers in San Lorenzo Park* Robert Norse and Becky Johnson, "Grass Busts Downtown Criminalize Young and Poor," *Santa Cruz Indymedia,* October 1, 2004.

CHAPTER TWELVE

173 *Maja told the Portland Oregonian* Maxine Bernstein, "Two Paths to Street Life and Arrest in Street Death," *Oregonian,* June 30, 2003.

180 *Nelson was complaint with parole officers* Jim Redden, "Street Killing Sets Off Grisly Echoes," *Portland Tribune,* June 17, 2003; also, police records.

CHAPTER SIXTEEN

239– *The Oregonian had a small article* Maxine Bernstein, "Woman Found Slain near
240 Eastbank Esplanade," *Oregonian,* May 24, 2003.

242 *"Jessica was labeled as a liar and a snitch"* Abe Estimada and Jim Parker, "Former Inmate Leader of Violent Street Family," *KGW News,* kgw.com, June 13, 2003.

242 *The streets "aren't dangerous if you're not stupid,"* Charles Boardman, "Painted into a Corner," *Street News Service,* June 9, 2003.

251 *"I heard you got adopted into a street gang,"* Maxine Bernstein, "Two Paths to Street Life and Arrest in Street Death," *Oregonian,* June 30, 2003.

257 *Kathy Oliver said, "The majority of homeless youth are good kids"* Israel Bayer, "Arrests Put Spotlight on Homeless Violence," *Street Roots,* June 13, 2003.

258 *A particularly nasty blogger* Betsy, *My Whim Is Law: Someone's Talking Trash,* May 25, 2004, at www.echonyc.com/~lizbet/blog/archives/000140.html (accessed April 10, 2006).

259 *Chuck Currie suggested Jessica was forced onto the streets* Chuck Currie, "Jessica Williams Did Not Have to Die," originally published for the *National Coalition for the Homeless,* 2003. http://chuckcurrie.blogs.com/about.html (accessed May 19, 2006).

259 *An opinion piece blamed lack of funding for youth shelters* David Rubin, "Open Hearts to Homeless Street Youth," *Oregonian,* June 16, 2003.

261 *It was all the fault of the "corporate whore media centers"* Posting, *Portland Independent Media Center,* July 21, 2003. http://portland.indymedia.org/en/2003/07/268438.shtml (accessed May 19, 2006).

261 *Twenty-one-year-old complained* Charles Boardman, "Painted into a Corner," *Street News Service,* June 9, 2003.

263– *Portland Riders* Nick Budnick, "Leader of the Pack?" *Willamette Week,* October
264 20, 2004; Maxine Bernstein, "Street Group Faces 21 Charges," *Oregonian,* October 21, 2004; Anne Saker, "Three Guilty in Portland Crime Wave," *Oregonian,* March 31, 2005.

CHAPTER SEVENTEEN

272– *Joshua was treated sympathetically by the press* Lys Mendez, "Sixth Person Admits
273 to Role in Street Family's Assault at Riverfront," *Oregonian,* July 31, 2003.

274 *One national magazine article* Karen Catchpole, "The Only Family They Have Anything in Common with Is the Manson Family," *Jane Magazine* (December 2003).

275 *Edward Stokes* For more on Stokes, see Carol Lin, "Serial Molester Arrested in Oregon," *CNN Transcripts,* April 18, 2004. Stokes wrote to a prison therapist that he had victimized over two hundred children.

276 *Dennis Mothersbaugh* Stuart Tomlinson, "Police Arrest Four in Racial Confrontation," *Oregonian,* August 16, 2005.

281 *Reality will not be frustrated* Keith Ablow, "Speaking in the Third Person, Removed from Reality," *New York Times,* November 1, 2005.

282 *Randy Blazak* Also see Wayne Wooden and Randy Blazak, *Renegade Kids, Suburban Outlaws: From Youth Culture to Delinquency* (Belmont, CA: Wadsworth, 2001).

Index

PublicAffairs is a publishing house founded in 1997. It is a tribute to the standards, values, and flair of three persons who have served as mentors to countless reporters, writers, editors, and book people of all kinds, including me.

I.F. STONE, proprietor of *I. F. Stone's Weekly*, combined a commitment to the First Amendment with entrepreneurial zeal and reporting skill and became one of the great independent journalists in American history. At the age of eighty, Izzy published *The Trial of Socrates*, which was a national bestseller. He wrote the book after he taught himself ancient Greek.

BENJAMIN C. BRADLEE was for nearly thirty years the charismatic editorial leader of *The Washington Post*. It was Ben who gave the *Post* the range and courage to pursue such historic issues as Watergate. He supported his reporters with a tenacity that made them fearless and it is no accident that so many became authors of influential, best-selling books.

ROBERT L. BERNSTEIN, the chief executive of Random House for more than a quarter century, guided one of the nation's premier publishing houses. Bob was personally responsible for many books of political dissent and argument that challenged tyranny around the globe. He is also the founder and longtime chair of Human Rights Watch, one of the most respected human rights organizations in the world.

For fifty years, the banner of Public Affairs Press was carried by its owner Morris B. Schnapper, who published Gandhi, Nasser, Toynbee, Truman, and about 1,500 other authors. In 1983, Schnapper was described by *The Washington Post* as "a redoubtable gadfly." His legacy will endure in the books to come.

Peter Osnos, *Founder and Editor-at-Large*